THE WILL TO RESIST

THE WILL TO RESIST

SOLDIERS WHO REFUSE TO FIGHT
IN IRAQ AND AFGHANISTAN

DAHR JAMAIL

Haymarket Books
Chicago, Illinois

First hardcover edition published in 2009 by Haymarket Books.
This edition published in 2010 by Haymarket Books.
©2009 Dahr Jamail

Haymarket Books
P.O. Box 180165
Chicago, IL 60618
773-583-7884
info@haymarketbooks.org
www.haymarketbooks.org

Trade distribution:
In the U.S. through Consortium Book Sales, www.cbsd.com
In Canada through Publishers Group Canada, www.pgcbooks.com
In the UK, Turnaround Publisher Services, www.turnaround-uk.com
In Australia, Palgrave MacMillan, www.palgravemacmillan.com.au
In all other countries, Publishers Group Worldwide, www.pgw.com

This book was published with the generous support of the Lannan Foundation and
the Wallace Global Fund.

Cover design by Eric Ruder.

ISBN-13: 978-1608460-95-3

Printed in Canada by union labor on recycled paper containing 100 percent
post-consumer waste in accordance with the guidelines of the Green Press Initiative,
www.greenpressinitiative.org.

Library of Congress CIP Data is available

10 9 8 7 6 5 4 3 2 1

CONTENTS

IRAQ

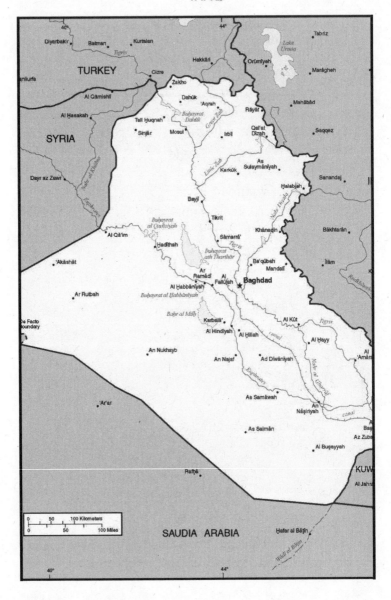

To the memory of Francis Macy (1927-2009).
If resistance is not from the heart, it is not resistance.

Weapons are the tools of violence:
All decent men detest them.

Weapons are the tools of fear;
a decent man will avoid them
except in the direst necessity
and, if compelled, will use them
only with the utmost restraint.
Peace is his highest value.
If the peace has been shattered,
how can he be content?
His enemies are not demons,
but human beings like himself.
He doesn't wish them personal harm.
Nor does he rejoice in victory.
How could he rejoice in victory
and delight in the slaughter of men?

—Lao Tzu, *Tao Te Ching*,
translated by Stephen Mitchell

War is a poison. It is a poison that nations and groups must at times ingest to ensure their survival. But, like any poison, it can kill you just as surely as the disease it is meant to eradicate. The poison of war courses unchecked through the body politic of the United States. We believe that because we have the capacity to wage war we have the right to wage war. We embrace the dangerous self-delusion that we are on a providential mission to save the rest of the world from itself, to implant our virtues—which we see as superior to all other virtues—on others, and that we have a right to do this by force. This belief has corrupted Republicans and Democrats.

Barack Obama and those around him embrace the folly of the "war on terror" even as they seek to avoid the phrase. They may want to shift the emphasis of this war to Afghanistan rather than Iraq, but this is a difference in strategy, not policy. By clinging to Iraq and expanding the war in Afghanistan, the poison will continue in deadly doses. These wars of occupation are doomed to failure. We cannot afford them. The rash of home foreclosures, the mounting job losses, the collapse of banks and the financial services industry, the poverty that is ripping apart the working class, our crumbling infrastructure, and the killing of hapless Afghans in wedding parties and

Iraqis by our iron fragmentation bombs are neatly interwoven. They form a perfect circle. The costly forms of death we dispense on one side of the globe are hollowing us out from the inside at home.

Our troops also ingest this poison as they dispense it. They come home haunted by their experiences. They try to piece together their past lives and find them shattered by dark memories of violence out of place in a nation oblivious to the wars being waged "over there." We laud military service as the highest good, but do not properly interrogate what it is serving. And until a book like this one comes along, it's easy to forget that not all troops neatly conform to the stereotype of the trigger-happy warrior.

Declaring a war against terrorism is an absurdity. You cannot make war against a tactic. It posits the idea of perpetual, or what is now called "generational," war. It has no discernable end. There is no way to define victory. It is, in metaphysical terms, a war against evil, and evil, as any good seminarian can tell you, will always be with us. The most destructive evils, however, are not those that are externalized. The most destructive are those that are internal. These hidden evils, often defined as virtues, are unleashed by our hubris, self-delusion, and ignorance. Evil masquerading as good is evil in its deadliest form. And this is the evil we practice.

We are witnessing the twilight adventures of our dying empire. The decline of the American empire began long before the current economic meltdown or the wars in Afghanistan and Iraq. It began before the first Gulf War or Ronald Reagan. It began when we shifted, in the words of the historian Charles Maier, from an "empire of production" to an "empire of consumption." By the end of the Vietnam War, when the costs of the war ate away at Lyndon Johnson's Great Society and domestic oil production began its steady, inexorable decline, we saw our country transformed from one that primarily produced to one that primarily consumed. We started borrowing to maintain a lifestyle we could no longer afford. We began to use force, especially in the Middle East, to feed our insatiable demand for cheap oil. The years after the Second World War, when the United States accounted for one-third of world exports and half of the world's manufacturing, gave way to huge trade imbalances, outsourced jobs, rusting hulks of abandoned factories, stagnant wages, and personal and public debts that most of us cannot repay.

The bill is now due. America's most dangerous enemies are not Islamic radicals, but those who promote the perverted ideology of national security that, as Andrew Bacevich writes, is "our surrogate religion." If we continue to believe that we can expand our wars and go deeper into debt to maintain an unsustainable level of consumption, we will dynamite the foundations of our society.

"The Big Lies are not the pledge of tax cuts, universal health care, family values restored, or a world rendered peaceful through forceful demonstrations of American leadership," Bacevich noted in *The Limits of Power*. "The Big Lies are the truths that remain unspoken: that freedom has an underside; that nations, like households, must ultimately live within their means; that history's purpose, the subject of so many confident pronouncements, remains inscrutable. Above all, there is this: Power is finite. Politicians pass over matters such as these in silence. As a consequence, the absence of self-awareness that forms such an enduring element of the American character persists."

Those clustered around Barack Obama, from Robert Gates to Hillary Clinton to Richard Holbrooke to Dennis Ross, have no interest in dismantling the structure of the imperial presidency or the vast national security state. They will keep these institutions intact and seek to increase their power. We have a childish belief that

Obama will magically save us from economic free fall, restore our profligate levels of consumption, and resurrect our imperial power. This naïve belief is part of our disconnection with reality. The problems we face are structural. The old America is not coming back.

The corporate forces that control the state will never permit real reform. This is the Faustian bargain made between these corporate forces and the Republican and Democratic parties. We will never, under the current system, achieve energy independence. Energy independence would devastate the profits of the oil and gas industry. It would wipe out tens of billions of dollars in weapons contracts, spoil the financial health of a host of private contractors from Halliburton to Blackwater and render obsolete the existence of U.S. Central Command.

There are groups and people who seek to do us harm. The attacks of September 11 will not be the last acts of terrorism on American soil. But the only way to defeat terrorism is to isolate terrorists within their own societies, to mount cultural and propaganda wars, to discredit their ideas, to seek concurrence even with those defined as our enemies. Force, while a part of this battle, is rarely necessary. The 2001 attacks that roused our fury and unleashed the "war on terror" also unleashed a worldwide revulsion against al-Qaida and Islamic terrorism, including throughout the Muslim world, where I was working as a reporter at the time. If we had had the courage to be vulnerable, to build on this empathy rather than drop explosive ordinance all over the Middle East, we would be far safer and more secure today. If we had reached out for allies and partners instead of arrogantly assuming that American military power would restore our sense of invulnerability and mitigate our collective humiliation, we would have done much to defeat al-Qaida. But we did not. We demanded that all kneel before us. And in our ruthless and indiscriminate use of violence and illegal wars of occupation, we resurrected the very forces that we could, under astute leadership, have marginalized. We forgot that fighting terrorism is a war of shadows, an intelligence war, not a conventional war. We forgot that, as strong as we may be militarily, no nation, including us, can survive isolated and alone.

Barack Obama has shown that he is as capable of doublespeak as any other politician when he announced an end to the war in Iraq. Combat troops are to be pulled out of Iraq by August 2010, he said, but some 50,000 to 70,000 occupation troops will remain behind. Someone should let the Iraqis know the distinction. I doubt any soldier or marine in Iraq will notice much difference. Many combat units will simply be relabeled as noncombat units. And what about our small army of well-paid contractors and mercenaries? Will Dyncorp, Bechtel, Blackwater (which changed its name to Xe), all of whom have made fortunes off the war, pack up and go home? What about the three large super-bases, dozens of smaller military outposts, and our imperial city, the Green Zone? Will American corporations give up their lucrative control of Iraqi oil?

The occupation of Iraq will not be disrupted. Lies and deception, which launched the war in the first place, are being employed by the Obama White House to maintain it. This is not a withdrawal. It is occupation lite. Obama has allocated nearly a trillion dollars in defense-related spending and the continuation of our doomed imperial projects in Afghanistan and Iraq, where military planners now estimate that troops will remain "for the next fifteen to twenty years." Obama has expanded the war in Afghanistan, including the use of drones sent on cross-border bombing runs into Pakistan that have doubled the number of civilians killed over the past three months. And as long as American troops are on Iraqi and Afghan soil the wars will grind on, the death toll on each side will continue to mount, and we will remain a lightning rod for hatred and rage in the Middle East.

The occupations of Iraq and Afghanistan have not promoted U.S. security or stability in the Middle East; instead, they have furthered the spread of failed states, increased authoritarianism, and unleashed savage violence. They have opened up voids of lawlessness, including in the tribal areas of Pakistan, where our real enemies can operate and plot against us. These occupations have scuttled the art of diplomacy and mocked the rule of law. We have become an outlaw state intent on creating more outlaw states. The occupations have, finally, empowered Iran, as well as Russia and China, which gleefully watch our self-immolation. And, in the end, we cannot win these wars. We will withdraw all our troops in an orderly manner or see these occupations collapse in an orgy of bloodshed.

Iraq no longer exists as a unified country. The experiment that was Iraq, the cobbling together of disparate and antagonistic patches of the Ottoman Empire by the victorious powers in the wake of the First World War, belongs to the history books. It will never come back. The Kurds have set up a de facto state in the north, the Shiites control most of the south and the center of the country is a battleground. There are two million Iraqis who have fled their homes and are internally displaced. Another two million have left the country, most to Syria and Jordan, which now has the largest number of refugees per capita of any country on Earth. An Oxfam report estimates that one in three Iraqis are in need of emergency aid, but the chaos and violence is so widespread that assistance is impossible. Iraq is in a state of anarchy. The American occupation forces are one more source of terror tossed into the caldron of suicide bombings, mercenary armies, militias, explosions, ambushes, kidnappings, and mass executions. And perhaps as many as 1.2 million Iraqis are dead because of what we have done.

It was not supposed to turn out like this. Remember all those visions of a democratic Iraq, visions peddled by the White House and fatuous pundits like Thomas Friedman and the gravel-voiced morons who pollute our airwaves on CNN and Fox News? They assured us that the war would be a cakewalk. Our troops would be greeted as liberators. Democracy would seep out over the borders of Iraq to usher in a new Middle East. The oil revenues would pay for the reconstruction. Now, struggling to salvage their credibility, they blame the debacle on poor planning and mismanagement.

There are probably about ten thousand Arabists in the United States—people who have lived for prolonged periods in the Middle East and speak Arabic. At the inception of the war you could not have rounded up more than about a dozen who thought it was a good idea. And I include all the Arabists in the State Department, the Pentagon, and the intelligence community. Anyone who had spent significant time in Iraq, as I have, knew this would not work. The war was not doomed because Donald Rumsfeld and Paul Wolfowitz did not do sufficient planning for the occupation. The war was doomed, period. It never had a chance. And even a cursory knowledge of Iraqi history and politics made this apparent.

This is not to deny the stupidity of the occupation. The disbanding of the Iraqi army; the ham-fisted attempt to install the crook and, it now turns out, Iranian spy Ahmed Chalabi in power; the firing of all Baathist public officials, including university professors, primary schoolteachers, nurses, and doctors; the failure to secure Baghdad and the vast weapons depots from looters; allowing heavily armed American units to blast their way through densely populated neighborhoods, giving the insurgency its most potent recruiting tool—all ensured a swift descent into chaos. But Iraq would not have held together even if we had been spared the gross incompetence of the Bush administration. Saddam Hussein, like the more benign dictator Josip Broz Tito in the former Yugoslavia, understood that the glue that held the country together was the secret police.

Iraq, however, is different from Yugoslavia. Iraq has oil—lots of it. It also has water in a part of the world that is running out of water. And the dismemberment of Iraq will unleash a mad scramble for dwindling resources that will include the involvement of neighboring states. The Kurds, like the Shiites and the Sunnis, know that if they do not get their hands on water resources and oil, they cannot survive. But Turkey, Syria, and Iran have no intention of allowing the Kurds to create a viable enclave. A functioning Kurdistan in northern Iraq means rebellion by the repressed Kurdish minorities in these countries. The Kurds, orphans of the twentieth century who have been repeatedly sold out by every ally they ever had, including the United States, will be crushed. The possibility that Iraq will become a Shiite state, run by clerics allied with Iran, terrifies the Arab world. Turkey, as well as Saudi Arabia, the United States, and Israel, would most likely keep the conflict going by arming Sunni militias. This anarchy could end with foreign forces, including Iran and Turkey, carving up the battered carcass of Iraq. No matter what happens, many, many Iraqis are going to die. And it is our fault.

The U.S. agreement with Iraq, known as SOFA, or status of forces agreement, calls for all U.S. forces to be out of Iraq by the end of December 2011. But this seems very unlikely. The Pentagon has, despite the SOFA, built its long-range planning around the assumption that troops will be based in Iraq long after 2011. The U.S.-Iraq agreement (which was ratified by the Iraqi parliament but never brought to the U.S. Senate for ratification, as mandated by the Constitution) calls for a national referendum to be held in Iraq during the summer of

2009. Iraqis will supposedly be able to approve or reject the agree-ment. The some fifty U.S. bases in Iraq are, under the agreement, to be turned over to the Iraqis.

Will Obama defy the results of a referendum and ram the contin-ued occupation down the throats of Iraqi voters? It certainly looks like it. Of course, all this will be handled, I suspect, by having our client government in Baghdad "request" that we remain, making an even greater farce of our public commitment to democracy.

The neoconservatives—and the liberal interventionists, who still serve as the neocons' useful idiots when it comes to Iran and Afghanistan—have learned nothing. They talk about hitting Iran and maybe even Pakistan with air strikes. They applaud Obama's call to send an additional thirty thousand troops to Afghanistan. They cheer on the expansion of imperial slaughter in the Middle East, blind to the awful consequences. Strikes on Iran would ensure a regional conflict. Such an action has the potential of drawing Israel into war—especially if Iran retaliates for any air strikes by hitting Is-rael, as I would expect Tehran to do. Widening the war into Pakistan could turn Pakistan into the first radical Islamic regime with nuclear weapons. And the expanded war in Afghanistan will make Iraq look like a picnic. There are still many in the United States who cling to the doctrine of preemptive war, a doctrine that the post–Second World War Nuremberg laws define as a criminal "war of aggression."

The wars in Iraq and Afghanistan grind forward with their terrible human toll. The mounting bombing raids and widespread detentions of Afghans are rapidly turning Afghanistan into the mirror image of Iraq. But these very real events, which will have devastating conse-quences over the next few months and years, are largely ignored by us.

As the conflict in Afghanistan has intensified, so has the indis-criminate use of air strikes, including one in August 2008, which took place in the Azizabad area of Shindand district in Herat province. The air strike was carried out after Afghan and coalition troops were ambushed by insurgents while on a patrol targeting a known Taliban commander in Herat, the U.S. military said. Hundreds of Afghans, shouting anti-U.S. slogans, staged angry street protests in Azizabad to protest the killings, and the even the normally compliant Afghan president Hamid Karzai condemned American air strikes.

The United Nations and the Associated Press have compiled statistics showing that U.S. and Afghan troops are now killing twice the number of Afghan civilians as the Taliban. And the civilians killed in fighting between insurgents and security forces in Afghanistan has soared by two-thirds over the past year.

Ghulam Azrat, the director of the middle school in Azizabad, in a scene we should remember, said he collected 60 bodies after the August 2008 bombing. "We put the bodies in the main mosque," he told the Associated Press by phone, sometimes pausing to collect himself as he wept. "Most of these dead bodies were children and women. It took all morning to collect them."

Azrat said enraged villagers threw stones at Afghan soldiers who arrived and tried to give out food and clothes. He said the soldiers fired into the crowd and wounded eight people, including one child. "The people were very angry," he said. "They told the soldiers, 'We don't need your food, we don't need your clothes. We want our children. We want our relatives. Can you give [them] to us? You cannot, so go away.'"

The war in Afghanistan has not gone well. Karzai's government in Kabul controls little territory outside the capital. And our attempt to buy off tribes with money and even weapons has collapsed, with most tribal groups slipping back into the arms of the Taliban insurgents. The eight-year war in Afghanistan has seen the

Taliban re-emerge from the ashes. An additional thirty thousand troops will do little to prop up the detested and corrupt regime of Karzai. The U.N. estimates that the Taliban is now raking in $300 million a year from the expanded poppy trade to fund the resistance. The Taliban controlled about 75 percent of Afghan territory when we invaded eight years ago. It has recaptured about half of the country since its initial defeat, and its reach has expanded to the outskirts of major cities such as Kabul and Kandahar. The Taliban assaults are increasingly sophisticated and well coordinated. And the Taliban is exacting a rising toll on coalition troops. Soldiers and marines are now dying at a faster rate in Afghanistan than in Iraq. Clashes now take place less than twenty miles from the capital, Kabul. Hundreds of militants, aided by suicide bombers, have carried out attacks against some of the largest U.S. bases in the country. And even downtown ministries in Kabul have been briefly taken over by armed Afghan insurgents.

Al-Qaida, which we have also inadvertently resurrected, is thriving. It has plenty of recruits. It runs training facilities. It carries out attacks in London, Madrid, Iraq, and now Afghanistan, which did not experience suicide bombings until December 2005. Al-Qaida has moved on. But we remain stuck, confused, and lashing about wildly like a wounded and lumbering beast.

Do the cheerleaders for an expanded war in Afghanistan know any history? Have they studied what happened to the Soviets, who lost fifteen thousand Red Army soldiers between 1979 and 1988, or even the British in the nineteenth century? Do they remember why we went into Afghanistan? It was, we were told, to hunt down Osama bin Laden, who is now apparently in Pakistan. Has anyone asked what our end goal is in Afghanistan? Is it nation-building? Have we declared war on the Taliban? Or is this simply the forever war on terror?

But our interests, or the interests of those we occupy, are not important. There are huge corporations who are making a lot of money off the wars in Iraq and Afghanistan. Obama seems intent on not impeding the profits. We should have known better than to trust the Democrats after they rode to power in Congress in 2006 on an antiwar platform and then continued to fund these wars and approve increased troop levels in Iraq and Afghanistan.

George W. Bush shredded, violated, or absented America from its obligations under international law. He launched an illegal war in Iraq based on fabricated evidence we now know had been discredited even before it was made public. He is guilty, in short, of what in legal circles is known as the "crime of aggression." And if we as citizens do not hold him accountable for these crimes and demand an end to these wars, we will be complicit in the codification of a new world order, one that will have terrifying consequences. For a world without treaties, statutes, and laws is a world where any nation, from a rogue nuclear state to a great imperial power, will be able to invoke its domestic laws to annul its obligations to others. This new order will undo five decades of international cooperation—largely put in place by the United States—and thrust us into a Hobbesian nightmare.

We must not allow international laws and treaties—ones that set minimum standards of behavior and provide a framework for competing social, political, economic, and religious groups and interests to resolve differences—to be discarded. The exercise of power without law is tyranny. And the consequences of our continued violation of the law, the creation of legal black holes that can swallow us along with those outside our gates, run in a direct line from the White House to Abu Ghraib and Guantánamo.

Bush—we now know from the leaked Downing Street memo—fabricated a legal pretext for war. He decided to charge Saddam Hussein with the material breach of the resolution passed in the wake of the 1991 Gulf War. He had no evidence that Saddam Hussein was in breach of this resolution. And so he and his advisers manufactured reports of weapons of mass destruction and disseminated them to a frightened and manipulated press and public. In short, he lied to us and to the rest of the world. There are hundreds of thousands, perhaps over a million, who have been killed and maimed in Iraq because of a war that has no legal justification, a war waged in violation of international law.

We do not have the power or the knowledge, nor do we have the right under international law, to occupy Iraq and Afghanistan. It is not for us to debate the terms of the occupation. We divert ourselves in our dotage and decline with images and slogans that perpetuate fantasies about our own invulnerability, our own might, our own goodness. We are preoccupied by national trivia that pass for news, even as the wolf pants at our door. These illusions blind us. We cannot see ourselves as others see us. We do not know who we are or what we have become. "We had fed the heart on fantasies," wrote William Butler Yeats, "the heart's grown brutal from the fare."

We are propelled forward not by logic or compassion or understanding but by fear. We have created and live in a world where violence is the primary form of communication. We have become the company we keep. Much of the world—certainly the Muslim world, one-fifth of the world's population, most of whom are not Arab—sees us through the prism of Iraq, Afghanistan, and Palestine. We are igniting the dispossessed, the majority of humanity who live on less than two dollars a day. And until we dismantle our imperial projects and abide by international law we will continue to unleash a terrible destruction on others and ensure our self-immolation.

Dahr Jamail's human portrait of the men and women who turned away from the project of empire should serve as a beacon. These returning veterans know the essence of war, which is death, and have been maimed by the trauma of industrial warfare. They have found, despite their pain, the moral courage to recover their conscience. The truth they tell demands that we find the courage to make our nation accountable for the crimes committed in our name.

INTRODUCTION

As an independent reporter working at different points during the first six years of the occupation of Iraq, I had some of the most disturbing experiences of my life. The U.S. military, which I had been raised to admire, had for me morphed into the enemy. Reporting from the Iraqi perspective on a brutal, chaotic, violent occupation that was destroying millions of lives with the indiscriminate randomness of a hurricane, my sense of outrage had transformed into an anger that I often aimed at those same soldiers I had admired as a child.

This feeling of being violated and betrayed increased with my continued coverage of widespread military operations; the use of white phosphorous against civilians in Fallujah; the collective punishment of entire cities by cutting off their water, electricity, and medical supplies; the widely prevalent torture of Iraqis; and ongoing home raids. To date, the occupation has managed to displace one out of every six Iraqis from their homes, and has, directly or indirectly, killed more than 1.2 million people.[1]

I felt a solidarity with the Iraqis because I had no difficulty imagining how I would feel if my country had been invaded and occupied. My direct experience of this extremely unethical behavior, very common among those in the U.S. military in Iraq, and my rage at the heedless and deliberate devastation I saw them wreak upon the people of Iraq, fueled my rage and transformed my childhood heroes into beasts. I was dehumanized by the occupation.

On returning home, in the course of delivering lectures and presenting slideshows and providing testimony at various forums, I started to meet soldiers who had deployed to Iraq. As I got to know them, I was surprised to discover within them a familiar anguish. I found the same survivor guilt, the ongoing burden of living a normal life without while carrying the knowledge within that Iraq is burning and her people are struggling to survive on a daily basis. I could see in their eyes the same angst that I felt—the utter inability to reconcile what we had seen in Iraq with the fact of our own relatively secure existence in a country whose government was responsible for causing irreparable damage there.

This compelled me to dig deeper. I realized a desire to meet more of these veterans who had been placed in an untenable situation and examine the roots and implications of their resistance to what was happening in Iraq. Through conversations, I learned quickly that there was active resistance within the ranks to what the troops were being ordered to do in Iraq.

I found men and women to interview who had spent time in Iraq doing patrols, working on bases, running supply convoys, and even acting as snipers. Others worked as intelligence operatives gathering information by spying on cell-phone conversations. Along the way, talking with these men and women, I realized the bond I shared with them had become, in many ways, as strong as my bond with the Iraqis I interviewed abroad, a bond that inspires me to risk my life to work there time and time again.

While there is a widespread, mostly subterranean resistance movement in the military today, admittedly it is not yet nearly on the scale of that which played a critical role in bringing an end to the Vietnam War. More than ever, due to the faltering U.S. economy, people are joining or staying in the military because of financial necessity, despite the risks this decision entails.

In fall 2008, I spoke with David Cortright, a Vietnam War veteran who has served as consultant or adviser to agencies of the United Nations, international think tanks, and the foreign ministries of Canada, Japan, and several European countries. He has authored sixteen books, including *Soldiers in Revolt* (Haymarket Books, 2005), which is about the massive GI resistance movement against the Vietnam War. I was interested to know how he viewed the growing resistance movement in the military today. Cortright said he feels soldiers are not being as overt today when speaking out against what is happening to the military because "there is much more to lose now by being punished by the brass. I see that as the most fundamental change—the nature of the military today as an all-volunteer force, economic conscription."[2]

Another factor that serves to dampen GI resistance today is that nearly 50 percent of those serving are married, and many of them have children to support. This, according to Cortright, constricts the nature and scope of the movement. Another key difference between Vietnam and current-era GIs, he feels, is that today when someone joins the military, they tend to stay with their unit for their career. "Now there is much emphasis on unit loyalty and solidarity. You bond with these people, and these social horizontal linkages have an effect of binding people to each other within the military community … I talk with lots of guys who hate the war, yet they go back for a second or third tour out of their duty to support their fellow soldiers. They think they are helping their buddies." That has been my experience, too. I have had occasion to speak with veterans and active-duty soldiers totally opposed to the occupation who nevertheless agree to redeploy for the sake of their "buddies."

Cortright also underscores the lack of substantial civilian support as a reason for today's GI antiwar movement not being on par with the Vietnam-era movement. "During Vietnam there wasn't a real GI movement until 1968, so it took a few years, but that was supported by civilians who made enormous sacrifices to help them. At the time we had a couple of legal defense organizations set up to defend GIs which don't exist today.[3] Then we had groups like the Young Socialist Alliance, among others, that would back those of us who spoke up in those days—we knew we could get access to lawyers."

However, a network is gradually building up, of groups tasked with helping those in the military who choose to resist. One group, the Military Law Task Force, which is a successor to a similar group from the Vietnam era, is an example. Cortright is convinced that "though we haven't seen as widespread a phenomenon as during Vietnam," there is no denying that resistance exists and is spreading. "We've also seen individual cases of resistance, and the work that many veterans have done in reaching out to active-duty military personnel has been successful. This is another expression of the underlying sentiment in the military that the war is illegal and unjust."

With each passing day, more soldiers are speaking out against the occupation, and are receiving support from civilians. This was a key component of the resistance during Vietnam, says Cortright. "People in the military have great authority and legitimacy in speaking to the broader public in the political arena, and the more we as civilians can support them in doing this, the more effective they will be in bringing awareness to the movement and the need to end the war."

Of course, times have changed. During Vietnam, there was one main Winter Soldier event—when Vietnam veterans returning from the front lines held a weekend press conference in Detroit on January 31, 1971, to tell the media what was really happening in the war and why it should end immediately. "Winter soldiers" is a reference to what Thomas Paine, America's founding father, called people who stand up for the soul of their country, even in its darkest hours.

Today, we've seen several of these Winter Soldier events, sponsored by a group called Iraq Veterans Against the War (IVAW). Such events are spreading across the country, as well as internationally. By 2010, Winter Soldier events had occurred in Maryland, Washington, Florida, Wisconsin, California, Illinois, New York, Oregon, Texas, Massachusetts, and Washington D.C., Georgia, and Germany.

During the writing of this book, I was consistently and deeply moved and awed by the courage and fortitude of the veterans who were taking a stand, despite the long odds against them and the brute force the military is able to exert upon them for doing so. I learned from them that, as perpetrators, their post-traumatic stress disorder (PTSD) is far more incurable and difficult to treat than that of people like me who had only witnessed the horrors they had been instrumental in inflicting. They have to live with the consciousness of having killed Iraqis, participated in their torture, raided their homes with women sobbing in the background.

Surpassed only by average Iraqis, members of the U.S. military who have been deployed to Iraq are paying the highest price for the occupation—both while in Iraq and when they come back home. They are now part of an unfortunate, tragic segment of U.S. society that has been maligned and tossed aside, neglected, forgotten. Today, more U.S. war veterans are killing themselves than are dying in open combat while overseas. One thousand veterans who are receiving care from the Department of Veterans Affairs (VA) are attempting suicide every single month, and eighteen veterans kill themselves daily.[4] Not all of these veterans served in Iraq, but what these figures bode for the future is inconceivable, when we consider that 1.7 million soldiers have so far served in the occupations of Iraq and Afghanistan.[5]

As if surviving their deployment to Iraq or Afghanistan is not enough, upon their return home, soldiers face another battle—to obtain the services they are entitled to receive from the VA. A valid discharge from the military entitles all soldiers to medical care from the agency. In the six months leading up to March 31, 2008, 1,467 veterans died while waiting to learn whether their disability claims were going to be approved by the government.[6] Veterans who appeal a VA decision to deny a disability claim must wait an average of nearly four and a half years for their answer.[7] As of March 25, 2008, 287,790 war veterans from the occupations of Iraq and Afghanistan had filed disability claims with the VA.[8]

These facts partially explain the growing resistance within the military not just against the occupations of Iraq and Afghanistan, but also against the horrendous toll they are taking on troops, who suffer while they serve there and suffer even more upon returning home. Being virtually abandoned by the government they swore an oath to protect and serve often becomes the proverbial last straw for the veterans, forcing them to resort to suicide.

The deeper one digs, the more apparent it becomes that the military is in a state of near collapse. For years now, one retired general after another has appeared in the media to denounce the occupation of Iraq, and to expose what it is doing to destroy the military. With the occupations of Iraq and Afghanistan, more than 565,000 troops have been deployed more than once.[9] By December 2006, it was estimated that 50 percent of troops in Iraq were serving their second tour, and another 25 percent were on their third or fourth tour.[10] A horrific example of how this is affecting soldiers in Iraq occured on May 11, 2009, at 2 p.m. Baghdad time, when a U.S. soldier gunned down five fellow soldiers at a stress-counseling center at a U.S. base in Baghdad. Admiral Mike Mullen, the chairman of the U.S. military's Joint Chiefs of Staff, told reporters at a news conference at the Pentagon that the shootings occured in a place where "individuals were seeking help." Admiral Mullen added, "It does speak to me, though, about the need for us to redouble our efforts, the concern in terms of dealing with the stress … It also speaks to the issue of multiple deployments."[11] The military is so overstretched that troops being redeployed often have traumatic brain injury (TBI) from surviving roadside bombs in previous deployments, and more than 43,000 troops listed as medically unfit have been deployed anyway.[12] Soldiers already diagnosed with PTSD and other severely debilitating mental-health conditions that accompany it are being redeployed as the military dredges up troops to keep enough boots on the ground in Iraq and Afghanistan. By October 2007, the army reported that approximately 12 percent of combat troops in Iraq were coping by taking antidepressants and sleeping pills.[13] By January 2009, the army announced that suicides among U.S. soldiers had risen in the previous year to the highest level in decades. The suicide rate for 2008 was calculated roughly at 20.2 per 100,000 soldiers, which for the first time since the Vietnam War is higher than the adjusted civilian rate.[14] In addition, more active-duty marines committed suicide in 2008 than in any year since the U.S. invasion of Iraq was launched in 2003, at a rate of 16.8 per 100,000 troops.[15]

Prior to the recent and ongoing collapsing of the U.S. economy, which by raising national unemployment has driven more people to join the military, the armed forces were so short of troops that more than 58,000 troops have been "stop-lossed" since September 11,

2001. Under this policy, soldiers who have fulfilled their contracts are frozen into the military and redeployed to Iraq or Afghanistan.[16] Further deepening this crisis, more than a quarter of a million National Guard men and women, who joined the guard to provide aid at home in times of national emergencies such as hurricanes and earthquakes, have been deployed overseas.[17]

Attempting to keep enough boots on the ground for both occupations, on June 22, 2006, the army increased the permissible enlistment age to forty-two, from a previous limit of forty. This follows a previous rise in the age limit from thirty-five to forty in March 2005.[18] By summer 2007, the army had grown so desperate for recruits that it began to recruit indiscriminately in violation of its own criteria. It accepted individuals with health and weight issues, lower academic test scores, and even those with criminal records. By July 2007, the number of incoming soldiers with prior felony arrests or convictions had more than tripled over the previous five years, and in the first half of 2007, the army had accepted an estimated 8,000 recruits with rap sheets.[19] Former army Private Steve Green is one such example. He was awarded a waiver for previous involvement in criminal activity and was found guilty of raping a fourteen-year-old Iraqi girl, Abeer Qasim Hamza al-Janabi, and murdering her and three of her family members in the village of Mahmudiyah.[20]

Economics continues to work in favor of the military, assisted in no small measure by its all-out efforts at recruiting. By October 2008, the Army and Marine Corps had spent nearly $640 million in recruitment bonuses.[21] By the end of 2008, the military was once again making its recruiting goals. As unemployment rises, the military lures the desperate by offering a sure method of obtaining a paycheck. In addition, the military has resorted to a tried and tested tactic of enticing foreigners into the ranks by offering citizenship after service in the military. For example, on March 3, 2009, 251 U.S. soldiers from sixty-five countries became U.S. citizens in a ceremony held in one of Saddam Hussein's old palaces in Baghdad. Since 2004, active-duty immigrant soldiers can apply for citizenship without the normal three-year waiting period and without being inside the United States.[22]

The dramatic change in the political climate of the country following the election of Barack Obama as president, and his promises to bring the troops home, has expectedly caused the population to lose what interest they still retained in Iraq, despite the tardy coverage by the mainstream media. While President Obama promises to bring troops home, he aims to leave behind at least fifty thousand as a "residual" and "training" force indefinitely. The end of either occupation does not seem to be in sight.

Most veterans I spoke with while working on this book feel, despite a large section of the populace being opposed to the occupations of Iraq and Afghanistan, that the consenting majority in the United States has been complicit in pushing U.S. soldiers into an unsustainable position by not doing enough to end the wars. Today antiwar veterans have to muster all the support and resources they can, not only in an attempt to rebuild their lives, but also to affirm and intensify their dual resistance to the ongoing occupations of Iraq and Afghanistan, and to the inherently dehumanizing nature of the U.S. military system.

I have been impressed by the courage and inspired by the persistence of these veterans. I recognize the risk their resistance entails. Their actions jeopardize benefits they have earned, including health care and funds for college, and can even lead to incarceration.

Working on this book has made me privy to the individual as well as collective transformation that has taken place in a section of

the population that is commonly known for its rigidity and subservience to authority. While it was not my initial plan, the voices of
resistance in this work have led me to remain more of an observer in
the book. By often quoting their words at length, I have attempted
to retain the rage, despair, and rawness of their feelings without in-
terjecting my own.

The environment in the United States today is not one that can
support and sustain a GI resistance movement of significant proportions, giving it enough power to directly affect the foreign policy of
the country, as it did so effectively in the Vietnam era. There is much
in the military to prohibit a GI resistance movement from growing
anywhere near the proportion that helped end the U.S. war in Vietnam. Military discipline is much more repressive than in the past,
which makes organizing more difficult. There is less radicalization of
the GI movement, as compared to that in the late 1960s and early
1970s; therefore, passive resistance against the command is more
common than direct resistance. There is a much lower level of political awareness and analysis among soldiers as compared to that during Vietnam, when there were hundreds of underground newspapers
that served to inform troops while criticizing the military apparatus.
The all-volunteer military, rather than a draft, is also responsible for
stifling broader dissent.

Despite these factors, dissent in the ranks is happening on a
daily basis. While overall violence for soldiers in Iraq has dropped,
it is escalating dramatically in Afghanistan, since President Obama
"surged" another thirty thousand troops into that occupation. The
overstretched military is in a state of disrepair, full of demoralized,
bitter soldiers whose reasons for staying in are based on economics
and loyalty to their friends rather than nationalism or patriotism.
These elements, accompanied by the continuing neglect that sol-

Key!

diers experience upon their return home, are driving larger numbers toward dissent.

This is a book about average soldiers and their brave acts of dissent against a system that is betraying them. I decided to focus on the rank-and-file members who actually served in Iraq, rather than those giving the orders from within safe compounds. I believe it is those who have followed the orders who have had to pay the highest price. My main objective in presenting this book is to highlight the reality that oppressed and oppressors alike suffer the dehumanizing effects of military action. For soldiers and war journalists like myself who have lived with this, struggled with PTSD, and reintegrated ourselves into society, a light at the seemingly endless dark tunnel of the U.S. occupations of Iraq and Afghanistan is the possibility of the shifting of these individual acts of resistance into a broader, organized movement toward justice—both in the military and in U.S. foreign policy.

ONE

RESISTANCE IN IRAQ

Dissent starts as simple as saying this is bullshit. Why am I risking my life?
—**Former marine Bryan Casler, who served in Iraq**
during and after the invasion

The first U.S. soldier who served in Iraq to publicly object to the occupation was Staff Sergeant Camilo Mejía, who in early 2004, after five months of frontline combat, refused to fight. He did not redeploy with his unit after a leave in the United States. Mejía was charged with desertion and sentenced to one year in prison, ex parte. In March 2004, he turned himself in to the U.S. military and filed an application for conscientious objector (CO) status. Though his application remains open to this day, he was made to serve nearly nine months in jail after his court martial. It was the intervention of Amnesty International that secured him an early release as a prisoner of conscience.

Mejía discussed his journey of conscience while in and after leaving Iraq in an essay entitled, "Regaining My Humanity":

> I say without any pride that I did my job as a soldier. I commanded
> an infantry squad in combat and we never failed to accomplish our

mission. But those who called me a coward, without knowing it, are also right. I was a coward not for leaving the war, but for having been a part of it in the first place. Refusing and resisting this war was my moral duty, a moral duty that called me to take a principled action. I failed to fulfill my moral duty as a human being and instead I chose to fulfill my duty as a soldier. All because I was afraid. I was terrified, I did not want to stand up to the government and the army, I was afraid of punishment and humiliation. I went to war because at the moment I was a coward, and for that I apologize to my soldiers for not being the type of leader I should have been.[1]

In his book, *Road from ar Ramadi: The Private Rebellion of Staff Sergeant Camilo Mejía: An Iraq War Memoir*, Mejía described various forms of resistance to the occupation, some of a subtle, passive variety, but resistance nonetheless. He has written of the plummeting morale of his fellow soldiers as their time in Iraq dragged on and their prospects of going home "became a flickering light in the Iraqi night." Among regular duties like running patrols, emptying toilets and other mundane tasks, he writes:

We also had to provide personnel to work as radio-watch runners at the company's command post. The runners would deliver messages to people in the company whenever they couldn't be reached by radio. Although they were told otherwise, the runners used their post to gain late-night access to the Internet ... Runners could also, on occasion, avoid going out on missions. These privileges made radio watch a favored task throughout the company. Soldiers with minor injuries were often given radio duty, and there were a number of people who always seemed to be posted to the radio room, much to the disdain of the rest of the company.[2]

This routine cycled for three days, thus everyone was doing it, but as far as the roster went "some people were malingering." Mejía writes, "Ironically enough, one of the most humanistic members of my squad was one of them. He was always coming up with a pain or some other pretext to stay back for these duties. There were so many people doing it, and others who were abusing the system. It was hard to come up with a specific number, but maybe three or four people were regularly using it to avoid missions."[3]

From our safe locations this may seem like inexcusable dereliction of duty, but in the course of my interviews and discussions with war vets and active-duty soldiers I realized how difficult it is for team leaders to maintain troop morale in the face of obvious failed policy. It is even more difficult to contain acts of dissent, particularly of a subterranean nature.

"Search and destroy" was one of the principal tactics used by the U.S. military in Vietnam. The idea was for ground troops to enter hostile territory to locate and destroy the enemy forces and withdraw immediately. As the unwinnable war continued, demoralized soldiers took to "search and avoid" missions instead, at times as a means to avoid certain death and at other times to protest against pointless bloodshed. In an odd repetition of history, another generation of American soldiers has revived the practice of search-and-avoid missions in Iraq. Among several factors responsible for this is how the military is understaffed, undertrained, and ill-equipped to do its job.

Eli Wright, an active-duty soldier with the Tenth Mountain Division in Watertown, New York, on the outskirts of Fort Drum, said, "Oh yeah, we did search-and-avoid missions all the time. We would go to the end of our patrol route and set up camp on top of a bridge and use it as an over-watch position. It was a common tactic. We would just sit there with our binoculars and observe rather than sweep. We would call in radio checks every hour and report that we were doing sweeps. We would hang out, listen to music, smoke cigarettes, and pretend."

Former sergeant Josh Simpson, of Washington State, joined the military in 2001, and served as a counterintelligence agent in Mosul, Iraq, from September 2004 until September 2005. He spoke of many variations of search-and-avoid tactics adopted by U.S. military personnel in Iraq. "When I was out there, unit members would go and play soccer with Iraqi kids instead of going on patrol. I knew soldiers who learned to simulate vehicular movement on the computer screen, to create the impression of being on patrol. So in headquarters, where I worked as well, they would see the vehicles going on patrol when no vehicles were being moved, except on a computer screen in some Stryker somewhere."

While it was not his primary reason for not patrolling, Simpson supported this kind of resistance on principle because he believed that Iraqis were right in using armed resistance against the occupation. "Any American soldier will tell you, even the most right-wing fascists will tell you, if someone invaded my country, I'd be doing the exact same thing that the Iraqis are doing. And that's across the board. I don't think you can get anyone to say, 'No, I wouldn't be doing that.'"

For the low morale his fellow soldiers and he experienced in Iraq, Simpson blames the nature of their work, which involved the entire process from collecting intelligence to going on raids to interrogating the people arrested during the raids. He sums up the situation succinctly,

I pretty much saw the whole thing and it is fucked up. It doesn't make any sense. You realize that the whole system is flawed and if that is flawed, then obviously the whole war is flawed. If the basic premise of the war is flawed, definitely the intelligence system that is supposed to lead us to victory is flawed. What that implies is that victory is not even a possibility.

We would raid people's houses, and 95 percent of the time fail to find the remotest trace that could connect them to any sort of terrorist actions, but I would have to come back and interrogate these people. We are taught to figure out when people are being deceptive. I would know that the people I interrogated were honest and straightforward. I knew they knew nothing about terrorism, that they were barely surviving, terrified of what was happening, without us terrorizing them further. But I would be told, 'You go down there and'—this is a serious quote—'put the screws to them.' You know what I mean? I was repeatedly told, 'The reason they are not talking to you is not because they are innocent or because they don't know anything, it's because you are being too nice to them. You gotta go down there and be meaner to them. Treat them like shit.' And I was a soldier, so I would go down there and be meaner to them and shittier to them. I'm not really proud of my actions as an interrogator in Iraq for the most part.

On completing his active-duty contract of five years, Simpson joined the reserves, thinking he would not be deployed to Iraq again. His reserve unit near Olympia, Washington, however, transferred him to a unit in Texas pending deployment to Iraq. In the interim, he tried to educate himself by reading about the United States and imperialism. Noam Chomsky's books *The Umbrella of U.S. Power* and *Rogue States: The Rule of Force in World Affairs* convinced him that he needed to get out of the military. "I thought to myself, I can't do this shit anymore. I'm sick. First of all it's bad for me mentally. I'm doing something I loathe. Second, I'm participating in an organization that I wish to resist in every way I can."

After consulting with some GI rights activists, Simpson decided to stop attending drill. Once his unit was activated for duty, this would make him absent without leave (AWOL). "So I just stopped showing up for drill, didn't call my unit, didn't give them any reason for it. I changed my telephone number and they did not have my address. I don't know if technically I'm still in the reserves. I don't know what my situation is, but I don't really care either. If I go to jail, I go to jail. I'd rather go to jail than go to Iraq."

The military defines AWOL for more than thirty days as desertion, after which period the individual is discharged from the military. Since March 2003, there has been an 80 percent increase in desertions, as compared to the preceding five-year period, 1998–2003.[4] Of late it has been even higher. Thousands of soldiers have deserted the army alone (not including other branches of the military) since the invasion of Iraq was launched.[5]

During fall 2007, I met Phil Aliff, an active-duty soldier with the Tenth Mountain Division stationed at Fort Drum in upstate New York. He had been part of the mission to help the Iraqi Army "stand up" in the Abu Ghraib area, an extremely volatile and anti-occupation section of Iraq. His platoon, he revealed, had been operating independently. The Iraqis that it was supposedly training to take charge of the security situation in the area seldom appeared. "I never came across an Iraqi unit that was able to operate on its own. The only reason we were replaced by an Iraqi Army unit on occasion was for publicity."

Aliff explained,

During my stints in Fallujah and in the Abu Ghraib area of western Baghdad between August 2005 and July 2006, we probably ran three hundred patrols. Most of the men in my platoon were just in from combat tours in Afghanistan, and morale was incredibly low. Recurring hits by roadside bombs had demoralized us to such an extent that we decided the only way we could avoid being blown up was to stop driving around all the time. So every other day we would find an open field and park, and call our base every hour to tell them we were searching for weapons caches in the fields and doing weapons patrols and everything was going fine. All our enlisted people had grown disenchanted with our chain of command.

Geoff Millard had served nine years in the New York Army National Guard. For a year from October 2004, he worked under a general at a tactical operations center in Iraq. Part of his duty entailed reporting "significant actions," or SIGACTS, the military term to describe an attack on its forces. Although he monitored highly explosive areas like Baquba, Tikrit, and Samarra, he says,

We had units that never called in SIGACTS. When I was there two years ago, there were at least five companies that never had SIGACTS. The only way to explain this was to accept that "search and avoids" have been going on there for a long time. One of my buddies is in Baghdad right now and we e-mail all the time. He just told me that nearly each day they pull into a parking lot, drink soda, and shoot at the cans. They pay Iraqi kids to bring them things and spread the word that they are not doing anything and to please just leave them alone.

It is understandable when senior war vets talk of dissent and resistance. However, I was more than a little perplexed at the countless instances I heard of resistance on the ground from young, first-time soldiers. Cliff Hicks, who served in Iraq from October 2003 to August 2004 believes,

Search and avoid, yeah, we were doing that I think before it had a name. When we were doing it, we didn't know it was GI resistance. The best thing is that they are not possible without a senior NCO [noncommissioned officer] or staff sergeant. Our platoon sergeant, an E7 [military pay grade], was with us and he knew our patrols were bullshit, just riding around to get blown up. We were at Camp Victory, at Baghdad International Airport. A lot of the time we'd leave the main gate and come right back in another gate to the base where there's a big PX [post exchange, the shopping area on a military base]. They had a nice mess hall, and a Burger King. The BK is where we wanted to go and to the PX and look at DVDs and dirty magazines. We'd leave one guy at the Humvees to call in every hour, and we would spend the full eight hours doing this. We were just sick and tired of going out on these stupid patrols.

In the course of my investigations, I came across some innovative avoidance tactics. Marine Bryan Casler of the infantry was deployed to Iraq at the time of its invasion in 2003. After serving in Afghanistan from 2004 to 2005, he was posted in Iraq. He disclosed,

There were times we would go out there to fix a radio because it had been down for hours. It was purposeful, so we did not have to deal with the bullshit from higher. In reality we would go so that we could just chill out there, have maybe one person on lookout and let the rest of the squad get some much-needed rest ... Then it becomes mutual and people start covering for each other. I think everyone knows what the hell's going on. A big thing used to be squads putting up in some Iraqi's house for a day or two, just going there and staying. They insert themselves in a house covertly in order to watch a neighborhood without anyone knowing that they were there. But it is really not about watching, it is about sleeping. Hopefully the squad is well-accepted in the family. Sometimes they even make friends. A few soldiers keep watch, the rest of the squad catch up on sleep and relax for a change.

According to Casler,

There was nothing to be done, no progress to be made there. Dissent starts as simple as saying this is bullshit. Why am I risking my life? First off, marines always get crapped on, and then the infantry gets crapped on ... Our constant refrain was, why are we doing this? All the problems we are facing in Iraq become internalized because people are frustrated but unable to do anything about it. Squabbles and other interpersonal conflicts start happening. The reason I mention this is that it can no longer be ignored that people are just fed up with the situation over there. There is no mission, you are just surviving from day to day with this thought, let us just get home from the deployment, and until that can happen, let us keep our lives as civil as possible. So people end up deciding there just isn't a good enough reason to go out on a mission. It is not worth my sacrifice, not worth my guys' sacrifice. I'm going to declare I'm setting out on it, I'm going to call it in over the radio, but I'm going to sit here and we are going to chill in this house for the next however long.

Another infantryman, Ronn Cantu, served in Diyala province for a year, in 2004, and was redeployed in December 2006 to serve in and around Baghdad, for much of the time running supply convoys.

On my second tour I was going on search-and-avoid missions. The patrols wouldn't go up and down the streets like they were supposed to, they would just go to a friendly compound with the Iraqi police or the Kurdish peshmerga [Kurdish militia] and stay at their compound and drink tea until it was time to go back to the base … A more routine occurrence was for our commander to order us out on patrol but not inform the patrol leader. We would wait where we were told, on time, in the proper uniform ready to go, but because the patrol leader would not turn up, about 50 percent of the time we never went on that patrol. So that wasn't bad. And we never called that patrol leader to come pick us up. We kind of accepted that as fate. Like, whoops, they forgot about us, we're not going out, no big deal. We didn't care.

Technology has aided these acts of resistance. Seth Manzel, presently in the Individual Ready Reserve (IRR) in Washington State, had joined the army for economic reasons. Between November 2004 and September 2005, he drove Stryker vehicles in the northern cities of Tal Afar and Mosul. He managed to avoid running patrols through computer tampering. "I'm not trying to be an apologist for all the horrible things that happened there," he told me, "but if you are there and you intend on surviving, then you need to do certain things. And those things aren't always within regulations, and they are not always pleasant or legal. It is just the situation you are put into. When I was a driver, I was extremely aggressive. I ran cars off the road constantly. It was not the right thing to do, but it was the right thing to do to live."

After his vehicle was destroyed by another Stryker, Manzel became a dismounted machine gunner. He claims his resistance to the occupation grew in direct proportion to the Iraqi resistance and not because of any high-minded ideals. He insists,

No one wants to be the last guy to die for his unit, and it got to that point where it was pretty obvious that if we did our job, that is what we would be. It was better to just go and hide somewhere. Mosul was a dangerous area, and became more so toward the end when we were constantly getting in firefights. I was a vehicle commander at that time. So we would go and drop the dismounted people at some house with an air conditioner, where they could kick in a door and hang out and drink tea with those people, while we would proceed with the vehicles and bide time out of visible range.

Manzel, like Simpson, had figured a way to fabricate on-screen the movement of their patrol, and thereby run virtual missions.

Sometimes if they called us up to go and do something, we would swiftly send online reports to show that we were headed in that direction. We would manually move our icon on the map, to the location where we were being ordered to go, and we then move it back and forth to simulate real-time patrolling. And ours was not an isolated case—everyone did it. Everyone would go and hide somewhere from time to time. It may not have been as regular as in our case, but everyone did it because the workload was just too much to handle and we were all burnt out.

◆   ◆   ◆

Once I had thrown in my lot with the people of the occupied country and witnessed them being treated inhumanely by my own country-folk in uniform, it was never easy for me to sympathize with the latter. The lines have blurred somewhat in recent times. As I listen to the experiences of veterans and active-duty soldiers I am forced to appreciate their unenviable situation, their dilemmas, and the constraints placed upon them in a life-threatening situation. While this reversal has deprived me of a legitimate target for my rage about an unjust war, it has done more to heal me than all my PTSD counseling did.

At another level, my anger toward the establishment intensified and grew exponentially as I continued to discover how callously the men and women in uniform had been exposed with insufficient gear and inadequate training. A 26-year-old medic, Wright, who was stationed in Ramadi from September 2003 until September 2004, said, "Our vehicles had canvas doors and we would put sandbags on the floors. By the end of our tour, we were bolting any metal we could find onto our Humvees. Everyone was doing this. We did not get armored Humvees until much later, until after we left." From Nathan Lewis of the 214th Field Artillery Brigade, I learned, "We never received any training for much of what we were expected to do. We had a white phosphorous mortar round that cooked off in the back of one of our trucks because we loaded that with some other ammo. We were never trained on how to handle it the right way."

Yet others were forced to question the occupation on legal and ethical grounds. Through the opaque layers of conventional dutifulness, some soldiers began to sense that the invasion of Iraq violated the Geneva Conventions, and, by implication, the Constitution of America,[6] since the United States is a signatory to the Geneva Conventions.

◆   ◆   ◆

Soldiers I interviewed described cases of outright refusal from units in Iraq to follow orders. Perhaps the most famous of these occurred on October 13, 2004, when army reservists refused to drive a convoy of fuel tankers through hostile territory because their vehicles lacked armor plates. It was nothing short of a suicide mission to enter the area in damaged trucks without armor plating and without a combat escort. The refusal had led to claims of a mutiny. Specialist Peter Sullivan told a reporter, "I was convinced it would have been a death sentence," which is why he and his platoon, stationed in Tallil, had refused to carry out the order. The eighteen reservists in Sullivan's platoon, the 343rd Quartermaster Company, had unanimously agreed to face disciplinary measures rather than follow orders.[7]

The ordeal began when the platoon's commanding officer ordered the group to deliver fuel to Taji, a city two hundred miles from their base. Their unarmored tanker trucks were in dire need of repairs. The fuel they were to transport had already been refused by another base because it was contaminated. In addition, the convoy was not to be accompanied by the usual armed escort. Sergeant Larry McCook, a member of the platoon, told his wife later that the trucks were simply unsafe for the mission.[8]

In the aftermath of this refusal, the soldiers were confined in tents outside their regular barracks, under armed guard. During their detention, other soldiers helped to sneak out information so that the detained soldiers' families in the United States could be updated on their situation. Ultimately, the army chose not to court-martial the soldiers, and all were returned to active-duty status by November 11, less than a month after their action. Upon their return to the United States, members of the company were lauded as heroes for refusing an order they believed would have led to members of their unit being killed or maimed.

This first recorded refusal of a combat order clearly shook the brass in Iraq. Brigadier General James Chambers called a press conference in Baghdad to clarify that the mutiny was "a single event that is confined to a small group of individuals." But the refusal, as it turned out, was not unique.

The Second Platoon, Charlie Company, stationed in the Adhamiya district of northeastern Baghdad, had lost many men in the eleven months since their initial deployment. After an improvised explosive device (IED, roadside bomb) attack killed five more of their soldiers, the members of the platoon held a meeting and admitted that it was no longer possible for them to function professionally. Concerned that their anger could touch off a massacre of Iraqi civilians, they decided instead to stage a revolt against their commanders on July 18, 2007.

Kelly Kennedy, the medical reporter for the *Military Times*, who was embedded with Charlie Company in Iraq during the spring and summer of 2007, first reported an inside account of the event in a four-part series called "Blood Brothers."[9] On her second day embedded with the unit, it was hit by an IED and lost five men. Shortly thereafter, Kennedy was flown out of Iraq. A month later, she received a couple of e-mails from the men saying, "We just lost four more men, and they want us to go out on patrol, and we are not going to do it." Kennedy reported, "I could not get back to them when I was in Iraq, but when they returned home to Germany, I went to see them ... I hope that the story would show people exactly what soldiers in Iraq are dealing with. I'm not sure Americans understand exactly what this war looks like to our soldiers ... They were catching insurgents, and they were battling every day, but then they were exhausted, too, mentally and physically."[10] Charlie Company had 14 of its 138 members killed in twelve months. The battalion to which Charlie Company belonged lost 31 of its thousand men.[11]

In an interview aired on *Democracy Now!*, Kennedy recounted the death of First Sergeant McKinney:

First Sergeant McKinney was well loved by his men. He was Bravo Company. He was considered intelligent. When they had a question, he was the one they went to, because he could explain things. Everyone thought he was a great family man. One of the soldiers, Ian Nealon [phon.], told me that he used to ride to work with him every day and that he just loved him.

And one day, he went out on patrol with his guys, and they had just been called back into Apache, which was the name of the combat outpost where they were in Adhamiya, and he apparently looked—said that he had had it. He looked at a wall, he fired a round, and then he took his M4, and he put it under his chin, and he killed himself in front of his men. It left a lot of people just saddened and horrified. And then, the next week, Bravo Company was hit by an IED, and they lost four guys, too.[12]

This incident may have helped spark the rebellion that followed:

After Bravo Company's IED went off, Charlie Company was supposed to go back out and patrol the same area. When some of the members who had been patrolling with Charlie Company before the scout platoon went as the quick reaction force to the IED attack for Bravo Company, they were struck by how much it looked like the first IED attack that—the roadside bomb attack, and they reacted as if it were their own men, and they went right to mental health and they got sleeping medications, and they basically couldn't sleep and reacted poorly.

And then, they were supposed to go out on patrol again that day. And they, as a platoon, the whole platoon—it was about forty people—said, "We're not going to do it. We can't. We're not mentally there right now." And for whatever reason, that information didn't make it up to the company commander. All he heard was, "2nd Platoon refuses to go." So he insisted that they come. They still refused. So volunteers went out to talk with them, and then he got the whole situation. In the meantime, it was called a mutiny, which is probably a bigger word than should be used for it, but that's what the battalion called it.

And eventually, what they did was they separated the platoon. They said, you know, "You guys aren't acting well together anymore, so we're going to split you up, and we're going to have you work with other platoon sergeants, other squad leaders, and see if we can turn things around this way." But they also punished them, in a sense, by flagging them and saying that they couldn't get promotions and they couldn't get their awards for two months. So there was a feeling that there had to be punishment for these soldiers refusing to go on a mission, but there was also understanding that the guys may have acted properly in this case.[13]

◆　　◆　　◆

Chanan Suarez Diaz served in Ramadi from September 2004 until February 2005. His experience underscores the lack of preparation and training for what soldiers were expected to handle in Iraq.

When after his first firefight, immediately upon his arrival, Diaz heard that his commanding officer had resigned on the spot, he knew that things would be rough. He has vivid memories of the day they went into Hurricane Point:

It was the first time we were actually in an Iraqi town in broad daylight with Iraqis pointing weapons at us, and we didn't know what the fuck was going on. So in my second day in Ramadi we got into a huge firefight. The Iraqis knew there was going to be a transfer of troops ... and that's when they attacked. We got into a huge firefight and it was such a surreal moment because we are just driving down the main strip down in Ramadi that we call "Route Michigan," and we are by the souk, the marketplace, and all hell breaks loose. There were RPGs [rocket-propelled grenades], and there were small-arm fires—it was just very chaotic. We dismounted, and I took cover by a wall and pointed my weapon to the direction of the fire, thinking to myself, what the fuck am I doing here? It was just very slow motion, totally chaotic. And, after that firefight, we came back to base and our commanding officer resigned, which is something that I didn't know that officers could do until I was in Iraq. They can resign their commissions, right there, just like that. And this is the same guy who got the whole company—I was in Weapons Company—all huddled together and gave this bullshit patriotic speech like, "Look at everybody around you, they're your buddies, and blah blah blah, they are not going to come back, we are doing this for freedom in America, blah blah blah." Second day he is in there, he almost gets killed, and he's like, "I'm done." And it's because of the privilege that he has as an officer that he can do that.

Today Diaz laughs, "Isn't that crazy? And I literally, when my gunny came and told us, the platoon, I was like, 'Wait, he can quit and we can't? Where can we sign up?'"

Group morale in the unit, already low from the welcome they received upon their arrival, continued to plummet. For Diaz, things got worse with each new atrocity he witnessed. Passing through the city in a convoy, he once saw a platoon of marines behind him opening fire on a family that was walking home. The marines were reacting to gunfire. He recollects during our interview,

They brought an ambulance, and got the family to that base, and I saw this fourteen-year-old Iraqi girl who was shot in the stomach. She shocked me because I would imagine somebody that was shot in the stomach would be screaming, but she wasn't. She was on the stretcher, completely silent, and just looking. She was still alert and everything. And the rest of her family was hysterical. Her mom was shot in the leg with a .50-caliber round. And the exit wounds from .50-calibers are huge. So she has her leg shot up with that and it was both of them that got wounded. The father and the younger brother were there crying. And these are people that were just walking home.

Like many vets, Diaz initially had not supported the decision to invade, but "I thought it was my duty as a corpsman to save lives and take care of people." I can see how deeply the experience of watching fellow marines die and of witnessing atrocities meted out to Iraqis has affected him.

Diaz still had a month to go in his deployment when his platoon refused an order. They had lost ten people from the company, and many more had been wounded. Their first commanding officer (CO) had quit, the second one was killed by a vehicle-borne improvised explosive device (VBIED, a car bomb), and the third one had been plucked from an office job. Since the third CO was outranked by COs of other platoons,

they were going to give us the shitty detail and the shitty mission. Basically they wanted us to go down the same route that this squad in 2/4, the one that we had relieved in Ramadi, had been made to go. It was like the south end of Ramadi, from what I remember. They were ambushed, and completely wiped out. They wanted another squad of people to do the same route, me walking in with that squad because they are going to need a corpsman there, and then they positioned themselves in three different areas—far away, mind you, not that close—vehicles, just in case if something happened. And they wanted us to do that, and I was completely against it. When the order arrived, the platoon freaked out.

I said a lot of people have died for this, why are they sending us on this death mission? I was addressing everybody, and everybody was huddled in their own little groups and talking about it, and they all said, "We don't feel good about this." This is already so many months into being shot at and blown up every day, and mortars dropping on you all day. And we had a month left, and everyone was clear: "We're going to be extremely careful and not do anything stupid." And then this popped up. I remember specifically our gunny told us that he wanted everybody with all their gear ready to go by 11:45. We are supposed to get in the vehicles, get ready to do this crap at noon. By 11:45, no one was geared up … Everyone was thinking the same thing. And it was kind of scary because you are taught not to question orders, so you felt like you were doing something wrong, but you also felt you were doing something right, and it felt as if you were going through uncharted territory. You didn't know what was going to happen. And the platoon sergeant, who was well liked for the most part, he wasn't feeling good about the whole mission either … He saw what everybody was doing, and he just left and spoke to the gunny. I don't know what he told him, I don't know what the discussion was, but he came back and said that the commanding officer had cancelled the mission.

Diaz and his platoon also organized some search-and-avoid missions. "There were a couple times where my vehicle commander, Steve, would have us hang out by a house or in the back of a house, and just kind of chill there, and everyone would have their spots. I don't know if that would necessarily be considered 'search and avoid.' On such days there would be no form of communication with the Iraqi insurgents. If there was a day that we didn't want to do anything, we would hang out, but such occasions seldom happened in Ramadi, because there you could never relax, you were always getting blown up."

He revealed other individual subversive actions he had noticed in Iraq. "I saw in the bathrooms, people would leave 'Fuck the war' or 'Fuck the U.S. Marine Corps' or 'What is it the United States Marine Corps stands for? Uncle Sam's Misguided Children.'" He found out that there were plenty of soldiers in his unit who opposed the war and the missions they were sent on, but that they would not speak up about it, let alone dissent.

Diaz was wounded in February 2005, when an RPG struck his vehicle. Two shrapnel wounds in his back landed him in the hospital for three and a half weeks, after which he spent a year in Southeast Asia in order to complete his contract.

His eyes flashed at the mention of the reserve unit that mutinied in October 2004. "When I heard about that mutiny, it was a complete inspiration. This was a whole platoon saying, 'Fuck it! We're done.' That is inspiring, even just reading about that stuff. Imagine all the different forms of dissent and people rebelling that we never get to know about because the military, for one, does not want that to get out; for two, they do not want other people in the military to know that shit is happening because that in itself will give people some more confidence."

Addressing a crowd of more than eight hundred people in the Seattle Town Hall during a Winter Soldier conference in summer 2008, Diaz said, "Our commanding officer wanted us to go through a route that another platoon had done and consequently been completely wiped out in an ambush. We refused. They canceled that mission, and we did not go. I do not think these are isolated incidents. I think this is happening every day in Iraq. The military doesn't want you to know about this, because it's kind of like lighting a fire in a prairie."

Later Diaz told me, "The level of resistance that we need in order to bring the military to its knees is not going to happen unless there's a strong, vibrant antiwar movement that supports GIs and gives them confidence. No one wants to be the first and only one, but if they see others, and more importantly, if they see other military people doing it, that is what gives them the confidence they need to be able to resist."

One of the most blatant acts of resistance Mejía had participated in, prior to his refusal to redeploy, was refusal to go on a mission. He and a few fellow soldiers were openly critical about the tactics they were ordered to follow in a mission. The troops were being sent out on the exact same mission, in the same place at the same time night after night, to draw enemy fire. Mejía writes of a friend's reaction. "'Man it's fucked up,' said Rosado, 'This motherfucker didn't have enough with doing this shit for three straight nights, now he wants us to go out a fourth. He's not gonna stop until somebody dies in this battalion.'"[14]

On the fourth night, there were attacks that severely injured several soldiers and blew up a Humvee. Mejía had had enough and refused to go out the fifth night when the order came to continue the mission. He was vehement: "'No way!' I said to Demarest after Warfel left. 'I'm sorry sergeant. I have all the respect in the world for you, and I hope you don't take this personally, but I'm not going on the mission tomorrow.'" When his sergeant persisted in trying to convince Mejía why he had to take his men out on the mission, Mejía persisted as well, "'I'm not going, sergeant. And I hope you don't take it personally, but this motherfucker is using us to get medals and promotions, and I'm not gonna be part of it. Why doesn't he come with us if he's so interested in showing the enemy we're not scared? I have never seen his ass out there.'"[15]

He admitted in the book, "I did not want to disobey my orders and I was terrified, but I felt like I had to do it." The higher-ranking soldiers attempted to persuade Mejía to say that he was refusing the mission because he was afraid, in the hope that it would make his punishment less severe, but Mejía refused. "'No, Will,' I said, stubbornly, 'I have to let them know I value my life more than anyone's promotion. I'd rather go to jail than die, kill, or be injured for someone's personal glory. You tell them that's why I quit.'"[16]

Mejía wrote further of the incident:

Williams said he would, but he didn't. When he went to the platoon leaders' meeting with the commander later that day, he found a most unexpected situation. The soldiers of first platoon had gotten together upon returning to base after the fourth night of Operation Shutdown. They were very angry about what had happened and at how they'd lost four people in one night, plus a vehicle. On hearing that we were being ordered to follow the same procedure for a fifth consecutive night, they decided they would refuse to go unless the mission was reorganized in a way that was sensitive to our safety and that let us regain the element of surprise …

When Williams summoned the squad leaders to give us the briefing for that night's mission, he called on me as if nothing had ever happened. But important changes had been made …

The final night of Operation Shutdown went off without any incidents or injuries whatsoever. I went on the mission with the rest of my platoon, as first squad leader, and my original refusal to participate in the mission was never again spoken about, at least not in Iraq."[17]

Mejía tells me modestly that there was nothing remarkable about this incident. "If you really think about it, this is a different form of search-and-avoid missions … soldiers saying we're not going to do this shit because it's crazy, or for other reasons. There is a lot of overlap with the things that are happening. I alone have come across five or six instances. I think it's pretty widespread. I do think that a whole lot of people are saying there is no reason why we should go out on suicidal missions."

It is clear that such discontent is widespread in Iraq. It is also understandable why the military does not want more soldiers or the public to know about it. One of the prime causes of the spread of GI resistance in Vietnam was soldiers discovering instances of their fellows engaging in acts of dissent. Thus far with the occupations of Iraq and Afghanistan, the military has been largely successful in keeping acts of rebellion out of the public consciousness.

TWO

QUARTERS OF RESISTANCE

Find out just what people will submit to, and you have found out the exact amount of injustice and wrong which will be imposed upon them; and these will continue until they are resisted with either words or blows, or with both. The limits of tyrants are prescribed by the endurance of those whom they oppress.

—Frederick Douglass

In March 2008, as the U.S. invasion of Iraq approached its fifth anniversary, I was walking through a decrepit neighborhood of northwest Washington, D.C. I perceived it as a crime-ridden neighborhood; it had cars with cracked windshields, two-tone paint touch-ups, and flat tires. Many of the house and apartment windows had burglar bars. My destination, 715 Princeton Place NW, near Georgia Avenue, turned out to be an old brick building that wears the look of a halfway house for recovering alcoholics or drug addicts. The multiroom, multilevel house serves as a meeting place for veterans as well as active-duty dissenters. It is conveniently located two miles south of the now infamous Walter Reed Army Medical Center. Inside, I met Geoffrey Millard, a former sergeant in the Army National Guard, who joined the military at the age of seventeen and served for nine years in locations ranging from Ground Zero in New York City to Iraq. Most of his thirteen-month stint in Iraq was spent working for a general at a tactical operations center (TOC). Millard now runs his own TOC, the veterans' house.

Measuring an imposing six feet, and weighing more than 200 pounds, Millard has tattoos up and down both arms depicting the violence and chaos of war. Competing for space with these are more recent tattoos. A photograph of him with Michael Stipe, the lead singer of the band REM, has Millard wearing the flag on his uniform upside down. "That was on March 19, 2006 … I was already off active duty, so I was doing this antiwar stuff like crazy. On return from the Vet's Gulf March, I was the featured speaker right before Michael played in this big concert," Millard tells me.

His former unit members did not take kindly to the photograph. He was totally unprepared for the hostility he encountered on stepping into his new unit. He had gone to inquire what he was going to need for his next drill.

I found that picture printed out in seven different places in the unit with a target over my face, and they said I was going to the rifle range. So I beat a hasty retreat and called up my lawyer, Tod Ensign. I tell him, "I can't go to the range, they're going to fucking kill me, I know it." So he says, "Alright, we will file for conscientious objector (CO) status." So we faxed in the form that declares the intent to file for CO. When I started to write my CO file, I realized I wasn't a CO. I started thinking about Iraqis, and I started to think if I were an Iraqi, what would I do? If I was an American, and Chinese tanks were rolling down the streets, I probably would use that nine years of military experience to fucking kill somebody. So I couldn't say war in all forms was bad, because when you're defending your home, you're not a bad person, you're defending your home and family. It's hard to kind of think about because those guys are killing my buddies, but they're still defending their homes. It's a hard place for me to be in right now. I don't want them to kill my friends, but I don't want my friends to take their homeland either. I wasn't a conscientious objector.

I must confess I had never thought about this aspect of applying for CO status. It had seemed like a convenient, uncomplicated, and legally admissible way out for those who, with good reason, do not wish to go to war. Millard's dilemma raised a hundred questions in my own head. What would I have done in his place? Before my time reporting in Iraq, I believed I was a pacifist, but, similar to the mental machinations Millard articulated, my beliefs had changed. Meanwhile, I have accepted that it is easy to practice peace in the rarefied air of mountain peaks. The world looks very different when every moment is a miraculous escape from death and every day is a ledger of lost friends and family. I understood what Millard meant.

So why did he decide to leave the U.S. military?

You know what it was? Why I knew I had to get out? 'Cause I stopped thinking like a soldier. I couldn't follow orders anymore, so I was questioning every order they gave me. Why? Why? Why? From shining my boots to what I was guarding to why I was even coming to drill, it was *why* all the way. "Tell me why. Why are we doing this?" Not just because you told me to anymore. My president lied to me, my commanders lied to me, I got lied to every goddamn day in Iraq, so don't tell me I must do all this just because I have been told to. It doesn't hold true anymore. So in August 2006, I went UA [unauthorized absence] at a Veterans for Peace convention in Seattle.

Adam Kokesh, a former marine and cofounder of the veterans' house, and its only other permanent resident along with Millard, walks past us, chanting the popular military rhyme, "It's not for us to wonder why, it's just for us to do or die." Millard comments grimly, "That's what soldiers are supposed to think, but I was unable to, and so I knew. I knew that when I didn't think like a soldier anymore, it was time for me to move on. And I did. That is why I got out in August of 2006."

Millard was publicly AWOL for nine months before being honorably discharged. At the time he received his discharge order by mail, he was actively reporting for the online progressive web site Truthout.org and working with GI resisters. "I was making myself a threat to the military," Millard says, "so they mailed me my discharge because I was more of a threat for them to fight than I was to just let go."

Interestingly, Millard does not recognize his nine-month-long AWOL as an act of resistance. "It was merely what I had to do. I viewed Lieutenant [Ehren] Watada[1] as a resister, I viewed those who were speaking out against the occupation as resisters. These people were facing jail time. In the Guards, all you risk is getting kicked out with a less-than-honorable discharge, which is not exactly harsh in my view. That is not resistance. But if every national guardsman left, THAT would be resistance. It took me a long time to realize I was a war resister. It's still weird to think of myself in that role."

Millard is showing me around the house when a small beagle puppy trots over to him. He gingerly picks it up and says with a soft smile, "Her name is Resistance. She was a stray who showed up at the house one day, and we adopted her. Now she is a peer support counselor." I believe him, from personal experience. On returning from

Iraq, I too had procured a pet that played a critical role in helping me with my PTSD.

The veterans' house is the first of its kind in the United States, but could become a model for others to come. Millard describes the house as a training ground for radical political activism. "You spend time with us, be with others, and at the end of your stint, you are a different person. You are not merely exposed to radical ideas in this place, you also pick up skills through your participation here. Everything in the house is about organizing, from allocating housekeeping duties, to preparing meals, to ensuring that Resistance does not go outside."

The loft at the veterans' house is full of empty mattresses, at the moment buried under the empty sleeping bags of veterans who are in town to protest on the occasion of the upcoming anniversary of the invasion of Iraq. I meet Marc Train, a young, wiry man from Washington, D.C., who joined the army "bluntly and simply, out of poverty." Three weeks prior to my visit, Train landed at the house from New York, where he had been facing chronic underemployment. "I researched and found that the job market here was a lot more conducive to veterans. Also I wanted to contribute to the approaching Winter Soldier event. I decided to staff at the house to enable all veterans coming here to make it to the National Labor College for the testimonies. I ensure that the house remains comfortable and clean. A couple of nonveteran interns and volunteers help me maintain the place. On the side, I do job hunting."

The Winter Soldier hearings were an IVAW initiative, organized at a local college. Among the 200-odd vets who participated in the event, many presented testimonies of their experiences in Iraq, both as perpetrators and as victims of an unjust occupation.[2] Their incendiary testimonies categorically condemning the occupation were nearly completely ignored by the mainstream corporate media.

Train, who was in the Third Infantry Division, opens up:

> I had been thinking a lot about Hurricane Katrina and Rita and what the government's response to that was going to be. It happened, coincidentally, at the same time that I joined the army, in September of '05. I sat back and thought about things a little bit, and it became clear to me that the government was doing pretty much nothing to help the actual people. In fact, they were giving real estate developers sweetheart deals and a free hand to knock down public housing and homes where families had lived. Thinking about that ended up getting me in trouble because I started publishing my ideas, anonymously, on a blog. When it eventually came out in July of '06, my sergeant major wouldn't have it. He freakin' railroaded me, taking away my security clearance, claiming that I was a threat to national security because my beliefs made me susceptible to foreign espionage since I disagreed with my government. But I was still willing to defend and support my government, at least at that time. And I still am, although not in the context of supporting the rulers in the administration, because they don't deserve it.

Train went AWOL between March and July 2007, after an advanced individual training (AIT), "because I didn't want to go to Iraq ... I did not want to be complicit in war crimes."

It seemed that Train has given a good deal of thought to the concept and execution of the veterans' house. His responsibilities at the D.C. house included organizing actions, doing GI outreach, and hosting visiting veterans. He believes there can be no universal standard for an ideal house, but the D.C. house could serve as a good model for other veterans to adopt with certain modifications to suit their specific location and requirements. It is difficult to predict the shape of things to come, but the current style of decentralized functioning among most antiwar veterans allows them sufficient flexibility to plan and implement outreach in ways appropriate and effective in their local context.

The veterans' house in D.C. accommodates up to thirty-six people, although during peak action periods it makes room for as many as fifty. There are two guest rooms on the second floor, an attic, and a basement, all of which are basically crash pads. Train and I walked down creaky, cramped stairs to the basement, a dingy room with eight racks on the floor. There is a laundry room and a functional bathroom.

The props I come across include CDs, punching bags, tools, several air mattresses, a phone, a working fax machine, and a dead one. A poster supporting Indymedia adorns one wall, and on another is a U.S. map that shows all the nuclear sites located within the contiguous forty-eight states.

House rules are few but are enforced strictly. Train is emphatic: "First and foremost no holding of any kind. We are strictly legal, a peace house. We don't tolerate illicit materials or items. We get stuff done but we do it right."

Home Front Battle Buddies is a peer counseling process where veterans counsel other veterans. On Sundays, a mixed lot of eight to ten veterans of the wars in Iraq, Afghanistan, Vietnam, and Korea assemble at the house. The seniors are popular as mentors. Sunday is also the time for outreach. House members move in and around Walter Reed, especially neighborhoods where a number of veterans are concentrated. The choice of the house location makes better sense to me now. This lower-end residential area helps veterans meet two objectives. On the one hand, it enables the veterans to engage the lay public in their struggle to end the wars, and on the other, it allows them to help less-informed veterans access their entitlements and benefits, regardless of the manner of discharge that the military hands them. Train, like his colleagues, is convinced, "Anybody that comes back from hell deserves care and treatment."

We return to the living area, which is full of bookshelves that contain an eclectic collection, from *Inside the Red Zone,* by Mike Ferner, a Vietnam Veteran who reported from Iraq during the occupation, to *War Made Easy*, to a French dictionary, to *Zen and the Art of Motorcycle Maintenance.*[3] Behind Millard's room is a study also lined with overflowing bookshelves. "This is really kind of a decompression space," he tells me. "As you can see, there's the door through which to enter the rest of the world, and then there's the door and the wall to my room. This here is my sanctuary."

Millard presents the impressive array of books: "This section here is African-American studies. The top shelf is Black Power, the second shelf is slavery, the third and fourth shelves are general African-American studies, and the bottom shelf is African studies. We've got a small section here on Irish studies. We got a section on white studies, women's studies, native studies, a big section on general politics, a section on media studies, and then a small section on fiction, a section on religion, music, and there's my record collection, then over there, that's all war and peace."

In the middle sits an award. "It is kinda funny. This was an award they gave me when I got home from Iraq, and it had a flag in it. We needed an upside-down flag for an action, so we used this one. And I put a picture of me, holding the upside-down flag, into the nice, beautiful container that they gave me." I am amused by this little subversion, a slice of unpremeditated dissent, as it were.

I was curious to know the cause of Millard's shift from being a loyal soldier to an antiwar activist. In response he recalls,

I actually was really pissed as the war was starting, but I didn't know what to do about it because I was a soldier. I was starting to question things. I was really against the Iraq war, though I was still in favor of Afghanistan, which has changed over time, but from the beginning I was against the Iraq war. I bought a bus ticket to New York City for a protest. All I had was my camouflage jacket and the ticket. Everyone on the bus kept telling me, "You gotta march with the vets." When I got to New York I looked around and I found "the vets," which happened to be the Veterans for Peace. I marched the entire way with this older Vietnam vet—real tall guy, real bad voice. The whole time I just talked to him about all the stuff I was going through. I vented for hours. Finally at the end of the march, he assured me that he would respond if ever I needed. When I got home after Iraq, and was moving things into my new apartment, I found his card.

The card he brought down from its pride of place atop a shelf was David Cline's. National president of Veterans for Peace (VFP) from 2000 to 2006. Cline, like Millard, was born in Buffalo, New York. He was drafted into the army at twenty years of age and sent to Vietnam in 1967, where he served in the Twenty-fifth Infantry Division as a rifleman and machine gunner. Serious wounds brought him to the army hospital at Fort Dix, New Jersey, in 1968. He received three Purple Hearts and a Bronze Star during his service.

After returning to the United States, Cline became an antiwar activist, serving as a civilian organizer of active-duty servicemen at one of the first GI coffeehouses, the Oleo Strut, in Killeen, Texas. He started producing a one-sheet underground newspaper called *Fatigue Press*, on politics and veterans' issues. It used to be distributed clandestinely on the military base. He joined Vietnam Veterans Against the War in 1970, serving first as a coordinator and then as a national director. He remained a member until his death in September 2007. As a result of his stint in Vietnam, Cline had suffered from chronic health problems, one of which eventually led to his death.

Millard is still overwhelmed by the fact that he had marched with Cline and not known his identity. In a choked voice he says,

> And I didn't know who he was … I called him when I got home [from Iraq], and he was the first vet that I talked to as a vet. Not a day goes by that I don't miss him, and his card sits up there to remind me to be that person for somebody else. That is a big part of this house, to be for somebody else what Dave was for me. I can't even think about him without tearing up and he's only been gone a short time. I spoke at his funeral, and told everyone, especially his own family, that David was as much a dad to me as my own dad was. I wanted his son to know how his father had changed the world. It has really meant a lot to me, to get a chance to do that. He was extremely special to me. And he never tried to convince me not to go to Iraq. Yet he showed me how a three-time Purple Heart winner could be against the war.

Another significant influence on Millard was Colonel David Hackworth, author of *About Face: The Odyssey of an American Warrior*.[4] Millard reminisced,

> I had a lot of time to read in Iraq. I worked as secretary to a general, and I think of my sojourn there as 95 percent "What the fuck am I gonna do?" and 5 percent "What the fuck am I gonna DO?" Because in my job you did not get to do a lot, except when shit popped off right there, like there's a mortar round that comes right in or something like that. So I read a lot, and one of the books that I read was this one right here [*About Face*]. I'd carry it around with me every-

where in Iraq. Everyone would say, "That's a great book until you get to the end." Well at the end, he turns against the Vietnam War, as a full-bird colonel. At the time of his death, with 114 medals, he was the most decorated service member. If he could turn against the war and was able to do something about it, it really didn't leave me a whole lot of excuses as to why I was doing nothing. I would say, more than anything else, it is this book that turned me into a resister. Because if Colonel Hackworth could, with everything that he had to lose—his life, his reputation—what was I? I'm a guardsman, I'm already looked at as a shit-head by most of the military because I'm in the guard anyways and then I'm a POG [person other than grunt] because I work for a general. So my military credits were pretty much toasted the second I went to Iraq. After reading this, I was left with no reason to not start doing something. I would say that this book has had a lot to do with me starting to actually resist, not just to be against the war, but to do things.

More than by Millard's books, I am struck by the man's clarity of resolve and his ability to translate resolve into action. I find myself wondering, there must be others. If they were to come together, would it not be a force to reckon with, mightier than the mightiest army of the world?

By February 2009, the veteran's house in Washington, D.C., had moved closer to Walter Reed Hospital, and, according to Millard, "is stronger than ever." Geoff Millard and Adam Kokesh are hopeful that their house may serve as a model for similar houses to spring up in other communities around the country. With hundreds of thousands of Iraq war veterans coming home and beginning their struggle for VA benefits, untreated PTSD, and in desperate need of community support, it seems a realistic enough hope. At the time of this writing, a second veterans' house has opened in Boston, with another scheduled to open in Denver.

GI coffeehouses, akin to those that sprang up during the Vietnam War, may be making a comeback as well. The first one was the Different Drummer Café, on the outskirts of Ft. Drum in Watertown, New York. The Coffee Strong coffeehouse in Washington State, near Fort Lewis, and Under the Hood coffeehouse, just outside Fort Hood in Texas, are others.

THREE

SPEAKING OUT

Censorship pervades the environment of an average soldier. In May 2008, Admiral Mike Mullen, chairman of the Joint Chiefs of Staff and the nation's highest-ranking defense officer, next to the president, wrote an open letter warning everyone in military uniform to stay out of politics as the nation approached a presidential election in which the occupations of Iraq and Afghanistan were to be central, divisive issues. The letter advised, "The U.S. military must remain apolitical at all times and in all ways. It is and must always be a neutral instrument of the state, no matter which party holds sway."[1]

The occupations of Iraq and Afghanistan, in which U.S. involvement has already exceeded that in the Second World War, are currently the longest U.S. conflicts fought with an all-volunteer force since the Revolutionary War. It is understandable that the establishment feels threatened by dissent in the ranks and wishes to check it with an iron hand.

Even without such injunctions, soldiers are only too aware of the risks of expressing dissent in public. Killing and getting killed on the battlefield are occupational hazards that a soldier accepts knowingly. In sharp contrast, following one's conscience to speak out against injustice and excess in war is hazardous to a soldier's professional credibility and future security. Yet some manage to undertake this crucial first act of resistance.

The Socialism Conference in Chicago in June 2008 offered a platform for GIs to speak out. The objective of the conference was to create ways of affecting positive social change and ending the occupations of Iraq and Afghanistan. Participating veterans conducted panel discussions on issues like the future of GI resistance. They also talked of their direct experiences of the two occupations. It was here that I ran into former marine Bryan Casler. He did not kill anyone in Iraq, but he suffers from chronic PTSD. He has nightmares, and grinds his teeth so badly that he dislocated his jaw.

"I'm still on edge 24/7," said Casler.

I have trouble being in social environments. I never thought of myself as suicidal, and I still don't, but for the past few months there have been points where I was driving and I would close my eyes for fifteen seconds and just think about what it would be like to crash my car into a concrete barrier. That's not me. I never had these thoughts until after I got out. I just don't feel like myself. I was always a hopeless romantic and now I have relationship problems. I have the greatest girlfriend in the world and I know it's not her fault. I just have personal problems I have to work out. There are just so many issues. I'm not at rest. And there are these regrets. I think about the Iraq war way too much. I wish I could think about my family more than I think about Iraq. And it's draining me. I can't focus in class. I can't focus at a job. I was working for a union, and I was picketing for the union, and all I could think of was how to end this war. I cannot attend to things that are outside the realm of ending this war. And I don't think it will be complete relief, but once this war is over, that will be a healing moment for my PTSD.

Speaking out about the occupation is part of that healing for him.

I saw so many things happening and I knew they were wrong. I can't speak for everybody, but I think a lot of people have PTSD from regrets, about something they did earlier that they now have a problem with. It is immaterial whether you thought it was right or wrong when you did it. All that matters is that now you have a problem with your actions and there's this inner turmoil. I have this inner turmoil every day. I was indoctrinated into the military spirit and the perpetuation of lies.

Casler, who served in Iraq, then Afghanistan, then back in Iraq, claims that during the invasion of Iraq his morale was fine, but toward the end of his first tour in Iraq, things had started to look different. He began to feel that, "people were racist and dehumanizing, and always on a high pedestal as being better than everybody else, an attitude that carried over to Afghanistan and then back to Iraq. It wasn't any individual's actions, just a perpetual thing, and it was accepted."

He believes there is a deliberate dehumanization process set in motion and sanctioned by orders from above. He backs his perception with evidence.

Our entire first platoon was minorities, Mexicans and Blacks, with white squad leaders and a white platoon sergeant in charge of them. When I realized what the hell was going on, I thought this was ridiculous because it's not something they were being covert about. Every time you are marching in formation it stares you in the face. And right enough, the pattern of abuse started with the abuse and dehumanizing of marines around you. It spilled onto the larger frame. Every branch of the military is below the Marine Corps, and everyone who is in infantry is below the grunts, and everyone that is not in your unit is below the rest of you guys, all the way down to team level. Everyone else is beneath you. You are the most supreme team on this planet and you are better than everybody else.

He mentions friends who were passed up for promotions because they were a minority. For the same reason they also received harsher punishments. When they had injuries they were accused of shirking.

After the November 2004 siege of Fallujah, Casler was brought back to Iraq from Kabul, Afghanistan. In both deployments he was stunned at the level of racism directed at the local populations. "The primary objective appeared to be to mistreat and dehumanize your guys. I could not do it, not to my men and not to those people. I liked the Iraqis, I liked the Afghanis. Why were we treating them like shit? What are they doing to us to deserve this? That was when I really started questioning what the hell was going on."

Like other Americans, I too was under the impression that morale among the marines was highest and that their unofficial motto "gung ho" was for real. Casler dispelled that myth: "Really? Is that what they tell you? I was always told that fake morale was better than no morale. And we were encouraged to just fake it."

On returning home, Casler enrolled at the Rochester Institute of Technology in New York. At a peace rally, he met Matt Hrutkay, another Iraq veteran who introduced him to the idea of GI resistance. Shortly thereafter, Casler received a recall order from the marines stating that "the president had authorized some 1,400 IRR marines to be involuntarily mobilized." Unable to get a school deferment, he found himself shipped down to a warehouse where he was reunited with approximately 250 of his peers, mostly from the infantry, who, like him, had already served an average of two or more tours in Iraq or Afghanistan. A general began to lecture them, telling them to prepare to be deployed again. The memory of that day still makes him livid: "My hands were getting sweaty because I knew I was going to do it ... Every time you have someone high ranking speak up, they say something that grabs your lungs and just squeezes. I was like, 'I know I can't keep silent, I can't do this anymore. Fuck the Marine Corps. I'm so sick of it. Sick of this motivated, hoorah screw yourself over for nobody's good bullshit ... fucking sick of it.'"

It was not going to be easy, he knew, but decided it was time to let the group know he was now interested in GI resistance.

> I was nervous, probably not very articulate. It was a two- or three-star general up there, and when he says, "Does anyone have any questions?" I stood up and the gist of what I said was, "This is bullshit reactivating us and the threat of retroactively removing our honorable discharge, removing my health-care benefits, removing my GI Bill, what's going on here? This is absolutely insane. And also what do you think about the Petraeus reports?"[2] I wanted to know what this general had to say, because I thought the Petraeus reports were actually bullshit, just more of the Bush agenda. So I was that guy, and everyone instantly looks at the general. All I'm thinking is, I'm not going to get my deferment now. That was it, that guy's got my name and my number. I'm done. So he starts answering, talking about how we have to fight them over there and how Iraq's linked to 9/11, and I couldn't believe what I was hearing.

The tension of the moment is palpable in Casler's account of it, and I am transported to the charged scene. At this point, one of his friends, who was about to be redeployed despite having been diagnosed with both PTSD and TBI, stood up and asked the general, "Who in their right mind is going to send me back to Iraq? Put a rifle in my hands, send me out there? I'm supposed to lead marines? You want to put me around Iraqi civilians? I'm not stable, I can't do this. Who in their right minds is going to approve me to go back?"

After the meeting, several marines surrounded Casler and repri-manded him for being disrespectful to the general. While he was taking flak, another group encircled the group that was attacking him. He noticed strangers defending him against the others saying, "First off, what we're out there fighting for is his right to do or not, so even if I don't agree, and I do agree, he's got the right to say that, and if he's saying it, other people are thinking it." Others who seemed to be in agreement felt emboldened to join in. During the next two days he spent there, Casler says he received scores of compliments for speaking out as he had, which convinces him that "dissent is there in the military. It's just people are told not to speak up. If you speak up, it's a career killer."

At the time we spoke, Casler was still in the Individual Ready Re-serve. What if he gets reactivated? "I'm not going back." He feels it is imperative to continue speaking out against the occupation. It is more than resistance to him; it is his therapy. "On a personal level, my greatest healing moments have come from talking to GI resistance members, doing the Warrior Writers project,[3] organizing other vets to procure the resources that they need, and testifying at Winter Soldier in Silver Spring, Maryland. "That made me a person again. That was my anti-boot camp. That was me becoming human."

Scientists will have us believe that evolution is a natural process, and rulers will sell us the idea that the unfit must be eliminated, but a handful of us have stumbled upon the precious secret that the journey from "man" to "human" is long and arduous and fraught with risks. The cacophonous clamor for power easily drowns out our deep need to be human. But when it becomes a matter of survival, the natural inclination toward humanity again becomes clear.

◆   ◆   ◆

Eli Wright's discharge, which came as medical retirement with 40 percent disability due to PTSD, does not translate for him as a 100 percent discharge from the military.

> I'm facing a temporary retirement for up to five years, and then it could either become permanent retirement or I could be separated from the military with severance pay and no further benefits. I'm still hanging in limbo not knowing what's going to come out of that. For the moment, however, I have definitely been able to achieve some sense of closure with my time in the military. It feels like a massive weight has been lifted from me. All my friends and everybody that I've seen since my discharge say that I look different, that I seem different. I certainly feel human for the first time in a long time.

He had been active duty when he spoke to me about the search-and-avoid missions in Iraq. Following the publication of my news story about it for Inter Press Service, Wright was harassed and threatened by the military. It was not until summer 2008 that I heard of the fallout from his revelations to the media about resistance in Iraq. "The article was forwarded up the chain of command, to General Oates, the post commander of Fort Drum, and his office, to respond. Some people weren't very pleased with active-duty soldiers talking about the kind of things we discussed," Wright recalled.

The Army launched an investigation and brought me in for questioning a couple of times. I immediately sought legal support and, based on legal advice, decided not to comply with the investigation. I had violated no law in exercising my first amendment rights in talking to you about those important issues. I refused to answer any of their questions and they asked me if I wanted an attorney to talk to. I informed them I already had two and was fully prepared. They thought it best then to dismiss me and make the whole situation go away.

I wanted to know what had prompted Wright to grow so outspoken in his opposition to the occupation, especially since his discharge. His story makes another dent in my general distrust of Americans in uniform. I am reassured by fresh evidence that military service does not necessarily divest an individual of his sensibility and sensitivity.

Wright had gone to Iraq as a medic with the desire to help people. Upon arrival in Ramadi, he, along with another medic, was called to an "enemy detainment camp" because a prisoner there needed medical assistance. At the entrance to the detainment facility, Wright was pulled aside by his battalion surgeon and instructed, "Anything that you see in there, inside those walls, stays in there. You don't talk about any of it after you leave that place." The cell he was taken to was a dark and damp enclosure of bare concrete cinderblock walls with a concrete floor and no lights. His memory reconstructs the scene for me, and his experience is important enough to be quoted at length.

It was the scent of blood that hit me immediately on walking in there. It was a sort of old, stale scent of blood that had just permeated that place for a long time. And they walked us inside and there was this prisoner in there, completely naked except for a small little cloth tied around his waist, and he was standing up on top of a cinderblock that was placed on end. They said that he had been there for three days. His scabbed hands, tied with zip ties that cut into his wrists were purple and swollen. This guy had the most confused, glazed look on his face.

He was being interrogated by several men who were just grilling him. They said he had been up for three days in this interrogation process. He had not slept. He had been standing on this cinderblock for most of the time. They had this bucket of water, which they would splash on him whenever he dozed off. They took him off the cinderblock and stood him against the wall and told us to start checking him out. And I didn't even know where to begin. He was covered in bruises, his face was all busted up and bleeding. This other medic started to check him out. Our task was more or less to see if the guy was stable, to ascertain if he was in any condition to continue his interrogation. He had some cuts on his face, on his nose and his eyebrow, and we started taping those up, not really doing much, just kind of dabbing away blood clots and applying tape over it, not even cleaning his wounds or anything. He was complaining of pain on the side of his chest, on his back. He had a lot of bruising on his ribs, so the medic started feeling his ribs, and he pressed on a couple of his ribs and the guy just screamed in pain and sort of buckled. They picked him up and slammed him back against the wall. The other medic told me to feel his ribs so I could see what it felt like, said he's got a couple of broken ribs. I verified that his ribs were broken and the medic started feeling around the rest of the area around his ribs to feel if there were any more fractures, and then suddenly he cocked his fist back and punched him right in the broken ribs. And the guy just dropped and screamed. I was stunned. It shocked the hell out of me.

It was an important moment for me. Seeing a medic, a fellow care-provider, violate our code of ethics, which is first and foremost to do no harm, and to see one of my own doing that to a ... I guess he was just a prisoner to them, but to me ... I didn't see him that way; he was a confused, broken human being. And to see a medic do that to him, I don't know. I think it just kind of destroyed my perception of us doing anything good there for these people. That's when I realized that we weren't there to help anybody. Nothing that we could do would be good. After that point, I didn't feel like there was any further good I could do for those people. That was my first night there. I never talked to anybody else about it. I was going to testify about it in Winter Soldier[4] but was not able to. This is actually the first time that I've spoken about it.

The reason I did not speak out about what I felt all through my time in Iraq and later was fear of the consequences. Because I felt I was alone. It was that sense of isolation and fear that drew me towards GI resistance. Speaking out as a member of the military while still on active duty brought on a different type of fear, but it was a risk worth taking. There is no other way I could have learned about the history of the GI resistance movement. The oath we took on joining the army was a considered risk. We knew we were putting our lives on the line. In comparison, I do not feel the risks one takes as a dissenter are that huge. I was not necessarily risking my life for the cause [of ending the occupation], while I did risk my life for the situation that brought me to this. So I feel this is a bearable risk. Indeed I dealt with a lot of harassment and faced alienation from my peers in the military, but that pales into insignificance when I look at the support I have found for what I and other fellow active-duty vets were doing. We did not feel isolated anymore, and there were enough of us doing it together to ensure constant motivation. That solidarity with the other guys [involved in GI resistance] in the Fort Drum chapter gave me the confidence to not be afraid because I knew they had my back. Anything that came up, they would be right there to fight it with me. That enabled us to win some things. When I think through it all, I have no doubt that as much as I risked and sacrificed, it was all worth it.

Wright has since worked with the Combat Paper Project,[5] and become very active in organizing GI resistance around the country. When we met for the second time, a few weeks after his discharge, Wright was still in a state of shock over being released from the army. He has found partial peace through his attempts at building a GI resistance movement. As with Casler, speaking out about his experiences in Iraq has become part of his healing process, and he feels it is his moral duty to do so. "I was in the army for over six years and had forgotten what this kind of freedom feels like. In some sense it is freedom I never had even before I joined the military. The work that I'm now doing to build a GI resistance movement, that's where I feel I've really gained my freedom. It has allowed me to reconcile with all that I've been through in the last six years, including the year I spent in Iraq and my time at Walter Reed."

Is there a hope of GI resistance getting substantially stronger? In response Wright tells me about Eric Johnson, a "fresh-faced kid" deployed to Iraq at nineteen years of age.

Well, it was like he wasn't even a kid anymore. He was a nineteen-year-old kid when he deployed; he came back a twenty-year-old man that had undergone this profoundly horrific experience. Ever since then he has been at it, fighting this battle to get his health care, to be taken care of, and for his situation to be recognized and addressed by his chain of command. We've been helping him out with everything that we can, but he's been facing some pretty heavy odds, and he's fighting it. Yeah, through that I've become very good friends with him, and it's amazing to see that transformative process of a brand-new, young soldier to a seasoned Iraq war veteran after just a couple years in the military, accompanied by a massive change of consciousness. He is eating up every bit of education and knowledge that he can get his hands on, trying to learn more about the politics and the ethics and all the factors that go into this war, all in order to be able to speak out and start organizing vets. It has changed him radically, just like it has the rest of us. I've tended not to look at the big-picture aspects of this because when I focus on individual people's stories, like him, that's where I see the successes of what we have done. And so, yeah, it's extremely inspiring for me.

Admiral Mullen's directive may have succeeded for now in keeping active-duty soldiers from speaking out while overseas, but it has not been able to silence voices such as Wright's back home. When we met, he was on his way to Kansas to visit a fellow medic he had served with in Iraq, in the hope that his buddy, who had just returned from his second tour, would join him in his efforts to increase GI resistance to the occupation.

The risks of standing up to the might of the most powerful establishment in the world are high, but those who have chosen this path are following the dictates of their conscience. That alone makes the journey worthwhile regardless of its outcome.

◆   ◆   ◆

I interviewed another dissenting veteran, Liam Madden, in late 2008. The reason he gave for his change of stand came as a surprise. He said it was his own reactions when on sniper missions that had disturbed him the most. With some embarrassment, he recollects the first time he had an Iraqi in his scope sight:

My adrenaline had completely taken over my body and it was like an addictive feeling. It was almost enjoyable, the way my senses were suffused with adrenaline. Later, I felt really ashamed that I had had another human being in the palm of my hands and thought that was something to be excited about, that I was ready to take someone else's life for something I didn't even believe in. It just kind of goes to show that the situation you're in can drastically change you.

Madden is a former marine who served in Iraq's volatile Anbar Province from 2004 to 2005. Although he was against the occupation before it started, he deployed because he felt he had no option. He grew dispirited upon arriving in Iraq, and more so at being sent on sniper missions and convoy protection missions, neither of which, shockingly, he was trained to do. "I simply did not feel we were helping the Iraqi people. There was just so much sadness and anger and fear and frustration in their eyes. I couldn't speak Arabic, but I knew because I could speak human. I knew what they were thinking, you know?"

On being honorably discharged after fulfilling his four-year contract, Madden began speaking out against the occupation publicly, referring to it as criminal. Along with Navy Petty Officer Jonathan Hutto, an active-duty seaman also opposed to the occupation, he founded the Appeal for Redress, a website that helps active-duty and reserve troops ask their congressional representatives to withdraw troops from Iraq. The mission of the appeal states:

> Many active duty, reserve, and guard service members are concerned about the war in Iraq and support the withdrawal of U.S. troops. The Appeal for Redress provides a way in which individual service members can appeal to their Congressional Representative and U.S.

Senators to urge an end to the U.S. military occupation. The first Appeal signatures were delivered to members of Congress on January 16, to coincide with the Martin Luther King, Jr. Day in January 2007. Appeal for Redress will continue to collect signatures until all active duty, Guard, and active reserve soldiers are out of Iraq.

The redress statement is similarly simple: "As a patriotic American proud to serve the nation in uniform, I respectfully urge my political leaders in Congress to support the prompt withdrawal of all American military forces and bases from Iraq. Staying in Iraq will not work and is not worth the price. It is time for U.S. troops to come home." At the time of this writing, 2,227 members of the military had signed the appeal.[6]

On October 24, 2006, Madden talked about the Appeal on the television show *Countdown with Keith Olbermann*. He was stationed in Quantico, Virginia, at the time. Olbermann quoted Tony Snow, then–White House press secretary, on the Appeal for Redress: "It is not unusual for soldiers in a time of war to have some misgivings … The servicemen and women involved in the Appeal were going to be able to get more press than the hundreds of thousands who have come back and said they are proud of their service." Labeling the statement as a "gross mischaracterization" of how Madden felt about his service, Olberman asked Madden if Snow's description was accurate. Madden replied, "I think a gross mischaracterization is as well as you can put it, Keith. I feel that I'm participating in democracy, and that's what citizens of a democratic land should do. If Mr. Snow has a problem with that, then he should know that I feel I have protected democracy more by appealing to my congressman than I did when I defended Iraq."

"It's something I feel strongly about," he told Olbermann, "And if people don't step out of their comfort zones and speak up, then nothing will ever get done."[7]

Madden also appeared on *60 Minutes* on February 25, 2007, along with nine other signatories of the Appeal, to give his message to a national audience. He had been active duty at the time of the interview, but discharged prior to the broadcast. He told CBS correspondent Lara Logan, "Just because we volunteered for the military doesn't mean we volunteered to put our lives in unnecessary harm, and to carry out missions that are illogical and immoral."[8]

In spring 2007, Madden received a disturbing letter from the Marine Corps alleging that he had violated the Uniform Code of Military Justice by wearing his uniform at an antiwar rally. The letter accused him of being disloyal, and therefore recommended him for "other than honorable discharge."[9]

In response to the letter, Madden told the *Chicago Tribune*: "All this was because I have publicly opposed the war in Iraq since I came back from it."[10] At least two other Iraq veterans have received similar letters for wearing their uniforms to antiwar rallies. There appears to be an ongoing effort by the U.S. military to censor overt displays of dissent by veterans upon their return to the United States.

The twenty-two-year-old's exchange with the military on the issue is revealing and displays a mature and rational, if dissenting, approach that the representatives of the government would do well to appreciate.

They offered to drop the proceeding if I agreed to stop wearing articles of my military uniform at protests. I responded with a letter that I would agree to stop wearing my uniform if the Marine Corps admitted in writing that my statements were neither disloyal nor inaccurate, and apologized for accusing me of being disloyal, concluding with, "If you drop the case I will take that as a measure of your implied tolerance and support of protesting in uniform against war crimes. I understand men in your position have their careers to think about, as I'm positive many German Colonels did in 1939."

Ultimately, the Marine Corps dropped its case, but not until it had declared to the press "that I agreed to stop wearing my uniform." Madden had no way to refute "this blatantly inaccurate reporting [that] the press proceeded to regurgitate across the country and thereby [damaged] my reputation as an antiwar veteran activist." The Associated Press reported: "The Marines said in a statement that they weren't proceeding with the case because they had (received sufficient indication) from Liam Madden, 22, that he would no longer wear his uniform when engaged in political activities."[11] In defiance, Madden has worn his uniform at countless protests since.

Busy organizing GI resistance in the Boston area, he is hoping to start a veteran support house for organizing, and conduct a regional Winter Soldier event[12] as well. "I have a strong sense of responsibility because I think if you have the ability to make a difference, then you should. I wouldn't be able to live with myself very easily if I knew that I gave up. We live in a country that murders people. It's murdering people, it's facilitating mass poverty and starvation across the world. If people don't wake up, then I don't want to live in that world. There is an urgency I feel about this."

◆   ◆   ◆

Adrienne Kinne joined the army when she was still in high school, primarily to fund college. Her soft-spoken nature masks a fierce intellect. From 1994 to 1998, she trained and worked as an Arabic linguist in military intelligence before joining the reserves in order to finish college, graduating with a major in psychology. It was just after September 11, 2001, when she received a call from her unit telling her she was mobilized. She was stationed stateside as an Arabic interpreter with top-secret FBI clearance until she came off active-duty service, but was stop-lossed for six months while still in the reserves. In February 2004, she was released, but has continued in service, working in the Veterans Administration to help her fellow soldiers.

Kinne's task was to work as a voice interceptor with Military Intelligence at Fort Gordon, Georgia. Her job was to listen to satellite phone communications in Iraq, Afghanistan, and surrounding areas during the early months of the occupation of Iraq. She admits that she had decided to exit the military the first opportunity she had, "because I couldn't see myself serving in support of the wars in Iraq or Afghanistan anymore. I didn't agree with either of the invasions. I felt that the invasion of Afghanistan was unjustified and I felt that the invasion of Iraq was based on false pretenses. The supposed link to 9/11 and the quest for weapons of mass destruction of Iraq, I had a hard time believing any of it." Her own views are straightforward: "That America is a country that's well-off means that it has a responsibility and a duty to do right by other people. And to me that doesn't mean that you invade them."

Kinne became politically active during the 2006 midterm elections in the United States and helped in assisting the Democrats take control of the House, which they did by riding the wave of anti-occupation sentiment sweeping across the country at the time. "I had just moved to Vermont and was watching the news, really wanting to know what the Democrats were going to do to change things and that was when Bush announced the escalation and Congress went along with it. I decided that I had to do something."[13] She traveled to D.C. from Vermont to attend a protest, her first one, against the escalation of force in Iraq. There she met other veterans and joined them in their resistance.

There is no other way for veterans but to speak out against both occupations, feels Kinne. "We have one way or another witnessed what it's like to be in the military, what it's like to be a returning veteran. We must speak to the American public of our experiences and lay out reasons for immediate withdrawal to better educate them." She advocates immediate withdrawal of all U.S. military personnel from both Iraq and Afghanistan, and is very outspoken about the need for reform within the VA.

With striking clarity, Kinne asks,

> Who will talk of issues facing veterans in the VA if veterans don't? That is not something that affects veterans from Iraq and Afghanistan alone, it affects veterans from peacetime, wartime, the Vietnam War. The problems are so huge and astronomical, the lack of funding, the lack of resources that the VA's going through, and prioritizing veterans based on what war they fought in. I think it's absolutely atrocious that veterans of previous wars who have had to struggle for so long to get their benefits are now being graded as second-class veterans so they can push veterans from Iraq and Afghanistan to the forefront for these politically motivated purposes. I think our government, if they promise soldiers that they are going to be taken care of…, then they need to uphold that promise.

On April 8, 2003, during the U.S. invasion of Iraq, a U.S. tank shelled the Palestine Hotel in Baghdad, killing Taras Protsyuk, a Reuters cameraman, and José Couso, a cameraman for the Spanish television network Telecinco.[14] The Pentagon declared the deaths an accident, a claim Kinne has publicly refuted by disclosing that secret U.S. military documents she had access to listed the hotel as a possible target.

At the time of the shelling of the hotel, Kinne was at her intelligence-gathering job,

I never really connected what happened on the ground to what happened in my office. Frankly, I don't remember whether I was not following the news or if I just did not make the connection. It took me a long time to connect that list of potential targets to what happened on the ground in Iraq. It only indicates that it's really hard for a person to believe that their government can do something like that intentionally. By deceiving the American people and the international community, the administration pushed forward the invasion of Iraq and created an environment where any catastrophe can happen.

During an interview with me, Kinne divulged the details of the murder of the two journalists at the Palestine Hotel. She says,

Prior to the U.S. shelling, we were listening to journalists staying at the Palestine Hotel. During the buildup to shock and awe, which people in my unit were disturbingly excited about, we were given a list of potential targets in Baghdad, of which the Palestine Hotel was one. I remember this specifically because putting one and one together, I went to my officer in charge and told him there were journalists at the hotel who thought they were safe, and yet we have this hotel listed as a potential target, that somehow the dots did not connect. Shouldn't we make an effort to make sure that the right people know the situation?

Her officer in charge, Warrant Officer John Berry, reminded her that her job was not to analyze, only to collect and pass on information and that "someone somewhere higher up the chain knew what they were doing."

Kinne was outraged that the military was listening in on U.S. citizens, both journalists and NGO workers in Iraq, in violation of the

USSID (United States Signals Intelligence Directive) 18, a directive that bars the tapping of conversations of American citizens or people from allied nations. When she brought this violation to the attention of Berry, he responded with a verbal waiver to USSID 18 for an indefinite period.

Later, during an interview on *Democracy Now!* Kinne revealed,

And it was shortly thereafter that we were given a verbal waiver that we could listen to Americans and other ally citizens of allied countries for whatever—from whatever organizations, humanitarian aid organizations, journalists, NGOs, because—and then we were given two reasons that we could listen to Americans and these ally citizens. One was that they were eyes on the ground, and they could stumble upon the location of weapons of mass destruction, and if they should pass the location on over the phone to co-workers or what have you, that we would have to be listening in order to find out where the weapons of mass destruction were located, and we could pass that location on to higher-ups. The other rationale that we were given in order to kind of justify spying on Americans was that the organization or the individual could lose their satellite phone, and a terrorist could pick it up and then start using it. And we would have to monitor all these phones in order to make sure that if that took place, we could be there to listen to the terrorists.[15]

In the same interview, Kinne dwelt on how all this had pushed her to speak out.

I mean, I was a very low rung on the whole totem pole of the military intelligence, and I can speak to my experiences and what I saw and what I witnessed, but not knowing, I think, what is going on in the higher levels, and I think that's part of the reason why I did decide to speak out, because I really hope very strongly that other people who know a lot more than what I know will choose to do the same thing for the right reasons. And if by speaking out you can encourage other people to kind of follow suit, I think that's part of what's all about, as well.[16]

Kinne's experience as an intern at the VA in Augusta, Georgia, has also had a profound effect on her and propelled her into action.

That's when I first started seeing soldiers come back from Iraq. When people come back physically damaged or mentally damaged from the war, you start to think more about things. I eventually got a full-time job at the VA in Richmond and started seeing more and more people coming back with multiple injuries in the polytrauma unit, traumatic brain injury and PTSD.[17] It is never ending as the prolonged occupations continue. You start talking to more and more veterans from Iraq and Afghanistan, really hearing about their experiences. Working in the VA, you also know that we don't have enough resources or funding, and you see that people are slipping through the cracks. You know that the VA, at some level, is actively trying to create loopholes in order to avoid giving benefits or treatment. It seems clearer that our government is completely unwilling to end the occupations, particularly the occupation of Afghanistan, not even the most progressive of Democrats, to the best of my knowledge, are talking about withdrawing troops from Afghanistan. All this has convinced me that if I really want to help soldiers or veterans, I have to push harder and do more to try and help end the occupations.

I ask Kinne what she thought should be the fate of those responsible for initiating and perpetuating the war in Iraq. Her forthright opinion does not surprise me at all. "I think they should all be tried for war crimes," she says.

What solution does she propose for the two occupations?

I think that it's imperative for the United States to withdraw troops from Iraq immediately, and that's true of Afghanistan, as well. Part of me had felt, when we first invaded Afghanistan, that if we were going in to find bin Laden, then it could be justified, but I think the past seven years has really demonstrated that we are not there to find bin Laden. We're there to essentially secure pipelines to get natural resources out of the area. A friend of mine who was in Afghanistan when we decided to withdraw troops and start sending everything over to Iraq went to his officer in charge and said, "How in the hell are we supposed to find bin Laden if we don't have the personnel and resources necessary to do so?" And his officer said, "We aren't here for bin Laden, we're here to maintain a show of force and presence in Afghanistan." And Bush said in the beginning of 2002 that he wasn't really concerned about bin Laden anymore, he didn't really think about him. So I think we really need to reevaluate what's going on in Afghanistan and withdraw troops from both Iraq and Afghanistan.

What of the accusation that is leveled at her and others like her, of being unpatriotic and disloyal? The answer comes with the same force of conviction that seems to direct her every action:

The whole idea that we're betraying the troops is just absolutely absurd. Everybody I know who is resisting these occupations has been or still is in the military. We have many resisters who are active-duty members and we have those in the reserves and National Guard, and the idea that we are against them, or that we don't support them, is absurd. I think people who would want to continue sending soldiers on repeated deployments in a war for a prolonged period of time are the ones who do not support the troops. Fifteen-month tours are simply untenable. In no way, shape, or form should soldiers be sent to Iraq or Afghanistan or anywhere, for fifteen months. There are lots of research studies that show that an acceptable length is around six months. It is obvious that the people who don't care about the troops are [the Bush administration] that continues to send them to war zones for multiple deployments and then deny adequate resources for veterans' care when they get home. As far as patriotism is concerned, I think that people who are unwilling to stand up against those who would seek to, basically, take America down a path that is aligned with the use of torture, the use of spying on Americans ... detaining people without any reason, without any day in court, we're totally denying, we're restricting habeas corpus ... those people are unpatriotic and they are really bad for America. Those people stand directly opposed to anything I've ever been taught that America stands for. I don't think I have to justify my patriotism or my support of the troops. I mean, I have a brother who is in Iraq right now and naturally I support him.

Kinne has lost faith in 'business as usual' with the political system when it comes to a solution to the Iraq and Afghanistan quagmires. "As much as I would like for our government to withdraw our troops, I have seen that the Democrats have been supporting the wars in Iraq and Afghanistan just as much as the Republicans." Her hope for a solution lies in people, not the government. "Once the elections [of November 2008] happen and events unfold, I foresee that the unfortunate fact will become clear that we will have a prolonged presence in Iraq and Afghanistan. That is when Americans will finally start to realize that our government is not going to end the occupations, and that is when they, the people, will stand up against the occupations and bring them to an end."

Kinne has no doubt that veterans need to take the lead in making this happen. "It's important for us as veterans to be in the forefront of the movement and make sure our government knows we're going to hold them accountable."

◆   ◆   ◆

"I didn't see any combat, but a lot of combat saw us," Ronn Cantu told me as we talked about his time in Iraq, "We had multiple IEDs [improvised explosive devices] go off in our convoys, too many to even count. We never saw who detonated them." Cantu said morale in his unit declined drastically after his first tour.

> As time wore on, we realized that they didn't have a real mission any-more and morale started to decline. In the second tour, the morale was pretty low because the resistance attacks had been stepped up, [and] they were much more catastrophic. It didn't seem like anything we could do was going to bring a quicker end to the war. An additional setback was that, by the time of my second tour, some of us had already been deployed multiple times. So we were telling the first-ter-mers, as I call them, what the war was really like. It was having a detrimental effect on morale as a whole. The new guys, they came in believing in the mission—why else would they have come in while the war was going on—they were believing in it, they wanted to go, they were excited, and the people who had been there from before were taking that away from them, bringing their morale down. So there's a morale issue in the force right now.

Cantu's first act of resistance occurred in October 2004, when he was home on his first R&R and went to visit a former instructor at the school in California where he had studied journalism. He was asked to write a guest editorial. He laughs, but not in jest, when he says, "That was my first little act of resistance: an article about how killing people is wrong and how war is wrong."

He remembers that resistance within the military to the occupation spread rapidly when he returned to Iraq. "Then we saw a lot of resistance. There was a lot of drug use in Third Brigade, First Infantry Division in Germany. A lot of people got kicked out for drugs. And people were reenlisting because they believed if they did so, there was an unwritten incentive that they wouldn't be sent directly back to Iraq."

Cantu deployed to Iraq again, only to find that dissent in the ranks had spread even more. As I mentioned in chapter one, he participated in search-and-avoid missions. During his second tour, Cantu started giving media interviews. He felt compelled to tell the American public what was really happening in Iraq. He had already signed the Appeal for Redress, which led to an interview on *60 Minutes,* along with nine other soldier signatories. He was out of uniform, off duty, and off base. The interview was conducted in Washington, D.C., just before he redeployed. In that interview he asked, "What are we trying to accomplish over there? I mean, what are we trying to do in Iraq?" *60 Minutes* correspondent Lara Logan, addressing the soldiers, remarked, "There are gonna be a lot of people who don't like what you're doing," to which the stocky, deep-voiced Cantu sternly replied, "By volunteering, we've done more than about 99 percent of the population. And anybody who joined after 9/11, when the country was at a state of war, it's my opinion that nobody has the right to question that soldier's patriotism, nobody."

Logan had simultaneously interviewed some soldiers opposed to the Appeal for Redress. She asked Army Captain Lawrence Nunn, in Baghdad, if he understood why the signatories felt the way they did.

Nunn replied by stating he was 100 percent behind the "mission," and added, "You don't sign up to pick which war you go to," to which Cantu replied, "We haven't said that we're not going to war. By the time this airs, I'll be back in Iraq."

Logan asked Cantu what consequences of his signing the Appeal he visualized on redeployment, with troops knowing his feelings about the occupation. "All I can do is just convey to those soldiers that I do not want them to die in Iraq and that I will do everything I can to bring them home safe,"[18] he replied succinctly.

On April 8, 2008, Cantu filed to become a conscientious objector, and when we spoke last, he was in the process of trying to separate from the military. Still active duty, he continues to give talks to educate people about the occupation, and he was one of three soldiers who started a GI resistance chapter at Fort Hood, a chapter that by December 2008 had grown to ten members. Other actions he has been involved in include banner drops on the base, leafleting, and holding barbeques to recruit new members to the budding movement. Of his plans once he obtains his CO status and discharge from the military, Cantu says, "The first thing I'm going to do then is have a press conference and call George Bush a liar, because then I'll be able to."

Polls of the military in Iraq have long shown that a clear majority want a quick end to the occupation. In February 2006, 72 percent of troops thought the United States should exit Iraq within the next year, with more than one in four saying the U.S. should leave immediately.[19] No one can miss the unmistakable moral rectitude and consistency that shines through the resolve of those who have opted for dissent.

FOUR

ABSENT WITHOUT LEAVE

Fascist and Nazi totalitarianism was made possible by the methodical transformation of passive citizens into ardent followers, uncomplaining patriots, willing executioners, and, finally, cannon fodder.
—Sheldon S. Wolin, *Democracy Incorporated*

Before being deployed to Iraq, twenty-five-year-old Ryan Jackson was stationed in Korea where, for the first time, he began to question what purpose the U.S. military and U.S. foreign policy really served. After two and a half years of honorable service, he decided to write a CO application. The carefully considered letter said,

I feel ashamed every day. I feel ashamed for taking part in the killing of others, and for allowing my comrades to be killed. I can no longer be a part of the Armed Forces or any organization of a violent nature ... Once my beliefs started to evolve and change, I became a different person. It starts to take a hold of you, giving you hope that you can make a difference, that you can change what you are doing, and that it is not too late.

I've come to realize that my beliefs will not be valid or sincere, based on what any person reading my application says or thinks. My beliefs are valid because I say so and because they are my beliefs and they compel me to be a better person.

Jackson eventually opted not to file his CO application. He felt it would be an exercise in futility because the military's CO application process is "immoral, unethical, and wrong." Instead, he sought to gain an administrative discharge by accumulating as many negative counseling statements as possible, on minor issues, by not showing up in the morning or missing physical training. His attempts at getting ejected from the army were almost successful and his out-processing paperwork was nearly complete, when a local commander arbitrarily stopped his pending discharge in December 2007. Jackson went AWOL, secured the services of a lawyer and some GI support groups, and turned himself in at Fort Sill, Oklahoma, on April 4, 2008. He was ordered to Fort Gordon, Georgia, where he was incarcerated, which is an uncommon penalty in the military for someone who has not committed a violent offence. His trial commenced when he had already been in confinement for thirty days. It was during a break in his trial that I was able to conduct a short telephone interview with him.

How had Jackson's experience of confinement affected his convictions? "Martin Luther King said, 'Punish me, you know I don't deserve it, but I'll accept it to show the world that I am right and you are wrong.' I take that approach, and find it liberating knowing that what I am doing is right. Hopefully I can get out and prevent others having to endure the same thing." Talking of a friend from his unit who was working on getting out of the military, Jackson said, "In my experience, I would say that there's a large percentage [of soldiers] that are against the Iraq war, and a lot of people that are against war period ... A lot of them just do it for security, and their family, to pay the bills, and the economy is not looking too good right now either. There are definitely people in every unit that feel that way—just not that many speak openly about it."

On being released Jackson planned to dedicate at least six to twelve months working with different organizations, traveling around and doing public speaking. There is a need to focus on the youth he feels: "If a recruiter can go into a high school, then there is an equal right for the opposing side to do the same and be able to give their perspective. I feel a strong need ... to speak out and tell my story anywhere I can."

Jackson was sentenced to 100 days in confinement, a reduction of rank to E1, forfeiture of pay, and given a bad conduct discharge. Since he was credited with time served, he was released twenty-nine days later.

◆　　◆　　◆

A U.S. military court in Germany convicted conscientious objector army medic Agustín Aguayo of desertion and missing movement. He was sentenced to eight months in the brig for choosing not to participate in the occupation of Iraq. I met this mild-mannered thirty-five-year-old man in San Francisco.

Aguayo was sent to Iraq in February 2004, when his application for discharge as a conscientious objector was being processed. There was no ambivalence in him when he said: "Before I left for Iraq, I searched deep within me. I concluded that if I go over there, I can't take a life. I said, 'I'll go,' but declared myself a conscientious objector. I'm not willing to cross that line. No matter what, I can't take a life."[1]

What he saw in Iraq reinforced his decision. Out on patrols or doing guard duty, he never carried a loaded weapon. He would rather have died than shoot an Iraqi.

Back from deployment, Aguayo found his CO application had been seriously mishandled. He filed a habeas corpus appeal in the federal court challenging the ruling. It was denied a week before his unit was scheduled to deploy back to Iraq in August 2006. After nearly three years of struggling with the army to be recognized as a CO, Aguayo went AWOL on September 1, 2006, and missed his unit's deployment to Iraq. Instead of facing a court-martial when he turned himself in the next day, he was told that he would be sent to Iraq, even if it required forcibly putting him on the plane shackled and handcuffed or confining him until the deployment.

Unable to think of an option, he fled the military base in Germany and did not emerge until after he had made his way back to the United States. In September 2006, he held a press conference in Los Angeles, California, to express his views against killing and war. Courageously, along with a caravan of supporters, Aguayo drove up to Fort Irwin, in Barstow, California, and turned himself in once again. On October 3, 2006, First Infantry Division personnel retrieved him from California and took him back to Germany, placing him in pretrial confinement in Mannheim Prison, Coleman Barracks.

On March 6, 2007, Aguayo was court-martialed and convicted of desertion and missing movement, his rank was reduced to E1, the lowest possible, and his pay and allowances forfeited. However, rather than sentencing him to a seven-year imprisonment, the maximum allowed by his conviction, the judge only gave him eight months in the brig. With good-conduct time, Aguayo was released on April 18, 2007. His attorney, David Court, said about the early release, "I believe that Agustín in his closing comments was compelling enough that the judge probably came to the conclusion, 'He thinks he's a CO regardless of what the Army says, and because he believes he is a CO, that's why he did what he did.' I suspect that the judge thinks he did not act with dishonor. It appeared that at the end, the issue was what is the punishment for a conscientious objector who follows his conscience and not the dictates of the Uniform Code of Military Justice?"[2]

When Aguayo was in prison, Amnesty International declared him a prisoner of conscience. His attorneys tried to get his case to the Supreme Court in order for him to be recognized as a CO, but the U.S. Supreme Court declined to hear his case to win his discharge as a conscientious objector. It was a long shot to begin with, but Aguayo was insistent on pursuing all avenues, even after getting out of the brig. Aguayo struggles to make a living in Palmdale with his wife and two teenage daughters. Of his own situation, he told Jeff Paterson, who formed the group Courage to Resist that supports military resisters, "My bid to the Supreme Court was rejected March 18, 2008. This means my case will never be heard by the Supreme Court and my quest for justice failed and I will never be vindicated legally. Although I have come to accept this and knew of the possibility, it has been disheartening. I don't need outside sources to validate me. I know who I am and I know what is in my heart. And even though I know I am not defined by this outcome or by others' opinions of me I can't deny my disappointment." Today he and his family continue to work to inform the public and soldiers about their experience, and the need for GI resistance.

Agustín Aguayo and Ryan Jackson seem to have accepted all of this calmly. I am unable to reconcile this with the inappropriately excessive nature of what they were subjected to. These men are not rogues or mutineers. They were well within their rights in seeking the legal option of being released from an obligation their conscience bars them from fulfilling. Not only were they denied the right to do so, but they were actually threatened and punished for attempting to do so. Granted that the military machinery is authoritarian and demands subservience, it is still subject, at least to an extent, to the democratic norms that every institution in the country must follow. Can it be possible that the authorities wanted to make an example of these men by humiliating them publicly?

◆   ◆   ◆

There are instances of less sophisticated forms of resistance from soldiers unwilling to participate in the occupation of Iraq. People have resorted to desperate and sometimes creative methods to avoid deployment. In February 2008, Army Private First Class Matthew John Myers of Apple Valley, California, asked a friend to shoot him in the leg. He claimed he had been wounded in a holdup on a golf course. According to authorities at the scene, a gunman had stolen his wallet and military identification, and shot him in the right thigh. On interrogation, Myers eventually admitted to investigators that he had made his friend Daniel Dotterrer shoot him with a .32-caliber pistol, in order to avoid redeployment to Iraq.[3]

Apart from not reenlisting, arguably the second most prevalent form of resistance is of soldiers going absent without leave (AWOL). After a soldier has been AWOL for more than thirty days, he or she is listed as a deserter and discharged from the military. As of early 2008, U.S. Department of Defense records show that close to 25,000 soldiers have deserted the army since the beginning of the war in Iraq in 2003. This is an 80 percent increase from the number of desertions in the preceding five-year period.[4]

To understand this trend, I sought senior veteran Jeff Paterson, who had joined the service after high school in 1986, in the belief that as part of the military he would be able to help people and "protect freedom." By 1991, when the U.S. attack on Iraq was imminent,

Paterson had already served in Japan, the Philippines, and South Korea, and was serving his last year in Hawaii. What he experienced of the relationship between the people in these countries and the U.S. military forced him to examine the military myth. He witnessed locals protest his presence, saw the antagonism between the military and local populations living near the bases, and "encountered people in the Philippines who were willing to sell their daughters as sex slaves to soldiers in exchange for kitchen appliances from the PX."

I met the tall former marine for breakfast at a café in downtown Oakland. He described his first years in the military.

> It wasn't merely the Marine Corps that I was indoctrinated in. There were a lot of other things, too. Around the time I joined, the civil wars in Central America were going on. My entire training was focused on jungle warfare, intervening in El Salvador, Nicaragua, to stop the communists there. From what I read in the newspapers at the time, and gathered from other sources, it was clear to me that the people of Central America should be able to figure out their own situation. It didn't seem like we were going to help them at all. In fact, I was convinced it would be wrong for us to get involved.

His world began to crack and crumble as he started to question the ways in which the military was being used as it was. For a soldier, starting to think for oneself often is the first step toward resistance. It is on taking that step that many soldiers arrive at the conclusion that they are in fact engaged in doing the exact opposite of what they had joined the military to do. For Paterson,

> That was sort of a political awakening, when I first started thinking about politics in that kind of way. As I was still in the Marine Corps I kept my mouth shut, did my time, did my four years. I was soon to get

out of the service. I was unhappy when my discharge was halted, and I was stop-lossed.[5] In August 1990, when Iraq invaded Kuwait, we were ordered to prepare to deploy. I was a field artillery fire control person and had specialized training in battlefield tactical nuclear warheads. As I was packing my bags, my commander told me if anything went wrong, I would have to "nuke all the ragheads." I realized at that point that I was not just in political disagreement with the idea, but that I was also not willing to do it. We were not going to help the Iraqis, and I didn't think we were going to help very many Kuwaitis, and I didn't want to be a part of that.

Paterson was stop-lossed when he was being out-processed at the Marine Corps Air Facility, Kaneohe Bay, in Hawaii. He decided he was not going to go to Iraq. He held a press conference and made public his refusal to fight. He applied for conscientious objector status. When that was denied, he refused to board the plane that was heading to Saudi Arabia during the buildup to the war by literally planting himself on the tarmac, moving away only when his commanding officer yelled at him. Eventually, his unit left, "which is what I thought they were going to do. I was a sort of liability. Also I had been on a hunger strike the past week, and had at that point become a medical issue for them. So they left me behind, and I was taken instead to the Pearl Harbor brig, where I did the next two months in pretrial confinement. I was court-martialed for a number of offenses. Ultimately, they chose to cut their losses and give me a quiet discharge even before the court-martial ended."

Paterson received an "other than honorable" discharge, which meant loss of all his benefits, including access to the VA and his GI Bill benefits. Paterson was one of approximately 100 soldiers who went to prison for publicly refusing to fight in the 1991 Gulf War.

Another significant 300 active-duty soldiers made public statements against the war. "So it was actually an impressive mini-GI resistance movement that happened over a period of about six months, a very compressed timeframe," Paterson remembers. "You had a dozen marine reservists from the same unit seeking sanctuary in a church in New York, en masse refusing to go anywhere and refusing to fight."

Thereafter, Paterson became totally immersed in activism, opposing the war and the subsequent sanctions against Iraq. By the time the current conflict was launched in Iraq, he felt equipped to provide support to a new generation of war resisters. Initially he sought resources from the antiwar group Not In Our Name to help soldiers like Camilo Mejía, Stephen Funk, Kevin Benderman, and Pablo Paredes, other GI resisters who had stuck their necks out to resist the war.

> The aim was to create individual defense campaigns as the cases came up. In effect, it entailed re-creating a support structure over and over again. That is when "Courage to Resist" was conceived. About two years ago, I dedicated myself full-time to the project. Our stated goal is to provide political and material support to war resisters. With the help of ongoing donations from across the country, we are able to cover lawyers' fees and travel expenses for objectors and resisters who need to have their story heard. We have worked with roughly two-dozen resistors, making a serious effort to ensure they don't have to pay for their legal expenses. We have assisted another couple dozen to tell their story.

Founded and run by Paterson, Courage to Resist was a modest project until it took up the case of Lieutenant Ehren Watada, the highest-ranking enlisted soldier to refuse orders to deploy to Iraq.

Working on his campaign, the group was able to get Watada's message out to a very wide audience. Consequently, its network expanded across the country, making it possible to set up office and acquire staff and adequate resources to deal with the daily needs of military objectors. The organization regularly engages in letter-writing campaigns, one to pressure the Canadian government to permit U.S. war resisters to remain there. The campaign has generated more than 6,000 letters to Canadian officials. As of December 2008, the Canadian minority conservative government continued to disallow U.S. war resisters to remain. However, all but two trials resulted in allowing resisters to remain in Canada, rather than deporting them back to the U.S. into military custody.

I learned from Paterson that 85 percent of soldiers who go AWOL do not get court-martialed. This is astounding, particularly when one considers the fact that since the invasion of Iraq was launched in March 2003, army desertions, defined as being AWOL for more than thirty days, have increased 80 percent from before the invasion. The numbers have since increased. During the 2006 fiscal year, 7 out of every 1,000 soldiers deserted the army; by 2007, the number increased to 9 per 1,000. In gross figures, that means 3,301 deserted in 2006, and 4,698 in 2007.[6]

This is the highest rate of desertion since 1980, and while the totals are far lower than they were when the draft was in effect during the Vietnam War, they still show a steady increase over the past four years and a 42 percent jump just since 2006.[7] Since that time, the rate has slacked due to the drop in overall violence in Iraq.[8]

The reason that most deserters are not being court-martialed is that the military cannot afford to lose them. Says Paterson, "If one considers the raw numbers that go AWOL from the army, people who have been gone for more than forty-eight hours, the vast majority aren't court-martialed in any serious way. They are dealt with through nonjudicial punishment, given extra duty for a couple weeks, and they get bad conduct statements in their military record. But for the most part the military is trying to bring them back."

"I think tens of thousands of people are probably currently AWOL," Paterson speculates. "If you talk to the people returning to the personnel control facilities, you will find them riding Greyhound with two or three other AWOL soldiers who happen to be on the same bus heading to the same out-processing facility. And that's happening every day of the week. So it's a constant revolving door. That is why the army is not able to court-martial all these people. Sometimes there are extenuating circumstances—one may have spoken out too vocally and someone at the Pentagon has flagged their record. Or the AWOL individual is found to have prior legal issues pending. Among branches, the Marine Corps usually treats people more harshly than the navy or the army. There are also the differentials in service, rank, and pay grades. If you're a higher-ranking person, you're going to be punished more harshly to make an example."

What causes this reluctance among soldiers to go to war? Paterson explains, "From my personal experience, I can tell you that it is one thing to think about the 'what ifs' of life, but it is another when you're actually faced with killing someone in the very immediate sense. And naturally it is easier to crystallize your opinions when you're really faced with something that you're going to have to do the next day."

One of the challenges that Courage to Resist faces is the prevalent belief that speaking out against the war is detrimental to an individual who is going AWOL. It is largely accepted that the best strategy for an AWOL soldier is to lie low, keep quiet, and later turn oneself in and seek clemency. If an effective GI resistance movement is to be built, Paterson says, "It is going to take at least a few people who are compelled to do more than that. I think we've won a lot of them over in the last couple of years, in that we have an informed-risk resister policy so people know the benefits and the possible consequences of vocally speaking out against the war. We have successfully supported and promoted several [vocal] resisters, including Ehren Watada and Agustín Aguayo, and the majority of them have not gone to prison."

Clearly this work, for Paterson, satisfies a deep personal need, but there is more. Paterson is convinced that it is also "about how we, as a people who overwhelmingly oppose the occupation, take a stand and undermine this policy being imposed on us by the government. There is no doubt that supporting military resisters is going to be the key to end this war."

His personal goal? Obviously to work himself out of a job by building a mass movement of resistance that will lead to the end of the wars and subsequently leave him with no resisters to support. In the meantime, his campaign continues to grow in both resources and impact. "We've come a long way," he says, as we conclude our interview.

> I think if at this point somebody comes up and says, I need help with legal fees, I want to speak out, we can say OK, here's five hundred bucks for a retainer. Work with us, and I'm sure we'll raise a few thousand more. It's much different than where we were a couple years ago. Our overarching political goal is one of seeing empire and occupation held up by pillars—the industrial military complex, and the corporations, and the Blackwaters, and the KBRs—end. But one of those is still military personnel. And we hope to weaken that pillar by supporting GI resisters. We know that has had an important impact historically. Clearly in the Vietnam War it played a major role, and though we realize it's not going to happen the same way this time, we still maintain that it's going to be a key part in ending the war if we're going to have any chance of success in doing so.

◆   ◆   ◆

It is estimated by the War Resisters Support Campaign that more than two hundred Iraq war resisters are AWOL in Canada, a small echo of the massive exodus of Vietnam War resisters who had fled to that country.[9] At the time, approximately fifty thousand Vietnam War resisters had found refuge and overwhelming support in Canada, primarily because Canadian prime minister Pierre Trudeau, who was in power at the time, believed that Canada should be a haven from militarism and open its borders to war resisters. Once again, Canadian citizens and communities have taken on the task of supporting the resisters financially, morally, and with legal aid and safe houses, just as they had done for the Vietnam War resisters.

The number of resisters in Canada this time around is small, but the support structure for GIs is still largely in place. As of late 2008, at least 64 percent of Canadians supported the resisters, and even believe they should be granted permanent resident status.[10] However, it is yet to be determined how the Canadian government will treat resisters in the future. During the Vietnam War, the government of Canada maintained a relatively open-door policy with resisters, but today the Canadian government is less welcoming.

The case of Iraq war resister Jeremy Hinzman illustrates the changed circumstances. In 2004, Hinzman became the first war resister to seek asylum in Canada, rather than going to fight in Iraq. He fled to Canada with his wife and two children. Like countless others, Hinzman had joined the military for the usual reasons: patriotism, adventure, and college money. In an interview aired on *Democracy Now!* in August 2008, Hinzman spoke of what had caused him to change his stance:

When I went to basic training, I, you know, started chanting, "Trained to kill! Kill we will!" and realized over the three years that I was in the Army that I just couldn't become a killer, because the Army screens out people with psychological problems, and it has normal, humane human beings come in, and in order to be a killer, you have to be able to desensitize yourself and dehumanize those who you're going to kill. And I, for whatever reason, wasn't able to do that, and so I applied for conscientious objector status. And when I did that, my command threw my application away. And I was made to reapply, and my application was subsequently turned down.

So, after serving in Afghanistan, I came back to my unit, and it became apparent that we were going to come to Iraq. And I felt that since I had already acted within the provisions of the Army to try to remedy the situation, we had no other option but to refuse service and take a court-martial or go to Canada. And I felt that since, again, we had tried to work within the Army, it really wasn't fair to take a court-martial at first.[11]

During June 2008, the Canadian parliament passed a nonbinding motion by a vote of 137 to 110, saying U.S. war resisters should be allowed to remain in Canada. But the minority conservative government has refused to enact the legislation. In August 2008, Canada's Border Services Agency ordered Hinzman to leave the country with his family by September 23. Amnesty International issued an alert on his behalf, listing Hinzman as a "possible prisoner of conscience," asserting that "the right to refuse to perform military service for reasons of conscience is part of freedom of thought, conscience, and religion, as recognized in Article 18 of the Universal Declaration of Human Rights and Article 18 of the International Covenant on Civil and Political Rights, to which Canada is a state party." Amnesty also argues that "conscientious objection is a valid ground for recognition as a refugee under the 1951 Convention relating to the Status of Refugees, to which

Canada is a state party."[12] If Hinzman is extradited by the Canadian government, he faces a court-martial and up to five years in prison.

On September 23, 2008, a federal court judge in Canada granted a stay of deportation to Hinzman and his family. The ruling allowed him to remain in Canada until the federal court decides whether it will hear an appeal of a rejection of the family's case on humanitarian and compassionate grounds. On February 10, 2009, Canadian Federal Court Justice James Russell heard that appeal. On April 24, 2009, Hinzman lost his appeal.

This outcome has far-reaching implications for other Iraq war resisters already in Canada, as well as those hoping to seek refuge there in the future. For both groups, it makes their task all the more difficult.

◆   ◆   ◆

A father of two, forty-one-year-old Peter Jemley is a fiercely independent-minded history major. The Arabic-speaking soldier wants Canada to accept him as a refugee on the grounds that he opposes torture. The *Toronto Star* reports on his case, "Jemley argues that as one of a small number of Arabic linguists with top security clearance, he could be forced to violate international law by participating in the interrogations of terrorism suspects. It was something he had not considered when he enlisted in 2005 and was handpicked to undergo two years of intense training due to his adeptness with languages."

In February 2008, Jemley discovered his government had sanctioned new rules on how terrorism suspects could be interrogated, which legitimize the use of torture. When he realized this, he decided to flee to Canada so as not to be party to violating international law, as well as his own morality. "It's a soldier's obligation to say 'no' if their commander is doing things that are criminally complicit," Jemley told the *Toronto Star*. "I think everyone is agreeing now that torture is really what has been going on … I have every reason to believe that from my small pool that I belong to, with my credentials, I will be ordered to do such things."

Jemley's moral stand has forced the Canadian government to address Washington's use of torture. In deciding Jemley's case, Canada must acknowledge whether or not the U.S. government has sanctioned torture. According to Jemley's lawyer, Jeffrey House, "There are specific rules for soldiers, and the basic idea is nobody should participate in torture, ever. Nobody should associate themselves with torture or violations of the Geneva Conventions because if we start to wink at violations of the Geneva Conventions, they're no longer law, they're just guidelines."

Jemley is unequivocal. "I did everything I was supposed to. I'm not afraid to be deployed. I'm not afraid to die. I'm ashamed about what's going on. I know it sounds glib but I mean it. If one less person gets tortured, then it'll all be worth it."[13]

If the Canadian government decides to send all U.S. war resisters back home, this will obviously make things far more difficult for anyone opting to flee to Canada seeking sanctuary. On the other hand, if the Canadian government does end up reflecting the will of the majority of Canadian citizens and opening its borders to war resisters, we will likely see an increase in the number of troops going AWOL rather than allowing themselves to be deployed to occupy Iraq or Afghanistan.

FIVE

ORGANIZED RESISTANCE

As aforementioned the name "Winter Soldiers" refers to people who stand up for the soul of their country, even in its darkest hours. Thomas Paine, the revolutionary who rallied George Washington's troops at Valley Forge, trying to keep them from deserting in the face of a bitter winter and mounting defeats at the hands of the British, said: "These are the times that try men's souls. The summer soldier and sunshine patriot will, in this crisis, shrink from the service of his country; but he that stands by it now, deserves the love and thanks of man and woman."

The phrase "Winter Soldiers" was adopted by Vietnam Veterans Against the War (VVAW) when they organized the first Winter Soldier event in response to the human rights violations that were occurring in Vietnam. The event, called "Winter Soldier Investigation," was held in Detroit from January 31, 1971, to February 2, 1971, and was intended to publicize war crimes and atrocities perpetrated by the U.S. Armed Forces in the Vietnam War. VVAW challenged the morality and conduct of the war by exposing the direct relationship between military policies and war crimes in Vietnam. The three-day gathering of 109 veterans and 16 civilians included discharged servicemen from each branch of military service, civilian contractors,

medical personnel, and academics, all of whom presented testimony about war crimes they had committed or witnessed during
1963–1970.

A smaller, modern-day incarnation of VVAW is IVAW (Iraq Veterans Against the War), which was founded in 2004. It seeks to offer
a platform to those who have served in the military since September
11, 2001, to speak out against what they see as unjust, illegal, and unwinnable wars in Iraq and Afghanistan. At the time of this writing,
IVAW had more than 1,400 members in 49 states, Washington, D.C.,
Canada, and on military bases overseas.

IVAW held a national conference called "Winter Solider: Iraq and
Afghanistan" outside Washington, D.C., in March 2008. The four-day
event brought together more than two hundred Iraq and Afghanistan
veterans from across the country to testify about their experiences in
both occupations. Although largely ignored by the corporate press,
the event was of historical significance. For the first time since the invasion of Iraq in early 2003, former and current members of the U.S.
military had organized with the specific purpose to make public the
truth of their experience. It was hoped, in vain as it turned out, that
the testimonies of veterans would provide the U.S. mainstream press
with sufficient information to report on the truly catastrophic nature
of the occupations and rouse people to take action.

At this first modern-day Winter Soldier event, I spoke with scores
of veterans during breaks in the powerful panels of testimony. A
constant refrain I heard was that individuals who had joined the
military for honorable reasons were disillusioned upon sensing how
they were being misused by the government of the country they had
sworn under oath to serve and defend.

Hart Viges had felt compelled to join the U.S. Army the day after
September 11, 2001, in the genuine belief that he could help make

the world a safer place. Like other speakers at the Winter Soldier event, he admitted that U.S. troops routinely detained innocent people during home raids. "We never went on the right raid where we got the right house, much less the right person—not once." He said it was common practice for troops to take photographs as war trophies. "We were driving in Baghdad one day and found a dead body on the side of the road. We pulled over to secure the area and my friends jumped off and started taking pictures with it, smiling. They asked me if I wanted to join them, and I refused. Not because it was unethical, but because it wasn't my kill. Because you shouldn't make trophies of what you didn't kill. I wasn't upset this man was dead, but just that they shouldn't be taking credit for something they didn't do. But that's war."

Speaking on a panel about the rules of engagement (ROE) was Adam Kokesh, whom I had met at the veterans' house in D.C. He had served with the marines in Fallujah for about a year from February 2004. He held up a small card for the audience to see, the ROE issued to soldiers in Iraq, which stated, "Nothing on this card prevents you from using deadly force to defend yourself." He elaborated on the condition of "reasonable certainty" that allowed for the use of deadly force under the ROE and led to countless civilian deaths.[1] "We changed the ROE more often than we changed our underwear. At one point, we imposed a curfew on the city [Fallujah], and were told to fire at anything that moved in the dark. I don't think soldiers should ever be put in situations where they must choose between their morals and their instinct for survival."

Kokesh testified that during two cease-fires in the midst of the siege of Fallujah, the military decided to let out as many women and children from the embattled city as possible. "For males to be released, they had to be below fourteen years of age. It was my brief to go over there and turn the men back, separated from their women and children. We thought we were being gracious."

Steve Casey served in Iraq for more than a year, from mid-2003. "We were scheduled to go home in April 2004, but due to rising violence had to stay in with Operation Black Jack. I watched soldiers firing into the radiators and windows of oncoming vehicles. Those who didn't turn around at checkpoints were neutralized one way or another. Well over twenty times I personally witnessed this."

Jason Hurd, posted in central Baghdad from November 2004 to November 2005, testified how, after his unit took "stray rounds" from a nearby firefight, a machine gunner responded by firing more than 200 rounds into a nearby building.

> We fired indiscriminately at this building. Things like that happened every day in Iraq. We reacted out of fear for our lives, and we reacted with total destruction. Over time, as the absurdity of war set in, individuals from my unit indiscriminately opened fire at vehicles driving down the wrong side of the road. People in my unit would later brag. I remember how appalled I was that we could be laughing about such things, but that was the reality ... We're disrupting not only the lives of Iraqis but also the lives of our veterans with this occupation. If a foreign occupying force came here to the United States, do you not think that every person that has a shotgun would come out of the hills and fight for his right for self-determination? Ladies and gentlemen, that country is suffering from our occupation, and ending that suffering begins with the total and immediate withdrawal of all of our troops.

Marine Vincent Emmanuel was posted near the northern Iraqi city of Al-Qaim from 2004 to 2005, and disclosed in his testimony that "taking potshots at cars that drove by happened all the time and were not isolated incidents. We took fire while trying to blow up a bridge. Many of the attackers were part of the general population. This led to our squad shooting at everything and anything in order to push through the town. I remember myself emptying magazines into the town, never identifying a target." Co-panelists nodded in agreement as he confessed to abusing prisoners he knew to be innocent. "We took it upon ourselves to harass them, sometimes took them to the desert and threw them out of our Humvees, kicking and punching them even as we did so."

Others testified that it was not uncommon to justify accidental killings of civilians by planting weapons on them. Corporal Jason Washburn of the marines served three tours in Iraq, the last one in Haditha from 2005 to 2006. "We were encouraged to bring 'drop weapons' or shovels, in case we accidentally shot a civilian so that we could drop the weapon on the body and make it appear like that of an insurgent. By the third tour, if they were carrying a shovel or bag, we were allowed to shoot them. We carried these tools and weapons in our vehicles, so we could toss them on civilians when we shot them."

In 2004, psychiatrist Robert Jay Lifton wrote an article for the *Nation*. Sharing his insights about the invasion and occupation of Iraq he writes about, "atrocity-producing situations," which occur when a power structure creates an environment where "ordinary people, men or women no better or worse than you or I, can regularly commit atrocities ... This kind of atrocity-producing situation ... surely occurs to some degree in all wars, including World War II, our last 'good war.' But a counterinsurgency war in a hostile setting, especially when driven by profound ideological distortions, is particularly prone to sustained atrocity—all the more so when it becomes an occupation."[2]

At the same hearing, an emotional Jon Michael Turner pulled his military medals off his shirt and flung them down as the audience cheered. He had served two tours as a machine gunner in Iraq.

> I was taught as a marine to eat the apple to the core. April 18, 2006, was the date of my first confirmed kill. I called him "the fat man." He was innocent. I killed him in front of his father and friend as he was walking home. My first shot made him scream and look into my eyes, so I looked at my friend and said, "Well, I can't let that happen," and shot him again. After my first kill, I was congratulated … I want to apologize for the hate and destruction that I and others have inflicted on innocent people. It is not okay, and this is happening, and until people hear of what is going on, it is going to continue. Today I am no longer the monster that I once was.

◆   ◆   ◆

The impact of the first Winter Soldier event inspired other veterans to organize similar events across the country. The first of these was the Northwestern Regional Winter Soldier at the Seattle Town Hall, in June 2008. The 850-seating capacity was nearly full on the occasion. Veterans from the U.S. occupation of Iraq had converged there to share stories of atrocities being committed daily in Iraq. Endorsed by dozens of local and regional antiwar groups, including Veterans for Peace and Students for a Democratic Society, the meeting drew local and some international media attention. The testimonies of the U.S. service members who had participated in the occupations of Iraq and Afghanistan were intended to establish to the public that the occasional stories of wrongdoing in both countries that the mainstream press chose to expose were not isolated incidents limited to a few "bad apples," as the Pentagon claimed.

"We've heard from the politicians, from the generals, from the media—now it's our turn," announced Iraq war veteran Kelly Dougherty, who served in Iraq as a military police officer in 2003. "It's not going to be easy to hear what we have to say. It's not going to be easy for us to tell it. But we believe that the only way this war is going to end is if the American people truly understand what we have done in their name."[3]

With a view to drawing mainstream media coverage, the earlier Winter Soldier event in D.C. had been closed to the general public. The hoped-for mainstream media coverage did not materialize, but IVAW experienced a burst of growth, its membership expanding rapidly in the months following the event. The strategy for the Northwest Regional Winter Soldier, in contrast, was to be inclusive. The organizers were keen to involve not just the community in Seattle, but also in surrounding areas, in the event. In order to energize public antiwar sentiment and capitalize on it, the veterans led a determined demonstration of hundreds through the streets of downtown Seattle, following the hearings at the Town Hall. Traffic was halted for nearly an hour by protestors chanting slogans of "U.S. out of the Middle East," "No Justice, No Peace," and carrying placards that read, "You Can't Be All You Can Be If You're Dead!"

◆   ◆   ◆

Iraq war veteran Chanan Suarez Diaz was stationed at Okinawa, Japan, immediately after serving in Iraq. Diaz started exchanging e-mails with his tenth-grade drama teacher to pour out his discontent about what he had experienced in Iraq. His teacher told him about a veterans' group, and Diaz joined the group online, while still active duty. Simultaneously, he launched into a self-education program, reading political books and progressive news online. By the time he returned to the United States, he was ready to begin organizing, giving talks and raising awareness about the occupation. He was involved in the first "Fund the wounded, not the war" protest outside his local VA in Seattle, and has also been involved in shutting down military recruiting stations around the Seattle area.

Of Bush, Rumsfeld, Cheney, and all others complicit in orchestrating the invasion and occupation of Iraq, Diaz says, "I think they should be tried, by members of the American community, and also by the Iraqi people. What they have done is inexcusable, and whatever is done to them, no matter how harsh, will still not suffice to bring justice to the Iraqi people and the American people after what they have suffered."

Diaz believes,

It is very important to read history and draw the lessons from other movements. We must learn from what worked then and what did not. We must know the facts and the depth of the G.I. movement in the '60s and '70s. That gives me hope. I also feel hopeful about the different forms of resistance popping up today, like more soldiers refusing to fight, the dissent, the more thinking that I see a lot of active-duty people do. The longer this continues, the riper the conditions for more soldiers to refuse to fight.

Despite what the Pentagon and its chief agent, mainstream American media, project about the overwhelming national and international support that legitimize the occupations of Iraq and Afghanistan, there is enough evidence to indicate otherwise. The question that begs introspection is whether the American public will put this evidence to use to build sufficient pressure on the government to change America's foreign policy.

◆   ◆   ◆

In the Seattle Town Hall gathering, Seth Manzel, who served in Iraq as a vehicle commander and machine gunner, told the audience, "I watched Iraqi police bring in someone to interrogate. There were four men on the prisoner ... One was pummeling his kidneys with fists and another was inserting a bottle up his rectum. It looked like a frat house gang rape." Another incident he narrated was of an elderly jaundiced man lying on the ground, writhing in pain at the detention center in Tal Afar. Manzel's medic colleagues had refused to treat him, saying that the old man was just being lazy and they were not authorized to treat detainees.

Army journalist Jan Critchfield, attached to the First Cavalry in Baghdad in 2004, said his unwritten brief there was to "counter the liberal media bias" about the occupation. He testified:

> I was with a unit that shot at a man and wife near a checkpoint. She had been shot through her shinbone, and that was the first story I covered in Iraq. Our target audience was in the United States, and the emphasis, we were told, should be on reporting on humanitarian aid missions the military conducted. I don't know how many stories I did on chicken drops, which were about distributing frozen chickens. I don't know what else to call it other than propaganda. I would find the highest-ranking persons I could get, and quote them verbatim without fact-checking anything they said.

Other veterans spoke about the lax to nonexistent rules of engagement that led to the slaughter of innocent civilians in Iraq. "Before being deployed to Iraq, we were told that we needed to be prepared to have little kids and women shoot at us," said former marine Sergio Kochergin, who served two deployments in Iraq.

> It was part of an attempt to portray Iraqis as animals. We were constantly told everybody there wants to kill you, everybody wants to get you. There was racism in every rank in the military. It seemed like a joke, but it was a joke that destroyed many lives in Iraq. We were supposed to do humanitarian work, but all we ever did was harass people, drive like crazy on the streets, pretending it was our city and that we could do whatever we wanted to do. I was in Husaiba with a sniper platoon on the Syrian border, and we would basically go out on the town and search for people to shoot. The longer we were there, the more lenient the rules of engagement got. So if anyone had a bag and a shovel, we were to shoot them. We were allowed to take our shots at anything that looked suspicious. And at that point in time, everything looked suspicious. Later on, we had no ROE at all. If you see something that doesn't seem right, take them out. Enough is enough. It is time to get out of there.

Doug Connor was a first lieutenant in the army and worked as a surgical nurse with a combat support unit in Iraq. Most patients he treated were Iraqi civilians. "There were so many people that needed treatment we couldn't take all of them," he recounted. "When a bombing happened and forty-five patients were brought to us, it was always Americans treated first, then Kurds, then the Arabs. It got to the point where we started calling the Iraqi patients 'range balls' because, just like on the driving range in golf, you don't care about losing them."

Despite the lack of major media coverage of most of the Winter Soldier events, the force of veterans coming together to speak truth to the occupations is not lost on local communities. As time passes, overall support for both occupations has continued to erode, and veterans organizing to give their public testimony has played an important role in this. These cases somewhat explain why our government goes to such inordinate lengths to propagate the "bad apple" theory each time it is faced with the threat of exposure.

SIX

RESISTING SEXISM

Maricela Guzman served in the navy from 1998 to 2002 as a computer technician on the island of Diego Garcia and later in Naples, Italy. She was raped in boot camp but did not talk about the assault for the rest of her time in the military. In her own words, she "survived by becoming a workaholic. Fortunately or unfortunately, the military took advantage of this, and I was much awarded as a soldier for my work ethic."

Guzman decided to leave the military on witnessing the way it treated the native population of Diego Garcia. Post discharge, her life became unmanageable. The effects of PTSD from her rape took a heavy toll. After undergoing a divorce, a failed suicide attempt, and homelessness, she moved in with her parents. A chance encounter with a female veteran at a political event in Los Angeles prompted her to contact the VA for help. She began seeing a therapist there who diagnosed her with PTSD from her rape. She told me in an interview that the VA denied her claim nevertheless, "Because they said I couldn't prove it ... since I had not brought it up when it happened and also because I had not shown any deviant behavior while in the service. I was outraged and felt compelled to talk about what happened. I do a lot of counter-recruitment[1] with high school kids.

Last year I spoke to over thirty thousand kids in the L.A. area about this specific issue. I am one of the sixteen cofounders of Service Women's Action Network (SWAN)."

Like countless others, Guzman had learned early that the culture of the military promoted silence about sexual assault. Her experience over the years has convinced her that sexual violence is a systemic problem in the military, "It has been happening since women were allowed into the service and will continue to happen after [U.S. involvement in] Iraq and Afghanistan. Through the gossip mill we would hear of women who had reported being raped. No confidentiality was maintained nor any protection given to them, making them susceptible to fresh attacks. The boys' club culture is strong and the competition exclusive. To get ahead women have to be better than men. That forces many not to report rape, because it is a blemish and can ruin your career." She is not hopeful of any radical change in policy anytime soon, but, "One good thing that has come out of this war is that people want to talk about this now."

◆   ◆   ◆

It is widely accepted that without unquestioning obedience from its ranks the military apparatus cannot sustain itself. Unless there is complete subservience soldiers cannot be motivated to follow any order, including those to use illegal weapons, torture prisoners, or kill civilians. Perhaps the first requisite is dehumanizing the individual. That process starts in boot camp and is directed at the soldiers themselves. They are addressed in derogatory terms like grunts, jarheads, and far worse.

The military is notorious for its sexist, homophobic, and misogynistic culture. Drill instructors indoctrinate new recruits by routinely calling them "girl," "pussy," "bitch," and "dyke." Pornography is prevalent, and misogynistic rhymes have existed for decades, like this Naval Academy ditty:

Who can take a chainsaw
Cut the bitch in two
Fuck the bottom half
And give the upper half to you?

Sexism, homophobia, racism, and misogyny are encouraged, and once soldiers excel in these lessons they practice them without discriminating between friend, foe, or colleague. Sometimes the colleagues happen to be women.

Tracey Harmon, who joined the Army Reserves in 2002 and served for six years, experienced the abuse of authority firsthand. Her sergeant ordered her and another female soldier to assist in a class he was teaching by processing soldiers for the course.

"My friend and I showed up at the range where he was teaching his class, and the entire class, who were all men, just started to laugh at us," she explained to me. "We realized we were only there to be "eye candy," and I was extremely offended. The next day I started to raise hell about it." Harmon reported the incident to her command major, "who took me in an office and shut the door, which he was not supposed to do since he's a man and I'm a woman. This in itself violated army regulations." Harmon, in her early twenties at the time, continued, "This command major was fifty years old, and he told me, 'Harmon, you are gorgeous, smart, and very competent, and if I were your age, I'd want to date you, and do a whole lot more than that.'"

Harmon told me she felt betrayed by this, but did not do anything about it at the time "because I accepted that as just being military culture." The "military culture" she refers to, as she explained to me, meant "you are either a bitch, a dyke, or a whore. If you sleep with one person in your unit, you are a whore."

Compared to countless other women in the military, including her best friend, who was also a soldier, Harmon's trials were light. She shared a story with me about her closest friend, whom she wished to remain anonymous.

"My best friend while I was in the military, she was raped," Harmon said, "One night, when she was in the barracks with two guys who had just gotten back from Iraq, they all got really drunk, and then they raped her. She told me just after it happened that she awoke remembering they'd also inserted a hair-straightener into her vagina, simulating a vibrator. I was the first person she told about this, since I was her NCO and best friend."

Specialist Suzanne Swift refused to return to Iraq, where she says she was sexually harassed by a commanding officer. Her charges of sexual harassment and assault went unaddressed, and instead she was arrested and confined for going AWOL. Her mother Sara Rich told *Democracy Now!*,

> What happened to her when she was in Iraq was she was sexually harassed by her platoon sergeant, and then she was sexually abused and used by her squad leader. She reported the platoon sergeant harassment to her equal opportunity officer, and he did nothing. And when she told her team leader about what had happened with her squad leader, nothing happened, as well. I tried to help her, going through our Congressman DeFazio, but she was too scared for her life to do anything. So I stayed silent. I stayed silent.[2]

Some women veterans' groups have coined the term "command rape," used when women are coerced by higher-ups to use their bodies in order to obtain generators, or even food, out in the field. This is one of the worst violations. Soldiers are taught to regard one another as family so this resembles incest since the higher-ranking soldiers are taking advantage of their authority to attack the people they are supposed to protect.

More than one hundred ninety thousand U.S. military women have served thus far in Iraq and Afghanistan on the front lines, often having to confront sexual assault and harassment within their own ranks. The VA's PTSD center claims that the incidence of rape, assault, and harassment were higher in wartime during the 1991 U.S. attack on Iraq than during peacetime.[3] Thus far, the numbers from Iraq show a continuance, and increase, of this disturbing trend.

Understandably, Department of Defense (DoD) numbers for sexual assaults in the military are far lower than numbers provided by other sources, primarily because the Pentagon only counts rapes that soldiers have officially reported. Revealing shocking statistics, in late April 2009, the BBC reported: "According to several studies of the U.S. Military funded by the Department of Veteran Affairs, 30% of military women are raped while serving, 71% are sexually assaulted, and 90% are sexually harassed. The Department of Defense acknowledges the problem, estimating in its 2009 annual report on sexual assault that some 90% of military sexual assaults are never reported."[4]

It is not difficult to ascertain the reason so few sexual assaults are reported in the military. Jennifer Hogg of the New York Army National Guard remembers,

I helped a woman report a sexual assault while she was in basic training. She was grabbed between the legs from behind while going up stairs. She was not able to pinpoint the person who did it. She was scared to report it to the drill sergeant, and I assured her that I would go with her and help her in the situation. During training, the position of authority the drill sergeant holds makes any and all reporting a daunting task, and most people are scared to even approach him or her. In this case, the drill sergeant's response was swift but caused resentment toward the female who made the report because her identity was not hidden from males who were punished as a whole for the one. After this incident many of the males said harassing things to her as they passed her during training, so much so that she regretted having addressed the issue. You can be ostracized as the woman who had dared to speak up. Women willing to speak up are trained to shut up, which results in an atmosphere of silence. After my experiences in basic and advanced individual training I never reported an incident again.

Hogg herself faced verbal sexual harassment, "When I removed my protective top in the heat I would often hear comments such as 'Where you been hiding them puppies?' in reference to my breasts." She did not even consider reporting.

To make matters worse, according to DoD statistics, 84 to 85 percent of soldiers convicted of rape or sexual assault leave the military with honorable discharges. Not only are they not penalized, they are honored.

Statistics of civilian sexual assault in the United States reveal numbers which, though much lower than those of sexual assault in the U.S. military, are also dismal. According to the National Institute of Justice Centers for Disease Control and Prevention, one in six women in the United States will be a victim of sexual assault in her lifetime.[5] In the military, at least two in five will.[6]

◆   ◆   ◆

Women in America were first allowed into the military during the Revolutionary War in 1775, and their travails are as old. April Fitzsimmons served in the air force from 1985 to 1989 as an intelligence analyst and an intelligence briefer for a two-star general. Early in her military career, she was sexually assaulted by another solider. The experience is still fresh in her memory,

> When the assault happened I was very frightened. I was at the NCO club and had a couple of drinks. I wasn't sure of my rights, and did not know what to do. I had no reference for it. I don't remember this ever being covered in training. I was so fearful, I said nothing. When I saw the perpetrator on base, I knew he was guilty, but still didn't know what to do until I was told by a security person on base to lock my doors. They knew of a woman in my dorm that had been raped. I had a woman boss, a senior master sergeant, guide me through the process of filing a complaint. I pointed him out in court, and he was removed from the base.

But that wasn't the last Fitzsimmons would see of the perpetrator.

Fitzsimmons was nineteen years old at the time, with two years of service behind her. After she reported her assault, she was offered counseling but declined as there is a stigma attached to it. Those who seek counseling are perceived to be at risk, as being too weak and vulnerable. Had Fitzsimmons sought counseling, she would have forfeited her top-secret clearance and also her access to the classified military intelligence she needed to do her job. Another reason for maintaining silence on the matter was that Fitzsimmons was declared "airman [sic] of the year," for the European command. "I didn't want to lose that. I wanted the whole thing to go away."

However, silence ceased to be an option for her in the wake of the events of September 11, 2001. "I began to see through all the double talk and heard Cheney and much of the administration saying things I knew to be untrue. We knew, for so many years, after … tracking Iraq for so long, what weapons they had. I knew what the administration claimed was untrue. I had been in the NSA and I knew what we had by way of information."

In an attempt to get accurate information out and prevent the invasion of Iraq, she began writing open letters. She then created a one-woman play, *The Need to Know*, which has been running for six years.[7] In the play, Fitzsimmons also addresses her own sexual assault in the military. "It is a visible assault," is how she described the scene to me. It lasts all of two minutes in a ninety-minute play, but after watching the performance, women who had been attacked, either in or out of the service, started coming forward.

When news of rapes and sexual assaults by U.S. soldiers in Iraq, against both other soldiers and Iraqis began to surface, Fitzsimmons became more active. It took her a long time to speak up but she says, "After reading about the fourteen-year-old Iraqi girl, Abeer Qasim Hamza, who was raped by several soldiers, and about Suzanne Swift, a soldier who after being raped by another U.S. soldier went AWOL rather than redeploy with the command that was responsible for allowing the rape to occur, I was convinced that there was a cycle of sexual violence in the military that was neither being seen nor addressed."

At the 2006 National Convention of Veterans for Peace in Seattle, Fitzsimmons met with forty-five other female vets and began compiling information. "I asked for a show of hands of women veterans who had been assaulted while on duty, and half the women raised their hands. So I knew we had to do something and we all started … sharing our stories." She, along with other women veterans like Maricela Guzman, founded SWAN to help military women who had been victims of sexual violence.

Jennifer Hogg, another cofounder of SWAN, told me that the organization focuses on leadership development of female veterans and makes it a point to have women of color and LGBT women veterans comprise a minimum of half of SWAN's staff. In addition to providing support to women who have experienced military sexual trauma, the group also works to support those who have been discharged under Don't Ask Don't Tell and women struggling to get their VA benefits.

Fitzsimmons noted, "When victims come forward, they are ostracized, doubted, and isolated from their communities. They are punished." Many of the perpetrators are officers who "use their ranks to coerce women to sleep with them. On being asked, all they have to do is deny it after which they are reprimanded and sent away. It's a closely interwoven community, so the perpetrators are safe within the system and can fearlessly move free amongst their victims. The crisis is so severe that I'm telling women to simply not join the military because it's completely unsafe and puts them at risk. Until something changes at the top, no woman should join the military."

◆   ◆   ◆

On July 19, 2005, Army Private First Class LaVena Johnson's body was found in a tent belonging to the private military contractor KBR in Balad, Iraq. LaVena's body was covered in abrasions; it had a broken nose, a black eye, burned hands, loose teeth, acid burns on the genitals, and a bullet hole in the head. The army labeled her death a "suicide," and told her parents she died of "self-inflicted, non-combat injuries." Her parents believe that their daughter, who was only nineteen at the time, was raped and murdered. In summer 2008 they demanded a full congressional investigation into her death.

In an interview on *Democracy Now!* Dr. John Johnson, LaVena's father, told Amy Goodman,

The first indication we got about the mode of death was from the casualty liaison officer at Fort Leonard Wood, Missouri. He told me
that LaVena was found dead in her barracks with a gunshot wound to
the head. I know a lot of people who knew people over there. A friend
of ours who is a police officer immediately e-mailed a friend posted
in Iraq to verify where she had been found and heard that LaVena was
found dead in a contractor's tent. My friend was so distraught over it
that he had a heart attack on his way over to our house. He didn't die,
but it was severe. The next day a relative brought me the message.[8]

Dr. Johnson was told by the military his daughter committed suicide by shooting herself in the head with an M-16 rifle.

First of all, my daughter was 5' 1" and that weapon is forty inches
long. Let's say, she did manage to get it into her mouth, then the re-
coil from that weapon would have blown her face off. Let's say, if she
was tall enough and she got it in her mouth pretty well, when that
bullet pops out of that barrel, it starts tumbling all over the place so
when it exits, it exits in a straight line, and tears a huge hole in one's
head. This bullet hit at the temporal lobe, bounced and ended up
going two-and-a-quarter inch[es] toward the temporal lobe and
popped out. And that can only happen with a hand revolver and not
an M-16 rifle.

When he examined his daughter's body he "could tell that her
nose had been broken, because plastic surgery had been performed
on it. She had makeup on but I could see an abrasion up under my
eye. I could see that her lips had been busted, because right near the
edges of both lips, I could see what looked like a cut. And her gloves
were glued on her hands, and I thought that was peculiar. So I was
pretty confident she had been beaten."[9]

When asked why he thought his daughter had been raped, Dr. Johnson elaborated, "It wasn't until we got the colored CD [compact disk of color photographs] that we could really look at that vaginal area, and it was torn—there were tears in the lip, just a numerous amount of tears. In addition to that, it had a substance running out of it, and it looked as if that substance may have been lye. So we assume they poured that in her to destroy DNA evidence."

LaVena's father has unearthed more stories that echo his daughter's. At least ten other families of female soldiers who the military claims took their own lives have contacted him, and the common thread among their stories is rape.

Ann Wright spent twenty-six years in the U.S. Army and Army Reserves and was a diplomat in the State Department for sixteen years before resigning in March 2003, in protest against the then-impending invasion of Iraq. Wright worked with the Johnsons in an attempt to find justice. At the families' request she was to have joined them in a face-to-face meeting with the army but the latter barred her from being present at the meeting.

"We have found, through investigations of other deaths—you know, there have been ninety-eight women, military women, who have died in Iraq, Kuwait, and Bahrain," Wright informed *Democracy Now!* in the same interview,

Forty of them have died of non-combat incidents, as the military terms it, nineteen of those forty under suspicious circumstances. Thirteen of them have now been termed suicides by the military. We know the military has misinformed many military families, to include the Tillman family; Karen Meredith, whose son Ken was killed by Iraqi trainees; Kamisha Block, who was shot in her barracks and the family told she was killed by friendly fire, one shot—it turned out she was killed by five shots, and her killer, a member of her unit, committed suicide right in her barracks but the family had no intimation about this for over eight months. So there's a lot of misinformation that's passed on to these families.

Quite obviously, a good deal of information is being withheld as well. The military's Criminal Investigation Command stuck to their story that LaVena Johnson's death was a suicide.

◆   ◆   ◆

In January 2006, I provided testimony about U.S. war crimes in Iraq at a Commission of Inquiry for Crimes against Humanity Committed by the Bush Administration in New York. Also presenting testimony was Colonel Janis Karpinski, the former commander of Abu Ghraib prison. She made one of the most shocking revelations, that it was by the order of Lieutenant General Ricardo Sanchez, former senior U.S. military commander in Iraq, that the cause of death of several female American soldiers in Iraq was covered up.

Karpinski testified that a coalition joint task force surgeon said in a briefing that women soldiers had died of dehydration in the one-hundred-thirty-degree heat. They refused to drink liquids in the latter part of the day because they were reluctant to use the latrines, which were located outside the barracks after dark, for fear of being sexually assaulted or raped by male soldiers. Generators at the camp were loud enough to muffle the sound of the women's screams as male soldiers jumped them and dragged them and sexually assaulted them.

Speaking of Lieutenant General Ricardo S. Sanchez, who was commander of coalition forces in Iraq from June 2003 to June 2004,

Karpinski said, "Rather than make everybody aware of that, because that's shocking, and as a leader if that's not shocking to you, then you're not much of a leader, what they told the surgeon is don't brief those details anymore. And don't say specifically that they're women. You can provide that in a written report but don't brief it in the open anymore."

Major General Walter Wojdakowski, Sanchez's top deputy in Iraq, saw "dehydration" listed as the cause of death on the death certificate of a female master sergeant in September 2003. But under orders from Sanchez, he directed that the cause of death no longer be listed.

Speaking at the Thomas Jefferson School of Law in October 2005 about sexual assaults in Iraq and their cover-up, Karpinski said, "It was out of control. An 800 number existed as a helpline for women to use to report sexual assaults, but no one had a phone, and no one answered the number, which was based in the U.S." She informed the audience that after more than eighty incidents were reported during a six-month period in Iraq and Kuwait, the rape hotline was still being answered by a machine that told callers to leave a message.[10] "There were innumerable such situations all over the theater of operations—Iraq and Kuwait—because female soldiers didn't have a voice, individually or collectively. Even as a general I didn't have a voice with Sanchez, so I know what the soldiers were facing. Sanchez did not want to hear about female soldier requirements and/or issues."[11]

Karpinski quoted Sanchez as saying, "The women asked to be here, so now let them take what comes with the territory."

◆   ◆   ◆

Catherine Jayne West got to experience firsthand what Sanchez meant when he spoke of letting female U.S. soldiers "take what comes with the territory." A member of the Mississippi National Guard, West served in Iraq from 2005 to 2006. "I was supposed to be a cook," she explained to me in an interview in May 2009, "But ended up pulling guard tower duty, going on patrols, guarding the front gate of the base, guarding Iraqi female prisoners, and filling tankers."

On the night of October 3, 2005, West was brutally raped by two other soldiers. "I was sent from my FOB (forward operating base) to another base because my doctor in the states sent a letter to my CO saying I needed to have an ob-gyn look at me because I had precancerous cells," she told me. "I arrived at Camp Anaconda with two other men who were sent for medical attention as well."

West did some shopping, had dinner, and caught a movie with her friend, then went back to her tent and they parted ways. "I went to the computer and e-mailed my family and told them where I was. Then I went back to my tent and went to sleep because I had the doctor's appointment the next morning. A little while later someone came to the back door of the tent."

West's commanding officer was aware of the fact that she was expecting a message from the Red Cross, "because my son back home was trying to hurt himself," she explained.

So the guy who came into the back of my tent woke me up and said I had a Red Cross message and to come with him because the chaplain wanted to see me. It didn't feel right, but I went on and followed him. I got to the door, and we walked to the tent where the chaplain was, and I shined a flashlight in there. It was empty so at that point I tried to escape, but he pushed me inside and I tripped and fell on some mattresses that were already on the floor. He then grabbed me, and put his hand over my mouth and told me not to scream, and that if I screamed he would kill me, and then have his friend in the tent next to this one come over and finish me off.

At this point the soldier rolled West onto her stomach and tied her hands behind her back. He then rolled her over onto her back and proceeded to take her clothes off. "I can still tell you exactly what he smelled like," she said, "I can see images of his face. Then he told me, "Uh huh, I know you like ass sex. The whore likes ass sex." I just laid there and cried. I couldn't say anything."

West vaguely remembers having her head slammed repeatedly against the ground, and knows that she went unconscious for a time but was aware that the other soldier the rapist mentioned came in and raped her as well. "The next day, I didn't shower and went and reported it. I couldn't find all my clothes, but had put on what I could find. The doctors used a rape kit and the doctor examined me—took semen samples, hair samples, and they were very thorough."

West described her experience with the criminal trial about her rape, which underscored how even then, the military appeared to be more concerned with covering up the incident, rather than bringing justice against the perpetrators. For starters, West had to fly to Alaska for the trial because one of the soldiers who raped her was based in Fort Wainwright, in Fairbanks, Alaska.

"I picked two guys out of the lineup, but for some reason they said they couldn't find the other guy. The reason the one guy was picked was that he went and bragged to guys in his unit what he'd done to me, so his buddies turned him in. In court, the defense asked why I didn't fight back, since I was in the army."

Since the defense was unable to find whom the second semen sample belonged to, they accused West of having sex with someone seventy-two hours prior to being raped. The rapist who was on trial ended up being found guilty for "kidnapping," but not for rape, despite having admitted to raping West. "I asked the judge how this could be possible, when he admitted to doing it," West said.

The trial required four trips to the courtroom, and just before the fourth, the rapist, Keven Lemieux, a PFC at the time of the rape, was promoted to specialist. "The military was trying to cover his ass," West told me angrily, "He was given three years for kidnapping, and spent some time in jail at Fort Lewis in Washington state, but they knocked off half his time."

After the rape, West was transferred out of her unit to another unit, comprised of 150 men and just seven women. "The view of most men in the military is that women have no place in the military," West said of her experience in the new unit. "I had a command sergeant-major who came up to me and said, "There aren't but two places for women in the military—in the kitchen and in the bedroom. Women have no place in the military."

West told me that, from her experience in the military, she believed sexual assault was rampant in the ranks. "In the hospital when I was getting checked out, there were three other marines there who had been raped by their fellow marines," she explained. "They were all men! Two of the criminal investigators who questioned me about my rape told me about these men being raped as well." West was also friends with a female medic who was also sexually assaulted.

I called the Pentagon and talked with spokesperson Cynthia Smith the same month I had talked with West. "We understand that one sex assault is too many in the DoD," Smith told me. "We have an office working on prevention and response." Smith shared with me an interesting approach the Pentagon is taking to work on "prevention and response." She explained, "We understand this is very important for everyone to get involved in preventing sexual assault, and are calling on everyone to get involved, step in, and watch each others' backs."

The "watch each others' backs" approach is not sufficient for West, who remains outraged by both her rape and the response by the military. "The military keeps sweeping it under the rug," West said. "The military is doing nothing about it. They are just pretending it never happens. They are only looking out for their own asses, rather than taking care of their soldiers."

Major reforms of the military around dealing with sexism and sexual assault are urgently needed to better the disastrous situation faced by women in the military. The U.S. military, upholding one of the most misogynistic cultures on the planet, needs a radical transformation to provide a safe, just, and healthy environment for women who serve. To date, most of what the military has done, instead of this, has been to cover up, deny, and propagandize about the crisis.

◆   ◆   ◆

At a House hearing of the Subcommittee on National Security and Foreign Affairs in July 2008, Representative Jane Harman exposed the way in which the U.S. military deals with the issue of sexual assault.[12] A recent visit to a VA hospital in the Los Angeles area had brought to her notice unbelievable horror stories,

> My jaw dropped when I heard from the doctors that forty-one percent of the female veterans at the hospital say they have faced sexual assault in the military. Twenty-nine percent say they were raped while in service. They speak of the continued terror and helplessness that they experience and of the downward spiral many of their lives have taken since. We have an epidemic here. Women serving in the U.S. military today are more likely to be raped by a fellow soldier than be killed by enemy fire in Iraq.[13]

Records reveal that in 2007 out of 2,212 reported sexual assaults in the military, a mere 181 were referred to court martial. Harman contrasted this with how in the civilian world 40 percent of those arrested for sexual assault are prosecuted.[14]

In December 2007 Lance Corporal Maria Lauterbach, a twenty-year-old pregnant marine was killed by a North Carolina Marine Corporal Cesar Laurean who had raped her earlier that year. Lauterbach's burned body, and that of her unborn baby, were found in a shallow grave in the backyard of Laurean's home. The young woman had filed a rape claim with the military against Laurean seven months prior to her murder. Protective orders were issued to keep him away from Lauterbach. Her mother, Mary Lauterbach, had warned the authorities that Laurean was a danger to her daughter, but the Marine Corps ignored her cautions.[15]

Testifying at the panel Mary Lauterbach said, "I believe that Maria would be alive today if the marines had a more effective system in place to protect the victims of sexual assault. The onus to generate evidence should not be on the victim. Maria is dead, but there will be many more victims in the future, I caution you. I'm here to ask you to do your best to help change the way the military treats victims of crime and to ensure the victims receive the support and protection they need and deserve."

In a sixty-day period during summer 2008, two more military women were murdered near military bases in North Carolina, and a Red Cross employee, Ingrid Torres, was raped at Kunsan Air Base in South Korea by an air force flight doctor.

Subsequent to the House Committee Hearing, Representative Harman, who is chair of the Homeland Security Intelligence Subcommittee, along with Representative Michael Turner, introduced legislation that made it obligatory for the Department of Defense to develop a comprehensive strategy to prevent rape and sexual assault in the military. "That a female soldier in Iraq is more likely to be raped by a fellow soldier than killed by enemy fire is sickening," said Harman, "This crisis has reached epidemic proportions and threatens our national security. Better training and rigorous prosecutions are needed to make clear to soldiers and to the command structure that bright red lines have been drawn."[16]

Aggravating the attendees at the hearing was how Dr. Kaye Whitley, the Director of the Sexual Assault Prevention and Response Office for the Department of Defense, was ordered by the military not to appear, despite the fact that she had been subpoenaed to testify.

On September 10, 2008, a second oversight hearing was held on the topic at the Rayburn House office building in Washington, D.C. This time, Dr. Whitley showed up. "I was given a direct order by my supervisor to get back in the van and go back," Whitley told the members of Congress present at the meeting, when asked why she failed to appear in the first hearing. Congresswoman Carolyn Maloney went on to tell Whitley:

> I'd like to ask Dr. Kaye Whitley, why do you think your superiors did not want you to testify? This committee had to subpoena four of your superiors before they allowed you to come testify. I can't think of any reason except that your testimony might show they haven't done anything. Eighteen studies have been done. And in this latest GAO report, there is talk about setting up a task force on sexual assault in the military in 2004, but they did not begin to do work until August 2008. Is this because DoD has not addressed the problem, they have ignored the problem, swept it under the rug? As men and women are overseas protecting our constitutional rights, the DoD has been so ineffective at protecting their personal rights.

Dr. Whitley replied, "I am not privy to discuss whether I would or would not testify. I know they [DoD] did know I was down here on the Hill a lot talking to Congressmen ... but I'm not privy to any discussion about this." Later in the hearing, when Dr. Whitley was pressured further to explain why she failed to appear at the first hearing, she stated, "We pulled up in front of the building and Mr. Dominguez [Principal Deputy Undersecretary of Defense for Personnel and Readiness] said, 'You will not be testifying,' and did I understand he was 'giving me a direct order?'"

Representative John Tierney, the Chairman of the Subcommittee on National Security and Foreign Affairs, also at the hearing, said of the DoD's effort to prevent Dr. Whitley from testifying at the previous hearing, "Dr. Whitley's office is, by the Pentagon's own acknowledgement, the, and I quote, "single point of accountability for Department of Defense sexual assault policy." Tierney later added, "But what kind of message does her and the Department's unwillingness, until now, to allow testimony send to our men and women in uniform?" and, "Just because the Defense Department's task force on sexual assault—after three long years—finally had its first public meeting in August, does not mean we can all collectively take a sigh of relief."

Congressman Christopher Shays was appalled. Earlier in the hearing he had stated: "The hearing held by this Subcommittee two months ago was a continuation of our ongoing efforts to curtail sexual assault in the military. However, instead of partnering with Congress, senior figures in DoD chose to prevent, for reasons beyond our comprehension, Dr. Whitley from testifying. This is one of many reasons why DoD has no credibility with me when it comes to protecting our women in uniform." Representative Shays continued, "The reluctance to allow Dr. Whitley's testimony is convincing evidence that DoD is still not serious about the problem of sexual assault."

Representative Maloney had opened the hearing by reading a written statement that concluded: "The DoD has made several promises that the Defense Incident-Based Reporting System (DIBRS), which collects statistics about crimes committed within the military services, would be up and running by now. Congress first mandated that the Pentagon collect crime statistics in 1988. Twenty years later, and DIBRS is not slated for completion until December 2008. This is unacceptable. If the DoD will not take it upon itself to make this a priority, we in Congress have a responsibility to see that our mandates are met."[17]

Since 2002, nearly sixty thousand female vets have reported being raped, sexually assaulted, or subjected to other forms of sexual trauma.

Exactly a year after the Johnson case, fourteen-year-old Abeer Qasim Hamza was raped in Iraq by several soldiers, who then shot her in the head, burned her corpse, and murdered her entire family in an attempt to hide the crime. If soldiers can commit sexual assault against their own, and get away with it, what is to stop them from doing the same (and worse) to an Iraqi "enemy?"

In the buildup to the invasion and in the years since, I have been privy to discussions in which well-meaning men and women of my country have expressed relief that, if nothing else, the invasion would help uplift the terribly oppressed women of Iraq. As it turns out, now Iraqi women, too, can enjoy the benefits women in the U.S. military enjoy, like freedom from sexual assault, true democracy, and justice.

SEVEN

RESISTING DISCRIMINATION

When I was in the military they gave me a medal for killing two men and a discharge for loving one.
— **Epitaph of Leonard P. Matlovich (1943–1988)**

Homophobia arguably manifests itself in the worst form of discrimination in the military, surpassing even racism. In the course of gathering material for this book, one important lesson I learned is that it is not merely an external enemy that soldiers fight. Far graver in consequence are the battles that soldiers wage with their inner demons. Instead of enabling recruits to vanquish their prejudices and strengthening the individual and the collective spirit, all military training seems to be geared toward invoking the darkest elements in human nature—fear, hatred, pettiness, insecurity, and similar aberrations. Under normal conditions, such an orientation legitimizes unacceptable behavior; under harsh and hostile conditions, it makes beasts of men. It is immaterial whether one is at the perpetrating end or the receiving end of unjust behavior. Of greater significance is the general air of violence and inequality that gets normalized in the process.

New York Army National Guard member Jennifer Hogg shares with me a deep unease. "Being a lesbian on 9/11 is what initially led me to begin to question my involvement in the military and the military's involvement in the world. If on 9/11, I did not have the freedom to hug my girlfriend goodbye before we left as a unit for NYC, then what freedom was I protecting? What freedom could we offer to the world if we treat it so restrictively based on who a person falls in love with?" It is a question that, with suitable modifications, is perhaps pertinent for each one of us to ask, even outside the military. We who never tire of vaunting the freedoms that America allows its citizens and feels authorized to export elsewhere at all costs.

Hogg confronted homophobia at all levels in the military. "During advanced individual training, after the conclusion of Bush versus Gore [election contest], a male E7 [higher ranking] teacher, during his introduction of the class for that day, stated that he was glad that Bush was going to be president because now we won't have all these fags in the army." She chose not to report the incident for fear of being singled out and picked on. "I felt as though physically I would easily fit the stereotype of a lesbian … not to mention that I was in a service position that was heavily male. I did not feel that even the full provision of Don't Ask, Don't Tell, Don't Harass, Don't Pursue (DADT),[1] would suffice to protect me. I heard the word 'fag' used on a daily basis by other soldiers in uniform. If the military does not stop or intervene in casual usage of a word as hate-filled as 'fag,' how could I expect them to take my accusation seriously or treat it as a violation? Besides, what I saw the military do to address DADT was a joke." Hogg explains, "In my unit, all briefings relating to sexism were treated as a joke and were never attended in full strength by the unit. Most people found ways to avoid briefings in general, or have a friend sign them in. Briefings on sexual orientation and DADT invariably had leaders who were embarrassed to give them, so it was never done in an effective or serious manner. Most had low attendance and the information offered was incomplete."

Like most homosexuals in the military, Hogg felt compelled to conceal her sexuality both in and out of uniform, so as not to face discrimination, or worse, though DADT officially only applies to soldiers while in uniform. "While it was not made into an issue for me while [I was] in uniform, I still felt heavily pressured to conceal my sexuality as a civilian for fear of being outed. So even if I served one weekend a month and two weeks in the summer, I was actively under DADT every single day of my contract. This caused considerable stress on my relationship and personal outlook." The fact that Hogg felt the need to conceal her sexual orientation at all times speaks to the dysfunction of the policy and the widespread homophobia in the military.

◆　　◆　　◆

Martin Smith, a retired Marine Corps sergeant who served from 1997 to 2002 as a Russian cryptologic linguist, also struggled with having to hide his homosexuality during his stint in the military. In an article for the *International Socialist Review*, he wrote:

> I remember my first visit to the chow hall in which three Drill Instructors (DIs), wearing their signature "smoky bear" covers, pounced upon me for having looked at them, screaming that I was a "nasty piece of civilian shit." From then on, I learned that you could only look at a DI when instructed to by the command of "Eyeballs!" In addition, recruits could only speak in the third person, thus ridding our vocabulary of the term "I" and divorcing ourselves from our previous civilian identities.

Our emerging group mentality was built upon and reinforced by tearing down and degrading us through a series of regimented and ritualistic exercises in the first phase of boot camp. Despite having an African-American and a Latino DI, recruits in my platoon were ridiculed with derogatory language that included racial epithets. But recruits of color were not the only victims, we were all "fags," "pussies," and "shitbags." We survived through a twisted sort of leveling based on what military historian Christian G. Appy calls "a solidarity of the despised."

Smith describes in the same article how the process of dehumanization of marines occurs concurrently with the dehumanization of the "enemy." The aim is ostensibly to train them to overcome all fear or qualms against killing: "Given the fact that Marines are molded to kill the enemy 'other' from TD (training day) One, combined with the bestial nature of colonial war, it should come as no surprise that rather than turning 'degenerates' into paragons of virtue, the Corps is more likely capable of transforming men into monsters."[2]

Smith told me he was aware of DADT before he joined the forces, but, for him, "part of joining was about trying to find myself. From my own internalized homophobia came the thought that I still needed to prove myself as a man." As with so many other recruits, there was in addition the economic factor, since Smith was in dire need of an income.

In boot camp, another recruit accused Smith of being gay. "It became a rumor and the drill instructors picked up on it, and I was ostracized from the beginning. There is a tendency to identify a handful to pick on and use that to build solidarity with the other guys." After transferring to Monterey, California, to study as a linguist, Smith hid his sexual orientation because "on base, being gay, you are vilified. But in the civilian world you're sort of a rock star because you are gay and in the marines. It's schizophrenic … so that was difficult. I would find other gay friends, marines, and we kept it secret because people would be suspicious of us just for being friends. So we would meet fifty yards from the barracks and sneak off base just to hang out as friends."

A hate crime in Laramie, Wyoming, in 1998, heightened Smith's survival instinct, forcing him to further hide his homosexuality. After Matthew Shepard, a gay University of Wyoming student, was brutally murdered, Smith found the NCOs starting class with vile jokes about gays and unabashedly declaring, "That fag deserved to die." It bothered him that no one protested.

After a transfer to Hawaii, Smith found a simpler method of disguising his orientation. "I had a boyfriend in town, and his brother's wife pretended to be my girlfriend, and we went to the Marine Corps ball together. She was a really attractive Asian woman, and it drew attention … People would ask us questions, and we improvised elaborate stories about what we were doing. My story was that I had this girlfriend out of town … when in reality I lived off base and was regularly seeing my boyfriend about a half-hour away."

While on base, Smith still found it necessary to maintain a facade of being "normal" by doing things like leaving copies of *Hustler* magazine lying around. "I would tell people I was going to stripper clubs on the weekends … constant lies. Don't Ask Don't Tell forces you to lie. It's not just about being gay, but who you are spending time with, who your friends are. Your whole existence becomes a lie. I turned to drugs, any kind of escapism. I made it a point to get out of my mind, which was the only relief I could get. That's the kind of toll it took on me."

While there are no hard numbers on the number of gays in the military, Smith believes that it is not dissimilar to that in the civilian population. "However, the difference is likely in who is 'out.' I think that far fewer people in the army are out to themselves and/or friends because of the extreme homophobic, masculine environment, and the obvious fear of losing your job and benefits."

Smith, who was honorably discharged on January 5, 2002, had numerous stories to tell about other gays in the military he saw gay bashed and discriminated against. He found it necessary to keep his orientation hidden for fear of negative consequences such as physical assault, loss of job, and discrimination.

◆   ◆   ◆

Jeff Key, a lance corporal in the Marine Corps Reserve, was deployed to Iraq in 2003. After coming out on CNN during an interview in March 2004, he was finally discharged two years later in April 2006. I spoke with him in August 2008, and found he had a lot to share from his experience as a gay man in the marines.

Why had he joined a military in which gays are openly discriminated against? His reply is profound in its transparency and simplicity: "I believe in representative government. I feel that we live in a world where there are those who fight against representative government and that it is something to be defended. Having been a disenfranchised, defenseless person for a lot of my life, then having grown into a big strong man, I wanted to defend those people, plus I had a general sense of love for my country."

Five years after his return from Iraq, Key admitted that on some levels his joining the military was an attempt to "sort of heal my internalized homophobia and to hopefully be accepted by my culture, because I never felt accepted by my culture and that was very much tied into the gender paradigm and homophobia. And so I thought to become that thing which is the paradigm of American masculinity: a United States Marine."

Key had expected and been prepared for abuse, but unlike most gays in the military, he did not experience any overt discrimination.

"I was pleasantly surprised that on the inside there wasn't very much homophobia. There's a lot of sort of homoerotic joking, which is kind of peculiar. Historically, since man has waged battle, there has been this homoerotic component to the whole military thing. But there's more joking around it than anything else, and that isn't necessarily malicious."

Nevertheless, he did feel constrained to keep his sexuality a secret, at least for a time. He decided to come out when he felt it was a lie to pretend to his fellow marines to be something he wasn't. "I have to say that I never had a negative coming-out experience when I decided to do so. I did not broadcast my homosexuality because, actually from a selfish point of view, I did not want it to harm my military career and I wouldn't have been put in a position of leadership—like I was—had the chain of command known … [and] if I had been more forthcoming about my sexuality."

Key contextualizes his vehement opposition to the U.S. occupation of Iraq. In the beginning, he believed,

> I brought to my country and to the Marine Corps what was, to me, a very noble, kind of sacred commitment. And it was based on a contract. And the written contract that I signed, which includes my willingness to give my life for our constitution, this country, and its people; to always follow lawful orders; and to never follow unlawful orders. And the stated part of the contract is that I'll be willing to give my life for you, I will dedicate myself as a marine to standing up for the principles of the country, and the unspoken part is that you will never use my blood for money.

For him the contract ended when "invasion and colonization, blackout prisons, and torture (began to) get portrayed and received as not only patriotic and democratic, but holy."

Key is candid about his experiences after returning from Iraq.

When I came back from the war, I was overwhelmed with depression. Becoming a marine was one of the very, very best things that had ever happened to me. I was very happy being a marine. I mean, just driving around on Camp Pendleton, I felt great. I loved putting on a uniform, and I loved hanging out with my fellow marines, who are funny, entertaining, sweet, awesome people. And finally, after all those years of struggling with this sexuality thing, I realized, I've got to let go of all that straight-acting bullshit, and live comfortably in a world ... where I've got to be myself. And so here I am with this epiphany, this waking up, realizing oh my god, this wonderful thing that's happened to me in my life has been betrayed and I cannot continue. Because, ultimately, as much as my commitment to my country means to me, and how much being a marine means to me, I am responsible for my own life to my creator.

The prospect of having to live the rest of my life and try to keep silent or in some way continue to be a party to the evil that is running the machine, the machine I call them, is perpetuating in my country, is in some ways worse than death. So when all these things came to light, out of a dark depression, I remember walking into that office and I remember raising my right hand, and I thought about what my oath meant to me. And that is that I'm willing to die to stand up for the principles that I believe this country stands for. So I decided to leave the military and use Clinton's stupid DADT policy to leave.

Key set out to do this on March 31, 2004. Being a ranking marine and easily accessible at Camp Pendleton in California, Key was invited on the *Paula Zahn Now* show on CNN to discuss soldier morale in the wake of the killing of the four Blackwater mercenaries in Fallujah that day. But Key had other plans when he walked into the Los Angeles bureau. After showing the video of the brutal treatment of the corpses of the mercenaries in the streets of Fallujah, Zahn asked Key, "I know I winced when I saw these pictures for the first time. When you saw these images of American soldiers[3] not only being brutally beaten and murdered, but dragged down the street, what went through your mind?"

Key responded, "Oh, I first saw it this morning when I was sitting at the computer. And, honestly, the first thoughts I had were a lot of intense anger. I wanted to go back there to find the people who did that and to hunt them down. It's the marine in me. I wanted to exact vengeance for it." Then, using the platform he had been offered, he proceeded to speak out against the U.S. occupation, quite unexpectedly:

> And then shortly after, I started to think about the families … There are several families today that are changed forever because of the events in Iraq today. I felt a huge amount of sadness for those people. I know that the American service members that lost their lives there, the Americans working there did so out of noble purpose, and its really—it's a shame. I've spent a lot of time and introspection and thinking since I came back from Iraq about our mission there, what it meant to me. I have very conflicting feelings about it. I'm still intensely committed to the reasons I became a marine four years ago and have decided this week to leave the Marine Corps, actually, and came out of the closet as a gay man. I had made sweeping rationalizations that allowed me to continue to lie about my sexuality and stay in the Marine Corps in attempts to stay true to my commitments, to the reasons I joined. And having come back and having received a lot

of information, things we didn't know when we were there, that we were never told about weapons of mass destruction, about our entering there in the first place, I just ...

Zahn cut him off, not knowing how to respond to his comments on Iraq and his sexuality.[4]

Key's action changed his life. He had let his marine buddies know in advance of the interview that he was going to come out on national television in front of millions of viewers, and had their support. He had even gone so far as to detail, in a seven-page letter to his commanding officer, what he was going to do and why. After the show, however, he was surprised at the lack of reaction from the military. "Sometimes with Don't Ask Don't Tell, people are discharged the next day, but I just wasn't getting any answers. Six months went by." He was told he would get an "other than honorable" discharge because he had not been showing up for drill at his base. He had made that choice in the hope that the military would immediately discharge him, as was usually the case with DADT.

It perplexed him. "I was under the impression that coming out of the closet as a big homosexual meant you couldn't be in the United States military anymore." That not being the case for him, he resumed service and started showing up to drill

as this out, queer, antiwar activist on Camp Pendleton, the largest Marine Corps base on the planet. It was awesome, because my being out of the closet to my buddies enabled us to have some really edifying conversations. They got to ask me questions, I felt [I] really made a lot of headway with regard to homosexuality and misconceptions about it, and about what gay men think, straight men think, and all that stuff. So that was sort of multiplied because I was very out of the closet, [and] five million people had seen the interview.

Key took advantage of not being ejected to not only be forthright about homosexuality, but also be "out of the closet about the fact that I thought that the occupation of Iraq was dangerous to my nation. And that I felt that it was immoral and believed that it was illegal. We were signers to the U.N. Charter and to the Geneva Conventions, and for all manner of reasons, it was illegal."

Marines began approaching Key to talk about both issues, and he was relieved to find that they were all "really, really cool about it. Even some very high-ranking enlisted men in my unit pulled me aside and said, 'We're going to take care of you, marine, you're still a marine and this is not going to be a problem for you, and if it is in any way, you come to me.'" Even his fellow marines in Iraq have written him letters of support. Eventually, the major of his unit told Key he needn't show up for drill anymore, that he had fulfilled his obligations. "And I said, OK, sir, if there is anything I can do for you or my marines, at any time, please don't hesitate to call. And then I drove off base for the last time."

It has not been easy. Key's departure began another period of depression for him. "I left Fort Pendleton that day and as I was driving … realizing I would never drive on that base again as a marine was horrible. I was so angry at the people who had stolen that from me and just disgusted, disgusted at the bloodbath that was going on in Iraq and continues to go on."

He wanted to just leave it behind, but his conscience compelled him to speak out. Today he does not advise anyone, gay or straight, to enter the military. "I would say don't. Do not join the United States military. In the foreseeable future, no matter which wing of the one party we have in this country happens to sit in the White House, their soldiers' commitment is going to be abused."

His advice to a young, gay person who may be considering joining the military is to "work through your homophobia in another way … If you think that your homophobia doesn't have any bearing on your wanting to join the military, then I would ask them to examine all the other good reasons somebody might want to join. If you need money for college, I promise you there are other ways. Money is not a justification for what you'll be asked to do. I would say to those kids, don't join."

For those already in the military, Key says, "I would tell them to take a long, hard look at how the military is being used now. If that resonates with their spirit in a good way, then God bless them and keep going. If I could ever help you, let me know, I will. But if it does not resonate with what you believe to be noble … then step up to the front, say, 'I'm a big, fat homosexual,' and leave the military today."

EIGHT

SUICIDE: THE RESISTANCE OF DESPERATION

We hear war called murder. It is not: it is suicide.
—Ramsay MacDonald, British prime minister 1931–1935

Sergio Kochergin, back home from his second deployment in Iraq, held a gun in his mouth, trying to muster the courage to pull the trigger. Untreated PTSD and accompanying nightmares and insomnia, heavy substance abuse, and several failed attempts at self-medication had taken their toll on him. He was in an apartment he shared with a friend in Texarkana, Texas. He had spent the past few months with his parents, where he "was drinking too much and causing too much trouble, breaking things, flipping out every day, and cursing at them." The decision to end his life came in early 2007, from a desperate need for relief and to avoid deployment back to Iraq. Although Kochergin's contract had expired, it would have taken more than six months for him to be medically discharged from the military, a period during which he was sure to be redeployed.

A year later, describing his aborted attempt to me, Kochergin said,

> I had a .40-caliber in my mouth for a long time, trying to figure out the right thing to do. Should I put an end to this suffering or should I allow

it to continue to torment me? Fortunately, I fell asleep and woke up the next morning. My roommate came in and fucking flipped out on me and took the gun away to his parents' house. I stepped out, and with a deep breath of air I was like, 'Man, this is way too good to just throw away.' After that, I decided I had to do something. That's when it sunk in that there's no point running away. I must start dealing with it and do something and that kind of pushed me up.

At the time we met, Kochergin was busy with antiwar activism and hoped to begin college soon. He seized the moment of hope that came his way and managed to find a constructive route out of his suffering and possible redeployment. Thousands of others never get or grab that chance.

There are numerous instances of veterans attempting to kill themselves after they return from their field postings. Some of these incidents seem to be an effort to avoid redeployment. Many more look like desperate bids to stop, once and for all, the internal pain that many veterans experience.

After witnessing the atrocities in Sadr City in Baghdad, Kristopher Goldsmith had returned home shattered, only to learn he was being stop-lossed and redeployed to Iraq. Testifying on the panel "Break-down of the Military" at a Winter Soldier event in Silver Spring, Maryland, Goldsmith gave an account of his response to the news:

The moment I learned that, I swung from being the happiest I had ever been in my life to the most depressed. My joy had come from the sense of relief I felt at the thought of being released from the prison called the army. When that prospect receded, I experienced the most depressing, most agonizing downward spiral I could imagine anyone going through. I was to be redeployed the same week as I had hoped to be discharged, as per my contract, and that was in May of 2007. The day before I ... was supposed to deploy, Memorial Day, I went out onto a field in Fort Stewart where there's a memoriam, a tree planted for every soldier in the Third Infantry Division that has died. I went out among those fallen soldiers and tried to take my own life. I took pills, and I went back to my regular poison of vodka, and drank until I couldn't drink anymore. The next thing I knew, I was handcuffed to a gurney in the hospital. The cops had found me and literally dragged my body into an ambulance, threw me in there, and locked me up. I spent a week in a mental ward—now mind you I was diagnosed because I had finally sought mental health. I thought I was having a heart attack. I believed myself to be strong, but on hearing I was stop-lossed I started having panic attacks and I couldn't admit that I was mentally or emotionally broken. So I went into the hospital complaining of chest pain and they had me seek a mental-health professional. They diagnosed me with depression and anxiety disorder, and adjustment disorder. But I was still set to be deployed, obviously [a] broken soldier, but set to deploy.

Goldsmith's ordeal did not end there. He ultimately obtained a general discharge from the military, but the papers cited the reasons for discharge as, "Misconduct, serious offense." The irony was not lost on the audience when Goldsmith said:

My serious offense was trying to kill myself because I was so damaged by the war—the occupation in Iraq. It was misconduct for me not to get on the flight while I was chained or handcuffed to a bed in the hospital. So I lost my college benefits, the one thing that had really given me hope in life that I was looking for—you know, I was gonna be a student, I didn't know where, I didn't know what I was gonna study, but I knew I was going to college in September of '07. That didn't happen. My money is disappearing between VA visits and personal instability. I've found it extremely hard to find a job. To tell you the truth, I haven't really looked because I'm having a rough time. So I deliver pizzas on Wednesdays, that's what I am now, a pizza delivery boy. I was a sergeant, I was a leader, I was a trainer, I was very well thought of. I was one of the most professional soldiers … I mean I got the paperwork right here in front of me if anyone ever wants to see the proof that I was a very good soldier. But now I'm a pizza delivery boy who works once a week because that's the only job where I can call in a couple hours before and say, "I'm still at the VA, I'm waiting in line. I'm sorry I can't come in for a couple hours."

I interviewed Goldsmith shortly after his testimony. "War is a really destructive thing," he told me. "It follows you home. And it doesn't go away." And what kind of homes filled with the specter of a distant war will this country be filled with as more of our broken, wounded, and destroyed soldiers are brought back?

◆   ◆   ◆

At the Northwest Regional Winter Soldier event at the Seattle Town Hall in June 2008, hundreds of symbolic headstones lined the walls of the hall in homage to U.S. soldiers killed in Iraq. One of the speakers on the occasion was Dr. Evan Kanter, the president-elect of Physicians for Social Responsibility, an organization that has vigorously opposed the occupation of Iraq since before the invasion was launched. The psychiatrist, who specializes in treating vets with PTSD, spoke at length to the 800-member audience about the crippling impact that the occupation has had on the mental health of the forces.

Panelists have mentioned that the most severely affected of our veterans are unable to participate in an event like this. One of the reasons that I'm here is to speak on behalf of those that I treat. Not only are they not able to come up here and speak publicly, many of them would be unable to tolerate being in a room with a crowd of this size. Their grievous condition is part of the true costs of the occupation, a very large proportion of which fall in the area of health care. As a doctor, I want to talk about these hidden wounds and hidden costs, many of which are intentionally hidden because if people knew the extent of the costs, maybe they would be less prepared to go to war.

We know that the death tally in combat is more than four thousand, represented by the headstones we see around this hall. What we do not know is that these do not include suicides or post-evacuation deaths induced by lethal wounds received in combat, nor even the deaths of over one thousand private contractors. If we include all the wounded, the injured, and the medically ill, we have a total of over seventy thousand, but the military intentionally camouflages and segregates the numbers in three categories that are extremely difficult to access. The ratio of wounded to killed in Iraq is much higher than in previous conflicts, and is a far more accurate measure of the scale of violence in the country than the tally of combat deaths. In Iraq, the ratio is 8 to 1, compared to Vietnam, where it was 3 to 1, or World War II, where it was 2 to 1. The reasons for this are the twofold advance in body armor and in battlefield medicine. Today we can stabilize and airlift people to Landstuhl Air Force Base in Germany within twenty-four hours, whereas in Vietnam it would have taken weeks for those treated in the field to be taken out for proper medical care. As a consequence, we now have service members with dreadful injuries who would never have survived similar conditions in an earlier battle. We, as a society, will be bearing the cost of caring for these grievously injured veterans for the rest of their lives.

Expounding further on this issue Kanter said,

We have a new word in the clinical lexicon, a terrible, sanitized word: polytrauma. We now have polytrauma clinics here in Seattle and in VAs and military health-care facilities around the country. The term refers to the condition of people who have been blown up and have multiple severe injuries, missing arms, missing legs, missing hearing, missing vision, [with] burns, fractures, and head injuries. We intensify armoring of our personnel and vehicles, and the insurgents keep increasing the magnitude of the explosive devices. The result is a huge number of people who survive with polytrauma from blast injuries and need to be cared for. In addition ... a new phenomenon we are witnessing but do not yet know how to deal with is the TBI, or traumatic brain injury. These are injuries brought on by atmospheric pressure caused by the great blasts. We do not know much about its pathology or its long-term impact. It's a new hidden wound that can be placed alongside post-traumatic stress disorder as one of the hidden wounds of war. Now if you think about the fact that we've deployed over 1,600,000 personnel so far [to serve in the occupations of Iraq and Afghanistan], looking at the PTSD and major depression cases alone will give you three to four hundred thousand psychiatric casualties.

These "psychiatric casualties" have a direct link with the high sui-cide rates in the military, says the doctor:

PTSD is no less a war wound than a shrapnel injury. It can be tremen-dously debilitating. Symptoms include nightmares and flashbacks, triggered physiological and psychological stress, social withdrawal, isolation, avoidance of any kind of reminders of the trauma, emotional numbing, uncontrolled outbursts of anger or rage, difficulty concentrating and focusing, and a state of hypervigilance, which the military calls the 'battle mind.' All these are symptoms that would make it impossible for a vet with severe PTSD to be in the room with us today.

Studies that go back to the Second World War have found that combat veterans are twice as likely to commit suicide as people in the general population. Other lesser-known distressing facts are that 9 percent of all unemployment in the United States is attributed to combat exposure, as is 8 percent of all divorce or separation, and 21 percent of all spousal or partner abuse.[1] The impact of all this extends to behavioral problems in children, child abuse, drug and alcohol addiction, incarceration, and homelessness, all of which have implications that go well beyond the individual and reverberate across generations.

◆   ◆   ◆

Currently, the number of veterans committing suicide is higher than those dying in combat overseas.[2] According to the *Army Suicide Event Report* (*ASER*), a total of ninety-nine soldiers killed themselves in 2006, the highest rate of military suicides in twenty-six years. More than a quarter of them were by troops in combat postings in Iraq and Afghanistan.[3] The figure does not include post-discharge suicides by military personnel.

The 2007 *ASER* contained worse statistics. The suicide figure rose from 102 in 2006 to 115 in 2007, and in 2008, rose to 128. By January 2009, the army announced that suicides among U.S. soldiers had risen in the previous year to the highest level in decades.[4] The suicide rate for 2008 was calculated roughly at 20.2 per 100,000 soldiers, which for the first time since the Vietnam War is higher than the adjusted civilian rate. In addition, more active-duty marines committed suicide in 2008 than any year since the U.S. invasion of Iraq was launched in 2003, at a rate of 16.8 per 100,000 troops.[5] January 2009 found as many as twenty-four soldiers committing suicide, a count that would be the highest monthly total since the army began tracking suicides in 1980.[6] If all these are confirmed, this suicide count would exceed the number of soldiers killed in both Iraq and Afghanistan during the same period. The number is six times higher than that for January 2008.[7]

In April 2008, the RAND Corporation released a stunning report revealing, "Nearly 20 percent of military service members who have returned from Iraq and Afghanistan—300,000 in all—report symptoms of post-traumatic stress disorder or major depression, yet only slightly more than half have sought treatment."[8] The situation continues to worsen. In the six months leading up to March 31, 2008, 1,467 veterans died while waiting to learn if their disability claim would be approved by the government. The average duration of an appeal pending a VA decision on disability claims is 1,608 days, which amounts to nearly four and a half years.[9]

The ill-equipped and underfunded VA has undertaken extraordinary efforts to hide the magnitude of the crisis. Indeed the VA staff are doing all they can to assist veterans, but the leadership of the VA, weighed down by the lack of adequate funding and support from the government, appears to be more interested in obfuscating the truth. Attempts have even been made to conceal the number of PTSD cases. A psychologist who led the PTSD program at a medical facility for veterans in Texas told staff members in 2008 to refrain from diagnosing PTSD because too many vets were pursuing government disability payments for the condition.[10]

Senator Patty Murray from Washington told reporters, "The VA's mental health programs are being overwhelmed by war vets from Iraq and Afghanistan but the department is trying to downplay the situation."[11]

When the Pentagon reports the number of U.S. troops wounded in Iraq (more than 32,000 at the time of this writing), it fails to mention that it tracks two other categories of injuries: "injured" (10,180) and "ill" (28,451). All three groups comprise soldiers who have to be medically evacuated to Germany for treatment.[12]

When the VA will not deliver the necessary care, many veterans turn to alcohol and drugs for self-medication. In the Pentagon's most recent post-deployment survey of health-related behavior, released in November 2007, of 88,235 soldiers surveyed three to six months after returning, 12 percent of active-duty troops and 15 percent of reservists acknowledged having problems with alcohol.[13]

The more fortunate among the troops do not need to self-medicate. The military does it for them, in order to keep enough boots on the ground. The dual objective of medicating soldiers is to steady their nerves and to enable an already troop-starved military to retain soldiers on the front lines. Mark Thompson reports in *Time* magazine, "Data contained in the Army's fifth Mental Health Advisory Team report indicate that, according to an anonymous survey of U.S. troops taken last fall, about 12 percent of combat troops in Iraq and 17 percent of those in Afghanistan are taking prescription antidepressants or sleeping pills to help them cope."[14]

Sergeant Christopher LeJeune has first-hand experience of this "treatment." He was diagnosed with depression, and the military doctor he consulted sent him back into the field with the antidepressant Zoloft and an antianxiety drug called clonazepam. He says in the *Time* article, "It's not easy for soldiers to admit the problems that they're having over there for a variety of reasons. If they do admit it, then the only solution given is pills." Two out of five suicide victims among troops in Iraq and Afghanistan have been found to be on antidepressants.[15]

◆   ◆   ◆

It is not hard to deduce that in addition to chemical clinical reasons, there are other factors that have led to suicides becoming an accepted and acceptable solution for soldiers desperate to liberate themselves from the military's vise-like grip. Consecutive deployment with little recovery time in the interim has affected veterans' mental health adversely.

It is common for soldiers to have only two weeks off between postings to Iraq and Afghanistan by rotation. Indiscriminate use of the "stop-loss" policy and widespread extension of deployments have aggravated an already critical situation. The length of combat tours has been extended from twelve to fifteen months, and there has been a dramatic rise in the number of "stop-loss" orders within the army. Soldiers subjected to stop-loss consider it a backdoor draft, and this has generated protest.

On May 9, 2008, the *Los Angeles Times* reported that the number of soldiers held in the army under the stop-loss program in March 2005 reached a high of 15,758. In August 2008, the House Appropriations Defense Subcommittee approved a $500 monthly payment for soldiers whose separations or retirements had been delayed by stop-loss orders since October 2001. The promised incentive has failed to boost morale.

Pentagon records expose one conspicuous result of the army's frantic stop-loss policy since 2003. More than 43,000 troops declared medically unfit for combat in weeks prior to their scheduled departure to Iraq or Afghanistan were redeployed anyway.[16] Army psychiatrist Colonel Charles Hoge told Congress in March 2008 that nearly 30 percent of troops on their third deployment are mental wrecks. He pointed to recent research that has proved that the year-long break that soldiers are currently permitted between combat tours is "insufficient time" for them "to reset" and recover from stress before proceeding back into combat,[17] the vast majority of soldiers today do not get anything near a year break between serving tours in Iraq or Afghanistan.

Too many soldiers now feel suicide is the only option, the last relief that they can find from their trauma and the only way to escape from further deployments.

◆   ◆   ◆

Many of those opting for voluntary death in the field do so when pushed to the extremes of their endurance, not by combat conditions, but in their struggle with their conscience.

Luis Carlos Montalván, a captain in the infantry division, served two long stints in Iraq. During his testimony at the Winter Soldier event in Maryland, he admitted to having witnessed war crimes.

In Iraq, I witnessed many disturbing things. I witnessed waterboarding. Two counterintelligence officers stopped a truck full of fake medicine being smuggled into Iraq and brought the driver in for questioning. They lifted his legs. They laid him down. They blindfolded him. Then they lifted his legs again and started pouring water down his throat. I knew that's something that we ought not to be doing. It's torture. Often I was given unlawful orders by superiors to not offer humanitarian assistance to refugees caught between the Syrian and Iraqi borders. I *disobeyed* those orders.

Montalván, justifiably proud of not having compromised his integrity during his service, remarked, "Perhaps the greatest lesson this country did not learn from Vietnam was that accountability is essential lest we allow history to repeat itself. Sadly, no generals or administration officials were held accountable at that time. That, I believe, is the reason that the current administration, its diplomats, and high-level military leaders got us into the Iraq, and now Middle Eastern, disaster and continue to proctor it with arrogant obstinacy and incredible incompetence."

Montalván dedicated his testimony to Colonel Ted Westhusing, the U.S. Army's top ethicist and a professor at West Point who volunteered for a deployment to Iraq in 2004. On June 5, 2005, Colonel Westhusing was found dead from a bullet to the head in what the army deemed a suicide, but the circumstances remain controversial.[18]

A note addressed to Generals Petraeus and Fil, to whom Westhusing was reporting directly, was found on his body. The army claims this was his "suicide note." It reads in part:

> You are only interested in your career[s] and provide no support to your staff—no [mission] support and you don't care. I cannot support a [mission] that leads to corruption, human right abuses and liars. I am sullied—no more. I didn't volunteer to support corrupt, money grubbing contractors, nor work for commanders only interested in themselves … I came to serve honorably and feel dishonored … I cannot live this way … Death before being dishonored any more … Why serve when you cannot accomplish the mission, when you no longer believe in the cause, when your every effort and breath to succeed meets with lies, lack of support, and selfishness? No more. Reevaluate yourselves, cdrs [commanders]. You are not what you think you are and I know it.

◆   ◆   ◆

A new form of suicide by veterans has come to be referred to as "suicide by cop." James E. Dean was an army reservist who had already served twelve months in Afghanistan and been diagnosed with PTSD upon his return. He was killed in Maryland by the police in December 2006. Dean had just been called up for a deployment when the incident happened. Depressed and angered by his orders to deploy to Iraq, the twenty-nine-year-old collected several weapons, and on Christmas barricaded himself in his father's home threatening to kill himself. The next day, after a fourteen-hour standoff with authorities, when Dean refused to negotiate, tear gas was fired into the house by the police. Forced out by the gas, Dean, who had fired several shots earlier, stepped onto the front porch and, according to the police, aimed a weapon at them but did not fire. He was then shot and killed by the police.

Wanda Matthews, a next-door neighbor, told a reporter, "His dad told me that he [James Dean] didn't want to go to war. He had already been out there and didn't want to go again."[19] According to his family and friends, Dean's time in Afghanistan had changed him drastically and dimmed his love for life, leaving him dependent on antidepressant medication, therapy, and alcohol. His wife tried to have the VA intervene, but to no avail.

Dean had been married four months at the time of his death, and was looking forward to spending the holiday season with his wife, Muriel, who he said was the best thing to have happened to him. Then he received the letter for his recall, instructing him to report to Fort Benning in Georgia, from where he would likely be deployed to Iraq. An outstanding soldier with the awards to prove it, Dean's recently diagnosed PTSD seems to have been triggered by the letter.

His drinking and rages immediately worsened. Family members said Dean would regularly break down in front of his wife and repeatedly tell her that nobody knew what it had been like in Afghanistan. Muriel said her husband had told her as he left their house for the last time, "The next time you see me, it's going to be in a body bag." "Our lives had just begun," she said. "He just couldn't go back to that war."[20]

A similar case is that of nineteen-year-old Marine Lance Corporal Andres Raya, who reportedly told his mother the one thing he wanted for Christmas was to stay home rather than return to military duty in Iraq. He was killed in a gun battle with police officers in January 2005 in Ceres, California. Homicide investigators declared that Raya was intent on dying at the hands of police when he entered a liquor store armed with a semiautomatic rifle. Lieutenant Bill Heyne, lead investigator for the Stanislaus County Sheriff's Department, said, "By the statements the suspect made at the scene, it was clear he wanted to die and take as many cops down as he could in the process ... As he ran from police, he was telling residents, 'Don't worry, you're a civilian. You won't get hurt.'"[21]

Two police officers were shot by Raya, and one of them died. Mental-health experts said Raya was likely suffering from PTSD when he was shot to death by the police. "He clearly needed to be assessed so it could be determined if he was in harm's way," Fred Gusman, director of the National Center for Posttraumatic Stress Disorder in Menlo Park, California, part of the Department of Veterans Affairs, told the *San Francisco Chronicle*.

Lalo Madrigal, a lifelong friend of the slain soldier, said that Raya, "just wasn't the same after the war—he couldn't hold a conversation anymore." According to Raya's family, on returning from Iraq, he was encouraging his relatives to watch Michael Moore's antiwar movie, *Fahrenheit 9/11*. His cousin Alex Raya said, "He showed us pictures of this guy's hand hanging off. He told us about going into homes and shooting them up, and he said he wouldn't pull the trigger a lot because he didn't want to kill anyone." On the Thanksgiving before his death, Raya told his family he had seen marines commit suicide rather than continue to fight in the occupation of Iraq. "He kept saying it was a war that had no point, that it was all for oil, and it made no sense that we were after (Osama) bin Laden but went after Saddam Hussein instead," his cousin recalled. [22]

Another incident of "suicide by cop" involved thirty-five-year-old Douglas Barber from Alabama, a former army reservist who since his return home had battled his demons from his time in Iraq and had started to secure medical help and counseling. Just before his death, though, in January 2006, he changed the message on his answering machine to: "If you're looking for Doug, I'm checking out of this world. I'll see you on the other side." He then phoned the police, stepped out on his porch with a shotgun, and, after a brief standoff with the former, shot himself in the head. [23]

Barber was clearly suffering from his experiences in Iraq, where he had spent seven months driving trucks. He was haunted by the deaths of fellow soldiers and the fear and desperation he had witnessed among the Iraqi people. In an interview after returning home, he said, "It was really bad—death was all around you, all the time. You couldn't escape it. Everybody in Iraq was going through suicide counseling because the stress was so high. It was at such a magnitude, such a high level, that it was unthinkable for anyone to imagine." [24]

Opposed to the Iraq invasion and occupation prior to his deployment, Barber had watched his life disintegrate upon his return. He separated from his wife of eleven years, and was prescribed clonazepam, an antianxiety drug that can cause depression. According to the *Independent*, just before his death, in an Internet article about PTSD, Barber wrote readers that his goal was

> to help you the reader understand what happens to a soldier when they come home and the sacrifice we continue to make. This war on terror has become a personal war for so many, yet the Bush administration do not want to reveal to America that this is a personal war. They want to run it like a business, and thus they refuse to show the personal sacrifices the soldiers and their families have made for this country.
>
> All is not OK or right for those of us who return home alive and supposedly well. What looks like normalcy and readjustment is only an illusion to be revealed by time and torment. Some soldiers come home with missing limbs and other parts of their bodies. Still others will live with permanent scars from horrific events that no one other than those who served will ever understand. We come home from war trying to put our lives back together but some cannot stand the memories and decide that death is better. We kill ourselves because we are so haunted by seeing children killed and whole families wiped out.

The article concluded: "This is what PTSD comes in the shape of—soldiers can not often handle coming back to the same world they left behind. It is something that drives soldiers over the edge and causes them to withdraw from society. As Americans we turn our nose down at them wondering why they act the way they do. Who cares about them, why should we help them?"

Until more of the general public in the United States fully comprehend the magnitude of the crisis affecting veterans, the overused slogan "Support Our Troops" will remain vacuous.

NINE

CYBER RESISTANCE

Need intro

If technology has transformed warfare into a spectacle of shock and awe, its contribution to the cause of dissent has been no less remarkable. It has enabled solidarities across borders and facilitated networks and forums dedicated to impartial communication of ground realities beyond the sanitized and often biased projection of mainstream news. True, technological advances have not brought an end to the occupation, but it has certainly helped alternative voices and views to be heard.

Many American soldiers in Iraq were confounded by the wall of censorship they confronted, jointly constructed by the military and the corporate media. The Internet offered them a convenient and powerful channel through which to get their stories out to the public. Constrained by slow military mail service from Iraq and Afghanistan, not to mention overt attempts by superiors to curtail their interaction with journalists, soldiers took to blogging, posting photographs, and uploading videos online, all related to their experience of the occupation.

"Fight to Survive," one of the first soldier blogs from Iraq, had its origin before the bloggers were deployed to the country. The site's mission statement declares, "The E-4 Mafia was a group of soldiers deployed in Iraq between January of 2004 and March of 2005. The posts from this period are an expression of our raw emotions and thoughts while serving in Operation Iraqi Freedom II. Since being honorably discharged in the summer of 2005, we've continued to post additional journal entries, poetry, and reflections from our time served and our current lives as veterans as we continue our fight to survive."

Garett Reppenhagen, Jeff Englehart, Ben Schrader, and Joe Hatcher were stationed in Germany, where they happened to attend a concert by a band called Bouncing Souls and befriended its members. Post deployment they were desperate to process the grief, violence, and frustration that they were experiencing in Iraq, so they started pouring their emotions into e-mails to the band members. The Bouncing Souls, impressed with the e-mails—which included powerful poetry—began posting them on their own website. In 2004, Hatcher created "Fight to Survive" (at http://www.ftssoldier.blogspot.com). Englehart later told a reporter, "We were opposed to the war before we went. And we got together and said, 'You know what we should do? We should write about this shit.'"[1]

Reppenhagen, the first active-duty soldier to have joined a veteran's group against the war, was pulling a shift at Tower Guard in Fort Collins, Colorado, in August 2008, when I phoned him. Tower Guard is an action designed to spread awareness about the occupation of Iraq. Veterans pull together scaffolding, cover it with camouflage, and donning their desert gear, take shifts atop the tower, this one twelve-feet high, to maintain a presence where people can ask them questions, and in response they can provide information. Reppenhagen and his friends are trying to hold a Tower Guard action every three months. Significantly they built one at the Democratic National Convention in Denver that they kept manned for four days. "Sometimes we get a smirk, but most folks are happy to talk with us, and ask us good questions. Old veterans come by and thank us," says Reppenhagen.

For him, the motivation for the blog had come from having to participate in an occupation he didn't believe in. "We were already against the war before going, and didn't know why we were going, and it didn't look good. There was no resistance to speak of within the military. But I found a purpose with the writing. I didn't want to let my friends down there by not serving, and nobody knew what would happen if you refused to go out, because nobody had done it yet. So the blogging began. As a high-school dropout I wasn't a strong writer," he tells me on the phone,

> but I had all these ideas I just couldn't stop, and writing them down was a huge release … Having people read them was therapeutic. This then became my mission, to have people read about what we were doing. After a while, Joe Hatcher, who we met in basic training, created the blog website. This was summer of 2004, and I'd never heard of a blog earlier. The idea caught on and sparked something, and as far as I know, ours was the only antiwar blog from soldiers in Iraq at the time. We used aliases; mine was "heretic" or "soldier X," Jeff Englehart was "hEkLe," Joe was "Joe Public." We used these because we were unsure of the consequences of revealing our identities.

Postings from Iraq on Fight to Survive ranged in content from asking people to sign petitions against stop-loss, to expressing disbelief at how persistent the military was in trying to get soldiers to renew their contracts, to posting graffiti and commenting on it. An entry posted in September 2004 by *heretic* titled "My Struggle For Reason" reads:

> Souls, Friends, and Conspirators,
>   The temperature dropped to sixty degrees last night while I huddled in a ditch near Diyala Bridge. The breeze off the river crawled

into my heart and the sudden chill reflects my current mood. I found out earlier that night that I had been extended an additional two months on top of my previous stretch. It now appears that I will be in the service until July, while my original date of release is supposed to be next month. All this, and my recent two week taste of the civilian world on leave, is leaving me empty and detached. It is so much easier to live in slavery if you had willingly accepted your fate. I am not sure if my mental fortitude is prepared for a whole extra year in oppression. And, I still don't have a certain time when I will be finished with this war.

Three soldiers in our unit have been hurt in the last four days and the true number of army-wide casualties leaving Iraq is unknown. The figures are much higher than what is reported. We get awards and medals that are supposed to make us feel proud about our wicked assignment. We feel privileged when we are given the smallest perk. Like a dog that is beaten everyday and then thankfully adores it's owner when he skips a day of punishment. I have more trust with some of the Iraqi locals than my own command sometimes. I know that my higher chain of command hates me for my political opinions and my moral views.

I am called a "faggot pink-o" or a "bleeding heart traitor". It doesn't take a liberal to realize the moral wrongs involved with this or any war. Why should I feel ashamed of caring about all of humanity, even the people that ignorantly hate me? Is wanting a better standard of living for all the world so negative? In a way, deeper than sexuality, I love my friends and brothers and for that I am labeled a deviant of some kind. Does everyone buy into this Arnold ideal of fear that they are not strong enough, so they have to over-compensate and become an asshole? I believe that all weapons should be laid down [by] choice of the individual. It is the same fear I have of my bigot neighbor that causes Americans to support a war against a possible U.S. threat. If we are all responsible enough to handle firearms, is it not sensible to allow countries like Iran and N. Korea nuclear weapons? If we think these countries are less responsible than the drunk driving redneck or the crack dealing gangster, I think we need to take a longer look at American society. Sure a nuke can destroy the world, but an automatic weapon can kill my daughter and she is the world to me. I don't believe that taking away people's rights is the proper step to world peace. However, we overspend on national defense and cut education when we need to be more concerned about raising a generation of problem solvers, instead of mindless warriors.

So I finally find the drive to get out and try to make a difference in the world, and I am stuck freezing in a middle eastern desert. What state will the earth be in if I ever escape this combat zone? What little changes I can make, I do through the networks I have built up with my close friends. The Bouncing Souls have given us soldiers a voice and forum to express the hardships and our feelings on the Iraq occupation. All my friends, some new and some old, listen and support our efforts and they have my deepest respect and thanks. I could not survive this in any sane manner without the backing of all of you. I cannot promise that I will have a positive effect on current issues that plague our planet, but I can promise I will never give up, if you never give up on me.

Another moving entry from August 22, 2005, titled "Finding Closure," posted by Jeff Englehardt (*hEkLe*) after exiting Iraq, reads in part:

There is nothing that I feel can alleviate the guilt for being directly involved with our illegal and immoral occupation of Iraq. I ask myself from time to time, "Why was I so afraid to resist the order to go to war? Why didn't I object to the whole damned thing?" I have been told many times not to be ashamed for my service to this country, but I can't help a genuine intuition that this war is not designed to promote freedom and our beautiful American way of life, but instead only carried out to proliferate Western imperialism and corporate profits every time a bullet is fired. My guilt is synonymous with the sentiment that I was indeed on the wrong side of the wire.

◆   ◆   ◆

As the blogging continued, the audience expanded. Radio personality Randi Rhodes, who at the time brought Air America Radio its largest audience to date, began reading their dispatches on air.

As was to be expected, the military began to crack down on the writers. "It was not difficult for them to track what base and unit the writing was coming from and they were able to narrow it down to me," says Reppenhagen. "My sniper section leader walked into my room and asked if I was writing something stupid on the Internet. I admitted I was posting writings, but whether it was stupid depended on the readers' views, and he told me to report to the colonel who wanted to ask me questions about this shit I was writing."

All along Reppenhagen felt he was leading a dual existence: "I was living two lives, going outside the wire, but still writing on the blog, all the time looking over my shoulder. I was afraid of our e-mails being monitored, and there was a lot of isolation." He rarely crossed paths with the other members of the E-4 Mafia, and knew that he would have to deal with the colonel alone. From his perch on the tower he recounted to me, "I did the whole thing, saluting him, doing the full pivot, and coming to at-ease, and he has a stack of everything we had written, and copies of personal e-mails I had written. He asked me if I had written it and I said yes. He told me I should stop writing, that I was going to be investigated by Military Intelligence and if found to have violated operational security, I would be tried for treason. I was scared."

Undeterred, he kept blogging, and was soon summoned by the colonel once again.

> I told him I had a right to continue. They pulled my computers, tried to limit my access, took me off sniper duty, and put me on guard duty of Iraqis on base. The last two months were lonely and difficult for me. I was afraid I would be court-martialed. In the end, it was determined that nothing I wrote had violated operational security and that I had committed no treason and, since there were no rules prohibiting blogging, I had broken no rules either. But I was continually hazed by my superiors as long as I was there…They were constantly looking for ways to trap me. I was made to fill sandbags and do other menial jobs. However I was finally awarded an honorable discharge in May 2005, and gained a lot of respect from most of my fellow soldiers. Many would give me the peace sign as they passed me by.

Reppenhagen dove headlong into activism after being discharged. He took a job with Veterans for America, in Washington, D.C., and volunteered at Walter Reed Army Medical Center. Coming full circle, Reppenhagen had one of his poems set to music by the Bouncing Souls. They called it "Letter from Iraq."

In 2007, he moved to Green Mountain Falls, Colorado, and enrolled in a community college to study to become a history teacher. He shares his plans: "I continue now to work at helping veterans get the mental and physical health care they deserve. And I want to teach history in high school … One of my dreams is to teach on a Native American reservation. After coming back from Iraq, I traveled around a lot, and saw many reservations, and saw this grinding poverty there similar to what I saw in Iraq, and decided that that is where I can help the most."

On being discharged, the other E-4 Mafia members also moved to Colorado: Schrader in Fort Collins, Hatcher in Cascade, and Englehart in Denver. They continue blogging, alongside antiwar activism.

◆   ◆   ◆

Soldier Voices (http://www.soldiervoices.net) is a site that originated as a forum for soldiers to speak their minds on the war and share their post-traumatic stress disorder experiences. It later expanded to accommodate service members (from all branches) and civilians alike in an open debate on the Iraq war. Members include current and former soldiers, marines, airmen, sailors, Iraq vets, Vietnam vets, their dependants, and civilians (American and foreign). The objective is to give a clear picture to the American people of what is being done overseas in their name. Who better for this task than the American service member?

The home page on the site encourages people to log in and "say whatever you want whether it's pro-war, against the war or just something you feel like sharing your opinions on." One woman, in a post titled "In Need of Your Stories," writes,

I am the mother of a soldier who like many of you has experienced the run around by the service, improper evaluations and treatment of medical and mental problems. I would like to compile all of your stories to show others what you have been through and how you have been mistreated. In my field that is called neglect. Please contact me if you will with a message on this site and I will reply. I would appreciate it. With much thanks, A disgraced mother.

Another post, titled "Scrutinize Depleted Uranium," reads: "Hi everyone. My name is Peter Dearman and I joined this forum for one main reason. I believe the use of depleted uranium munitions is an unnecessary and extremely callous act of warfare that, in most instances, amounts to using "dirty bombs" against innocent civilian populations." The post goes on to provide a brief description of DU and its effects, and gives a website to encourage people to educate themselves about it.

Casey J. Porter, a specialist from Austin, Texas, served one year in Iraq and in fall 2008 was on his second deployment after having been stop-lossed. His contract ended January 21, 2008, but he was redeployed on March 9, although diagnosed with PTSD by a civilian doctor. As he says on a YouTube video, "I am making the best of it by making short films about what really goes on over here."

A post from him on Soldier Voices reads, "Some of you might already know me through my films. I am a Stop-Lossed Soldier currently in Iraq." There is a website for his work: http://www.youtube.com/caseyjporter."

Porter's films feature raw footage coupled with a compelling background score. Scenes include mortar attacks against bases, military personnel running for cover during mortar attacks as explosions echo in the background, gun battles, destroyed Humvees, and soldiers talking about their low morale. One film, *Area of Operations*, reveals a new weapon of the Iraqi resistance, Lob-Bombs, which are created by cutting open an oxygen tank and packing it with ball bearings, screws, and bolts as shrapnel before welding it back together and pressurizing. The film also shows a Lob-Bomb attack that killed two soldiers, which the Associated Press reported as having been caused by small-arms fire. I spoke with Porter by telephone when he was at Forward Operating Base Rustamiyah. He told me there were two versions in the military and corporate media reportage of the deaths: "One reported it as small-arms fire and the other as indirect fire. Indirect fire is obviously a very general term, so the army can say, 'Oh, it is indirect fire, it's not an accurate weapon.' But when the public hears of indirect fire, they think some guy is shooting at you with a machine gun." There is a clip in the film that has audio recordings from military radios after the attack. It presents a soldier saying, "The K.I.A. [killed in action], I can't tell you who they are, they're in pieces, break …"

Later in the film a soldier in Iraq says to the camera, "Would this country be the way it is right now had we done anything close to what we promised before we came over? The Humvees we drive, they are not doing the drive over here as protection … not even the slightest. The MRAP [mine resistant, ambush protected] still won't stop an EFP [explosively formed penetrator]. But it's a big vehicle and makes a lot of noise and that's what the American people want, apparently." The camera goes on to show Humvees destroyed by roadside bombs, then returns to the soldier who says, "I won't be surprised if they turn this place into a duty station. I mean look at all the nations that we've liberated. Look at Germany, Korea. I'm pretty sure at one time somebody thought, 'Hey, we're only going to be here for a couple of months.'"

Another of Porter's films, *What War Looks Like*, shows scenes of destroyed military hardware. Pictures of blown-up tanks and Humvees crushed by roadside bombs are seen flashing across the screen. Other scenes show burnt-out Bradley fighting vehicles atop transport trucks, decomposed bodies of fighters, and then the names and photos of "friends we lost," U.S. soldiers killed in Iraq. After photos of a body being loaded for shipment back to the United States, the screen goes black as the text reads, "It's not politics, it is saving soldiers' lives, bring us home now."

I asked Porter what had made him decide to make the films.

After coming back from my first tour, I was so against the war that I started speaking out and showing videos I'd made from footage I'd shot during my first deployment. Then when I got stop-lossed, I decided I'm not going to be another American that complains about the situation and then does nothing. Going AWOL wasn't a realistic option for me, so instead of being complacent about something I feel is wrong, I decided to make films to show people what they're not seeing on television, and to show people that I'm not the only soldier that feels this way. Along with very realistic combat footage, I showed real threats facing soldiers, some of the financial traps, and other issues they must deal with during deployment.

Porter talks of the morale in Iraq being poor and more soldiers than ever before beginning to question the mission. However, he added, "One thing that disappoints me about American soldiers is the apathy, the 'what can you do?' mentality. But they are more or less speaking their minds by not reenlisting though they are afraid of the consequences of actively speaking up. More of them are doing it, but still not as many as should. The army seems like such a big giant, and the threat of, well, if you do this we're going to punish you, and we own you, and all this and that. Then this gets into soldier's heads."

◆   ◆   ◆

Adam Kokesh also maintains a blog, "Revolutionary Patriot" (http://www.kokesh.blogspot.com) where he has written about being assaulted by undercover FBI agents in Washington, D.C., about his thoughts on the Democratic and Republican National Conventions in 2008, and about dealing with PTSD.

Not a shy man, Kokesh did not hesitate to upload onto his blog a video of his speech during a march in D.C., where he is seen exhorting a boisterous crowd, "The time is now. The threat is clear. The bands of tyranny are tightening around America. It is our duty to resist!"

Kokesh was part of a team of vets who met with Representative John Conyers in July 2008 to push Conyers to file the Articles of Impeachment against George W. Bush. In a video of the meeting posted on his blog, Kokesh used his time at the microphone to tell Conyers, who was undecided about filing the articles,

> And I get the feeling that what you're doing and what the Democratic Party is doing is telling this country, as we are being bled dry by tyrants, that we're just going to be OK. That the only promises we get from Democrats are Band-Aids over these far deeper wounds that anyone is willing to admit to publicly. I hear one of the arguments against impeachment, that it would harm the Democrats in the upcoming elections. And I hope that you realize, because you didn't communicate this when I asked you the question, that there are real consequences to not impeaching that are far, far worse than not having Democrats in the Congress or Senate, or a Democrat in the White House. You said you've made thousands of decisions, many of them very respectable, many of them very courageous. But by your own admission, it seems that what is holding you back from this one is your own indecision. You said that I might be surprised by your plans. You haven't put forth any. And frankly, I'm not surprised.

Aside from blogging, testifying to representatives, leading marches, and getting arrested, Kokesh has participated in Operation First Casualty (OFC), a tactic of street theater in which vets don their camouflage and take to the streets of U.S. cities to carry out public patrols, realistic mock arrests, home raids, and tower watches to raise awareness of the occupation.[2] After an OFC action on March 19, 2007, the fourth anniversary of the invasion, he received an e-mail from the Marine Corps Mobilization Command that oversees the Individual Ready Reserve (IRR) to which Kokesh reports.[3] The e-mail accused him of violating the Uniform Code of Military Justice (UCMJ) by wearing his uniform during a political event. "I was like, wait a second, I'm in the IRR, the UCMJ doesn't apply. This is bullshit." The scathing response that Kokesh sent back is posted on his blog. It concludes:

> I fail to see how reminding me of my "obligations and responsibilities" helps you achieve either of these. It seems that while accomplishing our mission in Iraq, every corner we turn sends us further down the spiral, but there is still much that you can do to bring our fellow Marines home alive.
>
> So no, I am not replying to your email in order to acknowledge my understanding of my obligations and responsibilities, but rather to ask you to please, kindly, go fuck yourself.

In the chain of events that followed, the military threatened to give him a less than honorable discharge, which would affect his education benefits, but so far the military has not followed through. His case was helped by appearing on several major media programs, including *Good Morning America*.

Kokesh has also talked with me about an action at Ansbach military base in Germany during the summer of 2007 that he later wrote about on his blog.

We snuck onto a U.S. base in Germany. I had gone there in May last year for two weeks with the Stop the War Brigade, a bunch of Vietnam Vets living in Germany, and we organized an action. So it was me and three other veterans, and only three of us were able to get on base with expired military ID cards and passports and whatnot to say that we were going to the PX. And we got up in the chow hall and read a letter from the people of Ansbach.

The letter was partly an appeal from the people in a nearby community to prevent a base expansion that would encroach on their land and have more helicopters flying over civilian areas, but it was more an attempt to reach out to more soldiers to encourage them to resist the occupations of Iraq and Afghanistan.

Kokesh thinks the future of GI resistance holds great possibility for social change. He told me, "It's kind of a battle for the hearts and minds of the troops between resistance and obedience. And if the military power structure keeps fucking up and putting people off, then resistance is going to start winning a lot more hearts and minds, you know, and we're doing what we can to further that." Yet he is realistic.

The forces at play here are far greater than any organization, bigger even than the military itself. It's social, it's cultural … and I think it is great in terms of what we can do to foster a broader civilian resistance, and develop a culture of questioning authority … Whether the GI resistance movement is actually going to be enough to end the war, I don't think you can consider it in those absolute terms. We're building pressure. And there are a lot of forces maintaining pressure to keep the war going. If nothing else, we need to be a countervailing force to those and, who knows, maybe that's going to stop the next war.

"Theoretically, you know," Kokesh says, "the war should have ended when we elected a majority Democratic Congress in 2006. If you assume that you have the full grasp of the relevant facts, every event coming down the pipe is just going to continue to defy logic, but we can work towards building a culture that lives up to American ideals, lives up to the ideals of humanity, and encourage people to live up to their own principles. And that's really the heart of it for me. GI resistance is just one particularly poignant area where that is happening right now and where I can be an effective force."

The use of the Internet has become as integral to our lives as other means of communication are. Some people use it in creative ways and for professional advancement. Others use it to connect with strangers and seek emotional sustenance in these stressful times.

This is probably the first time that we have available to us an inexpensive and extremely inclusive means to communicate and thereby advocate sustained resistance to unjust military action, on an international scale, without losing any gestation time. The implication this can have on the formation of alliances, networks, pressure groups (for the administration), and support groups for the resisters, is tremendous.

There is a need to appreciate the fact that these groups and individuals have dared to stick out their necks, and are fully conscious of the implications of doing so. They have done this in order to have their voices heard, and more importantly, to facilitate the participation of fence-sitters, members of the silent majority, and well-intentioned but resourceless individuals in the promise of a historical transformation.

◆   ◆   ◆

Other Iraq war veterans have used the Internet as a tool of resistance in other unique ways. Seth Manzel served with the army in

Iraq from November 2004 until September 2005, in the northern Iraqi cities of Tal Afar and Mosul. He is in the IRR and currently lives in Washington State, where he runs a radio station in his garage that broadcasts online for soldiers and can be heard by troops at nearby Fort Lewis.

During an interview at the Northwest Regional Winter Soldier event in Seattle he informed me, "We have a website, www.givoice.com, which is also an online radio station, and that's a place that has information for soldiers who are looking to resist or just looking to get out, just good information all around. It also has forums on it for families and soldiers to share their experiences, and a general forum where anyone can post."

Manzel describes the site as a "three-tiered approach to promoting GI resistance and GI rights. I kind of see those as two aspects of the same thing because if soldiers stand up for their rights … their units don't have the resources to both take care of soldiers and deploy them. So if soldiers stand up for their rights, there will be fewer units that are ready to go, and that'll slow down the pace of war."

On November 5, 2008, Manzel and several other veterans opened the Coffee Strong Internet Cafe on the outskirts of Fort Lewis. Shortly after this, Under the Hood coffeehouse in Killeen, Texas, near Fort Hood, and the Norfolk OffBase, near Naval Station Norfolk in Virginia, opened. Plans were under way to help seed funding for future coffeehouses.

In response to why he was dedicating so much of his time to these projects, Manzel said, "The cost of not ending this war, of not making broad, sweeping reforms to our government is that we continue on with these imperialist wars. When this war ends there'll just be another one. It's imperative to our survival as a planet that America gets checked somehow, and if it's not checked by its people, who's going to do it?"

TEN

ART AS RESISTANCE

Throughout history, culture and art have always been the celebration of freedom under oppression.

—Author unknown

Soldiers returning from Iraq have tough truths to tell, and it has been well demonstrated that the establishment media does not want to broadcast these. Given the lack of an outlet for antiwar voices in the corporate media, many contemporary veterans and active-duty soldiers have embraced the arts as a tool for resistance, communication, and healing. They have made use of a wide range of visual and performing arts—through theater, poetry, painting, writing, and other creative expression—to affirm their own opposition to the occupations of Afghanistan and Iraq.

The first Warrior Writers Project workshop was led by Lovella Calica. To help veterans deal with their experiences in Iraq, she encouraged them to write. Those who were willing to do so were asked to share their writings with the group. An anthology of these compositions was produced as the book *Warrior Writers: Move, Shoot and Communicate*.[1] Calica has since gone on to lead three writing workshops with veterans, and has published a second book, *Warrior Writers: Re-making Sense*.[2]

The goal of the Warrior Writers Project is to provide "tools and space for community building, healing and redefinition ... Through writing/artistic workshops that are based on experiences in the military and in Iraq, the veterans unbury their secrets and connect with each other on a personal and artistic level. The writing from the workshops is compiled into books, performances and exhibits that provide a lens into the hearts of people who have a deep and intimate relationship with the Iraq war."[3]

Warrior Writers has also created exhibits that showcase artwork by members, and photographs taken by them in Iraq. It is a largely self-supporting endeavor wherein the funds generated from the sale of books and artwork help sponsor veterans to travel around the country, read from and display their work, as well as to fund other workshops. It has now grown into the Combat Paper Project.

Iraq veteran Drew Cameron and artist Drew Matott cofounded People's Republic of Paper (PRP), a paper-making studio in Burlington, Vermont. PRP offers artist residencies and also houses the Combat Paper Project. Cameron's commitment to the unique venture is premised primarily upon the need he experienced "for catharsis and reconciliation," and upon his conviction that people must hear the soldiers' side of the story. As he wrote in one poem,

> If I say nothing, I have failed.
> If I do nothing, I am guilty.
> If I live by these ideals of democracy I can see that war is failure.
>
> A war of opportunity rather than necessity is unjust.
> War is the antithesis of peace, prosperity, democracy and freedom.
> Let us hear the stories of these young men and women.
> Let us see through the eyes of the Iraqis

and the minds of the soldiers
what has occurred under the auspices of freedom and democracy.
Let us then ask ourselves if conflict has brought peace.
Let us be challenged by the horrific atrocities that no one should
have to bear, and then ask ourselves if they were worth it.[4]

The idea of integrating the Warrior Writers and PRP into Combat Paper evolved from a workshop at Green Door Studio, which combined photography, artwork, and readings from the first Warrior Writers book. During an evening reading session, the participants realized there was a lot of potential to extend the intense experience to far more people than any workshop could include. On the second day of that workshop, Cameron assembled a group of veterans and began making paper of the uniform he wore during the occupation by shredding, beating, and pulping it to form sheets of paper, and his friends loved it. That was the genesis of the Combat Paper Project.

In Cameron's words, "The residual anger from being used as tools for an immoral and illegal occupation finds release when shredded pieces of the uniforms are cooked and macerated in a Hollander beater to produce paper pulp." Cameron told me,

The fiber of the uniform, replete with the blood, sweat, and tears from months of hardship and brutal violence in Iraq, tells its tale through these sheets, which are then turned into books, broadsides, personal journals, or works of art composed by the veterans. The entire process is aimed at enabling veterans to reclaim and transform their uniform as a piece of art. It is a step toward reconciling veterans with their traumatizing participation in the occupation. This symbolic act gives them the hope to carve a path through which to reenter civilian life, not by distancing themselves from their experience and the accompanying guilt, but by taking responsibility for their actions. In 2007 we put together the second anthology, *Re-making Sense.* The title comes from the goal of remaking sense of our relationship with the war, of our lives, of what we do now, as veterans.

He says that combat uniforms that just sit in closets or boxes in the attic can remain associated with subordination, warfare, and service. The Combat Paper Project redefines them as something collective and beautiful. The slogan for the project is "From uniform to pulp, Battlefield to workshop, Warrior to artist."[5]

Cameron, who hails from a military background, was raised by his father to value the ideals that the military professes: loyalty, integrity, and honor. His trip to Iraq altered everything, and

it wasn't until after I came back that the truth hit me. I would keep to myself, and try to block out my experiences in Iraq. In the course of processing my memories I realized we had destroyed … [Iraq's] infrastructure and were not there to help. I realized it was not about freedom and democracy, and recollecting the way we had conducted ourselves, and the way we had brutalized the people turned me against the occupation. We were trained to fight and win battles. I was in the artillery, trained to blow shit up. We were not there to rebuild anything or help the Iraqi people.

Cameron was frustrated and aghast at the whitewashing of the situation in Iraq that the corporate media was engaged in. At the massive U.S. air base Camp Anaconda, just north of Baghdad, he had access to satellite television and he realized that the images and stories coming out were different from what we were seeing on the ground. I remember intelligence reports that briefed us on attacks against us and how we were going to be hit were almost never in the news. I remember being hit for seven consecutive days by mortars, but that did not make news. As the violence escalated, we went from being able to go outside the gate to get sodas to not allowing Iraqis within two miles of the base because of fear of mortars and bombs. The American mainstream media coverage was always this spectacular type of reporting, full of the visual splendor of tanks and such, and not much content.

That discontent with the media influenced Cameron strongly, spurring his desire to bring out the truth about what the U.S. government has done in Iraq. "The fundamentals of civil society and infrastructure have been so changed and altered in Iraq that it is absolutely devastated. To get your mind around that is challenging."

The art projects have been instrumental in assisting Cameron to come to terms with his experience in Iraq and in helping him heal.

I can see it in my own writing, how the anger, gore, and frustration flows out graphically before transitioning into a deeper reflection and contemplation about how to approach the cultural relationship between militarism and our society. I have been able to purge all that stuff that made me so anxious, and now I'm more deliberate and patient in trying to understand what is happening in this country. It has helped me understand war-making and how this country works. My dad was in the military. It is so deeply rooted in us, it's in our subconscious, and we have to root that out and be able to transcend it.

He believes that the power of the written word and of artwork can achieve what few other channels of communication can. "You can tell people through a didactic political conversation or panel how brutal the whole thing is, but it is not the same. What we are now doing through our art and our writing gives people the full picture."

The Combat Paper Project is the culmination of collaboration between combat veterans, artists, art collectors, and academic institutions. It is mostly displayed in public places, even on the street, which often attracts other veterans. Cameron is hopeful that with continued touring of exhibits and ongoing outreach, more veterans will join in. "We are trying to reach out beyond that … Last weekend, we had art-hop [where businesses allow artists to showcase their work], and I met four vets. One was a Vietnam vet who remained AWOL for over twenty years before returning home. They all want to be part of the project."

Cameron intends to continue work with both the Warrior Writers and Combat Paper projects, and hopes that "eventually one of these is started with the veterans on the West Coast. The commonality of experience that connects vets is really eye-opening. We've worked with vets from Vietnam, Gulf War, Bosnia … and the paper-making ritual has been transformative for everyone who has participated in it. For some it is an end and a rebirth."

The co-facilitator of the project, Drew Matott, is not a veteran, but an artist who has been involved in paper-making since 1998. Matott is interested in creating a dialogue with the public about the occupation of Iraq. One method he uses is to juxtapose art pieces that veterans created before a workshop against post-workshop pieces by the same veterans to underscore the transformation that has occurred in them. "Usually the first pieces are very, very dark, when they first came in. Their latter projects reveal the healing that has taken place," says Matott, who hopes the project will soon go international. In September 2008, he was in dialogue with the Ottawa School of Art, which was interested in bringing the group up to do a Combat Paper Project with AWOL soldiers in Canada. "Then we're looking at taking some guys to the United Kingdom, to work with vets from Iraq and Afghanistan there, simultaneously opening the project up to wars other than the ones fought by the United States, involving soldiers from the United Kingdom who have been involved in other conflicts, also bring it near bases for active-duty folks to attend as well ... I think it is making a difference."

The project has had exhibitions around the country in cities such as Minneapolis, Chicago, and San Francisco, with many more to come.

◆   ◆   ◆

In a summer 2008 interview, Brian Casler spoke with me of the immense relief from PTSD that participating in the Warrior Writers had brought him. For the marine,

> That was the first "ah ha!" moment. We were sitting there, a small group of people at Fort Drum when Calica, who was leading the workshop, read out a letter written by a soldier to his family. She asked the group to guess where the letter was from. Everyone guessed Iraq or Afghanistan, and were stunned to hear that it was in fact from a French soldier in the trenches during World War I. He was an antiwar soldier and he was writing home about all the problems they were facing. It was verbatim the same crap we have going on. And then I read up on the Vietnam letters home, and that was also verbatim the same crap we have going on. Then, I listened to my fellow veterans at the workshop and said to myself, that's me. That's me. Those words feel like they're coming out of me. Your poetry speaks a piece of my heart. And every time I push Warrior Writers, I

say this is the antiwar veteran's heart right here on paper. Get it. I got
a piece of me in there, but you know what, every piece feels like it's a
piece of me in there.

Jon Michael Turner, a former U.S. Marine Corps machine gunner, became an icon of the antiwar movement when at the Winter
Soldier hearings in Silver Spring, Maryland, in March 2008, he
leaned into his microphone and said in an emotion-choked voice,
"There's a term 'Once a marine, always a marine.'" Ripping his
medals off and flinging them to the ground as the room exploded in
applause he added, "But, there's also the expression 'Eat the apple,
fuck the corps, I don't work for you no more." Turner was the first
veteran after Cameron to become part of the Combat Paper Project.
He was still in the military when he moved to Burlington and heard
about the effort. "My first night in Burlington I started to make
paper out of the stack of uniforms in my trunk."

It was an accumulation of his experiences over time rather than
any single event in Iraq that had turned Turner against the occupation. He remembers,

> Halfway through my second tour, things started to click with me. One
> of my close friends was killed, and another close friend, I don't know
> how the fuck he survived it, but he got destroyed by a mortar. It was
> also about how much we were pushing people out of their houses. We
> would kick them out of their houses and they had nowhere to go. See-
> ing this, and interacting with the people and seeing how our actions
> affect them did it. Plus, I was scared for my life each time I went any-
> where, wondering if that was going to be the day. Finally it hit me. It
> sucks that it took three years, but I realized things happening there
> were not right.

Turner has found a genuine conduit to release the havoc that his time and actions in Iraq have wrought upon him and to heal himself: "All the experiences I've gone through, and all my built-up frustration and thoughts and anger … instead of taking it out on another person, I can put it into my art, and this allows me to reclaim those experiences. I can take part of my military uniform and cut it up, and turn it into a piece of paper. On that blank piece of paper I put one of my poems for other people to experience it, and for that moment when they read it, they can see it all through my eyes."

He is not fully relieved of his trauma. "I still struggle. The problem is [that] there is so much I need to reclaim. The Warrior Writers Project has taught people that they can express themselves through writing, and as traumatic as the experience may be, it's coming out in a beautiful way." He is hopeful that the healing will continue as the project grows, and not for him alone.

◆　　◆　　◆

In January 2003, Aaron Hughes was studying industrial design at the University of Illinois when he was called up by his National Guard Unit. After being trained in Wisconsin, he was shipped to Kuwait, where he spent fifteen months with a transportation company hauling flatbed tractor trailers full of supplies to contractors, marines, and other units. He regularly took supplies from camps and ports in Kuwait to bases in Iraq, such as Camp Anaconda, Baghdad, and Talil Air Base.

After his tour, Hughes returned to college and decided to major in painting. He created more than fifty works of art from the nearly two hundred photos that he'd shot while in Iraq. Rather than attempting to provide a narrative of his experience in the occupation, he wanted his art to depict a deeper reality. Discussing his art with journalist Tatyana Safronova, he expressed the view that "narrative creates absolutes and I don't have one." Instead, Hughes sought forms of expression more similar to memory, with the "abstractions and complexities that exist in images or in poetry too."

Safronova describes one of Hughes's oil paintings, in which Hughes portrays a kneeling soldier, in black and white, in uniform and holding a gun, unaware of two silhouettes of Iraqi boys standing behind his shoulder. The children are ghost-like, faceless, their images blurred into the desert. "It was very huge disconnect between us and them," Hughes said.

A charcoal and watercolor piece titled "Do Not Stop ..." represents the consequences of the orders given to drivers in convoys not to stop when children were on the road. The painting shows a soldier's boot next to the body of a dead child. "Safwan is the city that you cross the border into, in Iraq, and I'd say there's a convoy going through about every ten minutes, or less actually ..." Hughes explains to Safronova, "and these convoys have between 20 and 100 trucks in them. So that's like between a quarter mile to two miles long convoys, and these trucks are huge trucks. And there's a lot of kids on the road and ... it was really hard to control those kids. So there were some things that happened there with kids getting hit by trucks." In a poem that accompanies the piece, Hughes writes: "Keep the truck moving and don't stop. Forget the kids! Now, now I can't forget the kids. Damn kid. I'm not even there. Hundred thousand miles away and it's still in my fucking head."[6]

Hughes uses his art in other ways, as well. During fall 2006, he went to a busy street intersection in Champaign, Illinois, and began "Drawing for Peace." In the performance, he set a sign in the street that read:

I am an Iraq War Veteran.
I am guilty.
I am alone.
I am drawing for peace.

Expanding on his action, on his website, Hughes wrote: "It is an attempt to claim a strategic space in order to challenge the everyday and its constant motion for a moment of thought, meditation, and PEACE." The video recording of the same action shows how Hughes had effectively shut down a street by drawing on it. Several buses stop for ten minutes. Many people exit the bus and stand on the street to watch him work before strolling away. Cars drive by him, seemingly unaware, but he works on, kneeling to draw, ignoring them, engrossed in his work. A motorcycle policeman appears and demands that Hughes leave the road and then pulls him off by his arm. Hughes returns and continues working on the dove he is drawing, until the cop again pulls him off the road, yelling at him. Hughes, dressed in his desert camouflage jacket, listens to the policeman patiently, then takes his sign and walks away. The camera pans back to show traffic resume, and cars and buses driving over the dove Hughes has left on the street.[7]

The veteran, who has participated in marches, rallies, and the Operation First Casualty program, is seeking to publish his book *Dust Memories,* a visual documentary of his journey through Iraq. His work has been exhibited in the National Vietnam Veterans Art Museum in Urbana, Illinois, as well as in galleries in Chicago, Champaign, and New York.

I asked Hughes why he chose art as his means of protest. "I see creative expression as one of the closest ways we can touch our humanity.

By finding outlets for this, we can break through the structures that have been set up to encourage us to dehumanize each other." Hughes believes that art can be used to create a culture of a politically educated democracy because, "As long as we have a culture that is depoliticized, we can't deal with the occupation of Iraq effectively."

When he was deployed to Iraq, Hughes carried with him the

> culturally constructed ideas of America as the great helper. But when I got there, I saw we were oppressing and dehumanizing the Iraqis. Seeing that firsthand, and recognizing the structures that allow this to happen, I had my perspective flipped around on me, and I saw how rooted in hate, greed, and racism this war actually was. People are making billions of dollars while other people are dying, and I don't know how to respond to that but through revolt and by finding a language to fight against it. And that is where art comes in. I can use this to speak out against what is happening in Iraq. Through my art I have even found ways to work with the population I used to oppress in Iraq. I now work with a group that gets prosthetics to Iraqi kids who need them, and kids who have lost their eyesight because of us. These children are still willing to embrace me as a human being. That degree of forgiveness is something that is difficult to reconcile without being pushed into finding ways to break through the hatred and sustain hope in humanity through love.

◆   ◆   ◆

Books are a crucial avenue that soldiers have used to express their resistance to the occupation of Iraq. Staff Sergeant Camilo Mejía wrote *Road from Ramadi* (Haymarket Books, 2008), soon after his release from detention. The book recounts his personal journey from serving in Iraq to becoming a conscientious objector to the occupation. Aidan Delgado, a soldier who managed to gain conscientious objector status during the occupation, authored *The Sutras of Abu Ghraib* (Beacon Press, 2007). In the book, Delgado, who continues to speak out publicly against the occupation, writes about being deeply disturbed by the brutality and extreme racism he witnessed while serving at Abu Ghraib. It crystallized his religious beliefs and made him a confirmed Buddhist.

Josh Key wrote *The Deserter's Tale: The Story of an Ordinary Soldier Who Walked away from the War in Iraq* (Grove Press, 2007). Key had enlisted only after receiving assurance from his recruiter that he would never be deployed abroad. A year later, he found himself in Iraq. In his book he recounts his first doubts regarding his presence in Iraq:

> I hadn't been in Iraq more than twenty-four hours and already I was having strange feelings. First, I was vulnerable, and I didn't like it. Even with all these soldiers and all this equipment, I knew that anywhere, at any time, any enterprising Iraqi with a gun, a wall to hide behind, and one decent eye could pick me off faster than a hawk nabs a mouse. Second, with hardly one foot into the war in Iraq, I was also uneasy about what we were doing there. Something was amiss. We hadn't found anything in this girl's house, but we had busted it up pretty well in thirty minutes and had taken away her brothers. Inside, another squad was still ransacking the house. I didn't enjoy being stuck guarding this girl under the carport, in the cool April air before dawn in Ramadi. Her questions haunted me, and I didn't like not being able to answer them—even to myself.[8]

Key later deserted and went AWOL in Canada.

Sergeant Kevin Benderman wrote in *Letters from Fort Lewis Brig: A Matter of Conscience* (Lyons Press, 2007) about his experience of serving in Iraq and receiving two Army Commendation Medals for his actions there and how after being told he would be returning to the occupation, he had applied for CO status. When his application was denied, he refused to deploy with his unit, was court-martialed and sentenced to fifteen months in prison, and subsequently given a dishonorable discharge.

Letters from Abu Ghraib (Athens, OH: Essay Press, 2008), by Joshua Casteel, chronicles Casteel's time working at the infamous Abu Ghraib prison as a member of the interrogation units sent to overhaul the prison after the torture scandal had become public. The book is a collection of Casteel's e-mails home from his time at the prison. *Letters from Abu Ghraib* is an exposition of how deeply Casteel is affected by the moral implications of working at Abu Ghraib. He was extremely moved by conversations with inmates. Most of the detainees he interrogated turned out to be innocent, but one of his more profound moments of clarity came from a conversation with an admitted jihadist. In an interview with Inter Press Service, Casteel explained: "I had an interrogation with a 22-year-old Saudi Arabian who was very straightforward that he had come to Iraq to conduct jihad. We started having a conversation about religion and ethics and he told me that I was a very strange man who was a Christian but didn't follow the teachings of Jesus to love my enemy and pray for the persecuted ... I told him that I thought he was right and that there was a massive contradiction involved with me doing my job and being a Christian."[9] He has also written two plays, *Returns: A Mediation in Post-trauma* and *Ishmael and Isa,* that document his experiences in Iraq. Currently he is working on a memoir entitled *The Book of Joshua,* which is a narrative account of his eight years in the U.S. Army and his eventual conversion from nationalist Evangelical Christianity to Catholic pacifism.

Another book, *My War: Killing Time in Iraq* (G. P. Putman's Sons, 2005) by Colby Buzzell, based on his blog entries from 2004, when he was stationed in Mosul, in northern Iraq, outlines daily life, along with observations and comments on his fellow "grunts" surfing the Web for pornography. Ironically, at the same time Buzzell was feeling pressure from U.S. military as it began to shut down blogs by soldiers serving in Iraq, he was awarded the Lulu Blooker Prize for the best book based on a blog. The Department of Defense announced it was blocking access to thirteen communal websites, which included YouTube and MySpace, from military computers and networks.

Buzzell's book has been translated into seven languages and secured for him a freelance writing assignment for publications such as *Esquire* magazine. Of the clampdown, Buzzell told the *Guardian*, "It's hard for them out there, and this will make it harder. It will lower soldier morale for troops who are on their second or even third tour ... This is a totally screwed up policy. The commanders are just really nervous because they can't keep control anymore."[10]

Once soldiers translate their experiences into books detailing the transformative process they have undergone through their resistance to the occupation, it becomes impossible for the military to control who reads those books and the effect they have on the readers.

◆   ◆   ◆

Theatre has been a tool for resistance and social transformation across cultures and ages. American soldiers too have used it with the objective of exposing the reality of the occupation to the general population and partially to exorcise themselves of the dark experience.

I interviewed Jeff Key while he was driving from his home in Salt Lake City to Denver to perform *The Eyes of Babylon*, the one-man play that he has developed from his Iraq war journals. Writing down his experiences in a notebook he carried in the cargo pocket of his uniform kept him sane, says Key. For entertainment, he would read his entries aloud to fellow marines. After returning home, Key was inspired to turn his entries into a play when friends who heard him read encouraged him to do something with his writings. He wrote the play, and a workshop version of it opened at the Tamarind Theatre in Hollywood, California. It ran there for eight months and closed to full houses. Since then, Key has toured *The Eyes of Babylon* nationally and internationally.[12] As his car sped along the highway toward Denver, where his monthlong performance would coincide with the 2008 Democratic National Convention, Key mentioned that he had two more plays in the works. "We're going to continue touring this one for a year, and I've just been busy with the charity foundation, but the play is my principle form of activism." The charity is the Mehadi Foundation, a nonprofit organization founded by Key that serves "as a support network providing assistance to United States Armed Forces veterans" enlisted during the invasion and occupation of Iraq "who seek help dealing with issues of PTSD, drug and alcohol concerns and other issues." The organization also provides "aid and assistance to Iraqi civilians as they attempt to rebuild in the wake of the conflict, with specific emphasis on the alleviation of hunger and rebuilding homes and schools destroyed by the War."[13]

The lack of coverage of the occupation of Iraq worsened in December 2008, when major U.S. television networks ceased sending full-time correspondents to Baghdad.[14] The door is now left open wider for veterans to use alternative methods to get their message out. With countless stories to tell, in increasing numbers, veterans stirred by their conscience are using creative outlets and artistic expression to articulate their opposition to the occupations of Iraq and Afghanistan.

Art and literature sublimate the human experience. They have the power to transform those who create as well as those who experience the creation. It is not short of any miracle that despite having been through some of the most life-threatening and morally appalling experiences so many soldiers and veterans have retained their sanity and emotional intelligence. It is even more commendable that they have found within themselves the energy and resolve to deploy those precious assets to accomplish the two-pronged objective of healing themselves and reclaiming the ideals of democracy by making public their resistance.

ELEVEN

STANDING UP

Your silence will not protect you.

—Audre Lourde

Geoffrey Millard, Adam Kokesh, Sergio Kochergin, Kristopher Goldsmith, Luis Montalván, and other veterans assembled on Capitol Hill on the occasion of "Winter Soldier on the Hill," which was held in the Rayburn House Office Building on May 15, 2008. They came to offer testimony to members of Congress about what they had seen and done in Iraq, and to call for an immediate end to the occupation. This was the first time on record that lawmakers were exposed to this level of direct and honest account of the occupation.

Former marine Jason Lemieux testified.

> Throughout my three tours, I was present on numerous occasions when platoons of Lima Company were ordered by commissioned officers to shoot any Iraqi who seemed suspicious or made us feel uncomfortable with the assurance that the chain of command would, quote-unquote, take care of us. Taking care of us meant that the chain of command was loyal to their marines more than to the laws of war or the rules of engagement and would protect them from legal

prosecution even if it meant providing false information to investi-gators. Many of the marines serving on their second or third tours showed signs of psychological trauma and as deployments dragged on and friendly[-fire] casualties mounted, morale plummeted and use of excessive force became routine. To cover up [such actions] we were ordered to falsify reports. I was involved in fire fights during which the rules of engagement were lifted by the chain of command or were simply ignored, resulting in needless and strategically coun-terproductive civilian deaths. I was ordered innumerable times by commissioned as well as noncommissioned officers to shoot un-armed civilians if their presence made me feel uncomfortable. The understanding was that the immediate chain of command would protect subordinates from legal repercussions.

Scott Ewing, who served in the Tal Afar area of northern Iraq, confessed to witnessing several civilians being slaughtered by his fel-low soldiers. "During my deployment, I saw far more civilians in-jured and killed than insurgents. There has been virtually no explicit reporting by the mainstream media of civilian casualties caused by U.S. troops in Iraq. Anytime a suicide bomber kills civilians, it is highly publicized, but my personal experience in Tal Afar has been that the number of Iraqis killed or injured by U.S. forces far out-number those killed by insurgents or suicide bombers."

During September 2005 Ewing was part of a large-scale mission involving thousands of soldiers whose goal was to clear an entire city. "We were told to search aggressively, and we smashed windows, broke open and threw furniture, scattered the contents of drawers onto the floors, stepped on dishes, and left graffiti in Iraqis' homes." As evidence, he showed the members of Congress photographs de-picting vulgar anti-Arab graffiti.

There was scarcely any reportage of the historic "Winter Soldier on the Hill" event by any media outlet other than C-SPAN. Soldiers who have decided to take a stand against the occupation are fully aware that doing so imperils their financial security and professional credibility, yet they have felt compelled to protest.

The corporate media, in contrast, remains tied to its corporate interests, and thus, continues to misrepresent reality to the gullible news consumer.

◆　　◆　　◆

After a year-long deployment in Iraq, Ash Woolson returned stateside, determined to do more than just speak against the occupation. The honorable discharge that came at the end of his contractual obligation with the army did not help his attempts to reintegrate into society. I heard of his trials when we met near Seattle.

> When I was in Iraq I saw how the value of human life was nothing. We lose our humanity during war. And it's not just the soldiers … everyone loses in war. The civilians in Iraq, a million of whom are believed to have died, and the veterans who return, eighteen of whom are believed to be committing suicide every day. No one that I saw was benefitting from this war. So then I started asking myself, who is benefitting? And I started seeing the conglomerate corporations that are benefitting and not the people. So the natural question was, Why am I fighting? Why am I here?

After returning from his deployment, Woolson said, "I did not talk about Iraq at all. When I got back I got arrested a bunch of times on account of … drinking, getting into fights, and then I drove across the country. Just left my family and school, and took off one day. I was having mental breakdowns. I was really depressed. And when I came out to Washington, where I moved from Wisconsin about two years ago, I started talking to other veterans for the first time."

Through a friend of a friend, Woolson became involved in anti-war activism. He created an action group that performs guerilla street theater. His other major undertaking is to turn Bellingham, Washington, where he lives, into a sanctuary city for soldiers refusing to go to Iraq. Toward this objective he has become active in a political group that works directly with the city council and the mayor. He also participates in Operation First Casualty in Bellingham. He was invited by Buddhist monks for a walking tour in Japan to promote peace. He embarked on this 1,200-mile walk to talk about what was happening in Iraq. Over a period of seventy-two days, he gave fifty speeches along the way, sometimes to crowds as strong as four hundred. He was shocked to see the extent of influence the U.S. government exerts on Japan and felt all the more obliged to bring to the notice of the Japanese people the critical implications of their country's involvement with the occupation of Iraq. Japan has maintained a troop presence in Iraq since the beginning of the occupation. The peace walk from Hiroshima to Tokyo aimed at drawing attention to Japan's constitution, Article 9 of which, at least on paper, prohibits the country from going to war. Woolson was invited back in August 2008 to conduct a series of lectures about how the United States is conducting this war and how, like any other war, this too is a poor man's war.

◆   ◆   ◆

Camilo Mejía had been incarcerated for taking a stand against the occupation. When I met him a second time after several years, I was eager to know why he still persists so staunchly in his efforts to organize GI resistance, spending more time on the road than at home. He has no choice: "Having seen and participated in the amount of destruction and death that was brought upon the Iraqi people has created a need in my life to undo some of the damage that we have created there," he calmly explained. "This is a lifelong mission. I feel that in order for me to be comfortable with myself, to live with myself, I have to live my life outside of my own interests. And I think that a big part of that is going to be doing antiwar organizing, just doing everything I can to stop the war in Iraq. And at the same time to connect that to other struggles and to basically go after the system that's responsible for what is happening in Iraq and other parts of the world right now."

Mejía is convinced that discussions about ending the war are pointless unless we are willing to look at its roots. "I don't think it's possible to end the war in Iraq without really denting the system a whole lot, as at the time of Vietnam, when the proper connections were being made. There was a lot of talk about racism, there was a lot of Black Power involvement in the GI resistance movement, and there was class consciousness … I fear that if organizations today don't make connections between the different struggles we will accomplish nothing."

It is possible to build a GI resistance movement as large as that that existed during the war in Vietnam, he feels. "If we continue to do our work, and if we continue to do outreach, and go to the bases, and every now and then we obviously have to have these big events where people come together and we create that sense of cohesion, but that has to happen alongside a grassroots outreach movement … If we do that, I believe we're capable of building up a movement as big or bigger than what happened during the Vietnam War."

Mejía believes,

The brutality and flagrant nature of the U.S. government today is the best recruiting tool both for the GI resistance movement and for the larger movements to promote social change. The choice of the U.S. government not to be more proactive in assisting victims in the aftermath of Hurricane Katrina is very revealing. These are things that prepare the ground for radical ideas to flourish. And when you look at the military for that ground, it's been there for a long time. I mean, when I was in Iraq we were going out on missions without the proper radio equipment, without armor, without enough water to conduct patrols in the hottest hours of the day. So the ground is fertile for radical ideas to flourish, but a lot of work has to be done.

Drawing up a sober assessment of the depth of this country's crisis and the extensive and arduous effort required to affect the necessary change, Mejía connects the dots.

You need a conscious movement to take these people and explain to them how the factors that led to them being in the military—poverty, racism, lack of options, sexism, all these elements that deny them the right to a life with dignity—are also the factors behind the war and behind what is happening to the Iraqi people. That what we are doing to them would not happen if it wasn't done to us first. If we don't address poverty, we cannot address GI issues. And it's a struggle, it's an uphill battle. But I do believe that it can be done. I do believe that people can be radicalized. So it's an important task and it's something that we have to take very seriously and it's something that we can do, and I believe that we will.

He is unhesitant in declaring that those in the Bush administration responsible for the invasion of Iraq "should be tried and convicted for their war crimes," but insists emphatically that the task at hand runs deeper than that. With his impressive clarity he concludes,

> The brutality, the cruelty with which this government operates, is not new to American politics; it's not new to American government. So obviously they have to pay for their crimes, but we have to realize that these are just figureheads. We have a corporate government, and we have corporate interests behind everything that happens in the White House, behind everything that happens in Congress, and we need to go after that as well. We cannot just think that by changing politicians and trying a few of them we're going to change the system. We have to go after the actual structures of power that are behind the decision-making processes that explain the current state of affairs.

◆   ◆   ◆

The Democratic National Convention was held in Denver, Colorado, from August 25–28, 2008, at the Pepsi Center and INVESCO Field at Mile High Stadium. On August 27, dozens of Iraq war veterans converged there to lead a march of ten thousand people to the convention, in order to deliver to Democratic presidential candidate Barack Obama a message that appealed to him to call for an immediate withdrawal from Iraq, to provide full veterans benefits, and to pay reparations to the Iraqi people.

Fifty veterans formed two squads of twenty-five members to lead the march to the Pepsi Center. Led by members in dress uniforms and combat uniforms, and flanked by thousands of demonstrators, the procession arrived at the DNC and asked to meet with Obama. Instead, former Texas lieutenant governor Ben Barnes stepped out to accept a letter from the veterans. Veteran Jeff Key declared that he intended to remain there until a representative from Obama's campaign came out to talk. He told a reporter, "They are running a campaign based on an antiwar platform. We want to send one veteran to read [our] letter from the podium."

"We're here to hold the Democrat Party accountable," said veteran Jason Hurd. "We voted them in to end this war. They have not done that … We want our brothers and sisters to come home now. Not later. Now."[1]

Everyone who participated in the march, non-veterans included, were met by more than one hundred Denver Police Department officers clad in riot gear and armed with batons and pepper spray. Initially, the police refused to allow any veteran in to deliver the group's message, and the scene grew tense as hundreds prepared to engage in civil disobedience. Finally Key, and former marine Liam Madden, were escorted into the convention, where they met with Phil Carter, head of veterans' affairs for the Obama campaign. Inside the boisterous Pepsi Center, no mention was made of the demonstration or the concerns of the veterans about ending the occupation and providing assistance for veterans and the Iraqi people.[2]

A few days later a similar scene was enacted in Minneapolis–St. Paul, where the Republican National Convention was held from September 1–4. While the Denver story could be considered a partial success at least, there was nothing to redeem the RNC encounter. The day the convention commenced, a formation of about sixty Iraq and Afghanistan veterans marched in uniform to the Xcel Energy Center in order to deliver a briefing on veterans' issues to Senator John McCain, the Republican presidential candidate. The march was led by Wes Davey, a father of five and grandfather of seven who served twenty-eight years in the army, including a tour in Iraq. When Davey, also a former St. Paul police officer, attempted to deliver the briefing, he was escorted off the premises by the police on duty.

Aware that the environment here would be more hostile than at the DNC, the contingent chose to focus only on veterans' issues and to leave withdrawal of troops and reparations off the table. Veteran T. J. Buonomo told a reporter, "We actually chose not to pressure him on the issue of withdrawal. There's nothing that's very controversial about the things we were asking. There's nothing that's very controversial in asking that people get the discharge they deserve, that people with PTSD not have it held against them."[3]

The letter from IVAW focused on medical needs of soldiers returning from Iraq and Afghanistan, two occupations that McCain has given his vocal support to from the beginning. "It is often said that a nation's character can be judged by how it honors its veterans ..." it stated. "We honor veterans by offering them full benefits, adequate healthcare (including mental healthcare), and other long-term supports." Previous attempts to mail, fax, and personally deliver invitations to the McCain campaign requesting that he meet with veterans in order to discuss the recommendations had gone nowhere. "I'm not surprised that McCain is not responding ..." said Rebecca Hansen, a veteran from Madison, Wisconsin. "I don't think (Republicans) want the American people to know that vets and active-duty soldiers are not in support of the war anymore."[4]

The veterans at the protest felt insulted at being snubbed. Additional cause for their anger was the fact that McCain was running for office by exploiting his military service and his former status as a prisoner of war. There was also the inconvenient matter of McCain having voted against two components of an Iraq supplemental funding bill in spring 2006 that would have opened up more funding for veterans' health care. The following month, McCain voted against providing the VA with $430 million for "outpatient care and treatment for veterans."[5]

Despite excessive deployment of riot police and their strict biometric identification of attendees (retina scans and fingerprints), at least one Iraq veteran managed to slip inside the convention. C-SPAN covered the story. At the beginning of McCain's acceptance speech for his nomination as the Republican presidential candidate, the viewer can see Adam Kokesh holding up a sign that reads, "YOU CAN'T WIN AN OCCUPATION."[6] The footage with Kokesh yelling, "Ask him why he votes against vets!" shows McCain waiting with a smile as the crowd attempts to provide cover by chanting "USA, USA, USA," just as it did when other protesters had interrupted speeches. As the crowd chanted, Kokesh flipped the sign over to reveal the other side, which read, "McCAIN VOTES AGAINST VETS." A minute later, as McCain started talking about 9/11, Kokesh's voice can again be heard as he yells to get McCain's attention as the gathering roars to drown out his voice.

Subsequently Kokesh was led out of the Xcel Center by security, handcuffed by local police, and then briefly questioned while security debated whether or not the Secret Service would get involved, before escorting him off the premises and allowing him to go free. In an interview after the incident, Kokesh clarified, "Well I wasn't so much trying to interrupt the speech as make the point that McCain has a horrible voting record on veterans. What the Republican Party is doing with their take on the war in Iraq is spinning it in such a way that it's about victory or defeat. But they can't face up to the fact that you can't win an occupation. In an occupation, everybody loses. What we're calling for is an immediate withdrawal of all occupying forces in Iraq."[7]

◆   ◆   ◆

Among the innumerable factors that enable the U.S. government and military to continue the occupations of Iraq and Afghanistan are military repression, the faltering economy, soldiers' loyalty to their fellow soldiers, the absence of a draft, and lack of effective organizing. These same factors come into play to obstruct the formation of a larger, coalesced GI resistance movement.

Currently the GI movement lacks overall cohesion at a level that begins to approach that of the massive GI movement of the Vietnam Era. This is a subjective weakness, rather than an objective limitation. Meanwhile, the military has taken some cues from history. For instance, they no longer rotate fresh recruits into experienced units that have been in the field for long stretches. It is an established fact from the Vietnam days and has been noticed in Iraq as well that fresh recruits gain swift exposure to the most advanced resistance when placed in the field alongside more experienced soldiers. To keep the pace of radicalization in check, the military now uses "unit cohesion" instead, which involves rotating whole units in and out as a group.

However there is no denying the positive similarities in the overall situation of GI resistance today and during the Vietnam era, when the movement against the war burgeoned to inconceivable proportions. As during the Vietnam War era, there is today a growing sense among soldiers, in both Iraq and Afghanistan, that the mission, if there is one at all, is progressing poorly. This sense of futility acts as a major deterrent for soldiers to risk their lives and makes them more prone to resist. Another unchanged element is the military's callous disregard for soldiers' lives, both during service and post-discharge. This begins with the lies of the recruiters. Most practice deceit and rule-bending to get people to sign up. The military treats soldiers today as it did three decades ago, as nothing more than implements, tools and military hardware. The absolute disregard for their mental health care, during and after deployment, remains the same. The exposure to toxic chemicals and the accompanying denial by the establishment of adverse effects of the chemicals is also strikingly similar.

As before, the broader antiwar movement is welcoming and accommodating of all GI resistance. Activists understand the critical importance of a GI revolt to ending the war effort, and continue to warmly welcome GIs into the ranks of the movement. For these seeds to germinate into a full-blown resistance movement akin to that which helped end the Vietnam War, a vigorous antiwar movement will have to be revived among the general population. GI leadership will have to dedicate itself to grassroots movement-building and be willing and inclined to engage with the rest of the antiwar movement, which in turn must act as the most dependable source of support and sustenance for the GI resistance to rely upon.

◆   ◆   ◆

When First Lieutenant Ehren Watada of the U.S. Army stated on June 22, 2006, "As the order to take part in an illegal act is ultimately unlawful as well, I must refuse that order," he became the first and highest-ranking commissioned officer in the military to refuse orders to deploy to Iraq. It turned him into a symbol of resistance to the occupation.

Watada's court-martial in February 2007 garnered international media exposure, but ended in a mistrial. A second court-martial in October was aborted when a U.S. district judge issued a stay order, claiming that Watada's "double jeopardy claim is meritorious."[8]

The articulate and charismatic officer clearly posed a threat to the military when he chose to take a stand against the occupation. Decorated with awards such as the Army Commendation Medal, National Defense Service Medal, and the Global War on Terrorism Service Medal, among others, the exceptional officer was sure to attract followers if word of his rebellion spread.

In a speech at the Veterans for Peace National Convention in Seattle, Washington, on August 12, 2006, Watada laid out a blueprint of how to build widespread GI resistance. That night I was part of the crowd of five hundred others, mostly veterans of wars ranging from the Second World War to the current occupations of Iraq and Afghanistan. The mood was electric before Watada took the stage. Just as he began to speak, about fifty veterans from the occupation of Iraq filed in behind him. Surprised by this symbolic act, he turned again to the audience while the veterans behind him stood at attention, and the crowd hung on his words.

"Today, I speak with you about a radical idea. It is one born from the very concept of the American soldier or service member. It became instrumental in ending the Vietnam War, but it has been long since forgotten. The idea is this: that to stop an illegal and unjust war, the soldiers can choose to stop fighting it."

"For soldiers to resist," he said,

is not an easy task, but it is of utmost importance if they hold themselves responsible for their actions and remember their civic duties and supersede the ideologies of their leadership. The soldiers must be willing to face ostracism by their peers, concern over the survival of their families, and of course the loss of personal freedom. They must know that resisting an authoritarian government at home is equally important to fighting a foreign aggressor on the battlefield. Finally, those wearing the uniform must know beyond any shadow of a doubt that by refusing immoral and illegal orders they will be supported by the people not with mere words but by action.

Through his words and actions, Watada was publicly threatening the U.S. military. He was talking openly about building an antiwar movement. He was redefining resistance as a collective undertaking that entailed not only soldiers laying down their arms, but a massive support network of people and communities behind those who resisted. It was a well-detailed plan that he projected as he addressed the issue of the soldiers.

> They must realize that this is a war not out of self-defense but by choice, for profit and imperialistic domination. They must consider the lies used to justify the invasion and occupation of Iraq. WMD, ties to Al-Qaeda, and ties to 9/11 never existed and never will. The soldier must know that our narrowly and questionably elected officials intentionally manipulated the evidence presented to Congress, the public, and the world to make the case for war … Though the American soldier wants to do right, the illegitimacy of the occupation itself, the policies of this administration, and rules of engagement of desperate field commanders will ultimately force them to be party to war crimes. They must know some of these facts, if not all, in order to act.

Emphasizing that enlisting in the military does not absolve one from the responsibility of distinguishing between right and wrong, he proceeded:

> I was only following orders" is never an excuse. The Nuremburg trials showed America and the world that citizenry, as well as soldiers, have the unrelinquishable obligation to refuse complicity in war crimes perpetrated by their government. Widespread torture and inhumane treatment of detainees is a war crime. A war of aggression borne through an unofficial policy of prevention is a crime against peace. An occupation violating the very essence of international

humanitarian law and sovereignty is a crime against humanity. These crimes are funded by our tax dollars.

"Should citizens choose to remain silent through self-imposed ignorance or choice," argued Watada,

it makes them as culpable as the soldier in these crimes ... When we say, "Against all enemies foreign and domestic," what if elected leaders became the enemy? Whose orders do we follow? The answer is the conscience that lies in each soldier, each American, and each human being ... If we want soldiers to choose the right but difficult path, they must know beyond any shadow of a doubt that they will be supported by Americans. To support the troops who resist, you must make your voices heard. If they see thousands supporting me, they will know. I have heard your support, as has Suzanne Swift, and Ricky Clousing, but many others have not. Increasingly, more soldiers are questioning what they are being asked to do. Yet, the majority lack awareness of the truth that is buried beneath the headlines. Many more see no alternative but to obey. We must show open-minded soldiers a choice, and we must give them courage to act.

You must know that to stop this war, for the soldiers to stop fighting it, they must have the unconditional support of the people. I have seen this support with my own eyes. For me it was a leap of faith. For other soldiers, they do not have that luxury. They must know it and you must show it to them. Convince them that no matter how long they sit in prison, no matter how long this country takes to right itself, their families will have a roof over their heads, food in their stomachs, opportunities, and education. This is a daunting task. It requires the sacrifice of all of us. Why must Canadians feed and house our fellow Americans who have chosen to do the right thing? We should be the ones taking care of our own. Are we that powerless? Are we that unwilling to risk something for those who can truly end this war? How do you support the troops but not the war? By supporting those who can truly stop it. Let them know that resistance to participate in an illegal war is not futile and not without a future.

When the raucous applause subsided he continued:

Now, I'm not a hero. I am a leader of men who said enough is enough. Those who called for war prior to the invasion compared diplomacy with Saddam [Hussein] to the compromises made with Hitler. I say, we compromise now by allowing a government that uses war as the first option instead of the last, to act with impunity. Many have said this about the World Trade Towers: Never Again. I agree. Never again will we allow those who threaten our way of life to reign free, be they terrorists or elected officials. The time to fight back is now, the time to stand up and be counted is today.

Watada continues to report to duty every day.

In February 2007, military judge Lieutenant Colonel John Head put a stop to Watada's case following what he found to be possible inconsistencies concerning a "stipulation of fact" that was agreed upon prior to the hearing. The decision led to a mistrial that technically ended Watada's court martial, which the army then appealed. Nevertheless, a judge said Watada could not be retried on the same charges, as that would have been double jeopardy.

The Justice Department dropped its appeal of the double jeopardy ruling in May 2009. Watada, while continuing to report to his desk job each day, still awaits the army's decision on how it will handle two other court-martial charges (for conduct unbecoming of an officer) and the possibility of administrative punishment.

Watada's attorney, James Lobsenz, said in a press release concerning the decision, "Because there are no longer any criminal charges pending against Lt. Watada, and because [his] military service has been extended far beyond his normal release date, he anticipates that he will soon be released from active duty. He plans to return to civilian life and to attend law school."[9]

At the time of this writing, it appears as though Ehren Watada, the highest-ranking enlisted member of the military to publicly refuse orders to deploy to Iraq, will not spend one day in jail nor one day in Iraq.

AFTERWORD

Writing *The Will to Resist* was for me an act of expiation, among other things. Having experienced the occupation of Iraq at a close range I had come to see members of the U.S. military as the single most prominent agents inflicting and perpetrating brutal injustice on a civilian population, in addition to decimating a sovereign nation that had not displayed any visible signs of hostility toward the United States. That all this was done in the guise of liberating the said nation had only added to my anger toward American soldiers.

It was painful to replace my childhood awe and admiration of the military uniform, and all that it represented, with disgust and mistrust. I was able to do it by dehumanizing the uniformed men and women of my own country in a manner not dissimilar from the way I saw them dehumanizing the people of the land they had illegally invaded.

I have already placed on record in the introduction to this book when and how I came to sense the error in my judgment. Initial chance encounters with war veterans and active duty soldiers during my lecture and talk tours in the United States led me to discover an unexpected bond with them. I was struck by the knowledge that they, like me, were struggling with the debilitating effects of their experiences in

Iraq. Their complicity in the occupation only compounded their suffering. This realization left me determined to explore what I could of their lives. Several intensive interviews, participation in Winter Soldier events and intense sharings later, I was able to put out this volume.

I have sufficient evidence now to establish that the occupations are being sustained at the cost of irrevocable damage to the wellbeing of our soldiers and their communities.

Dr. Kernan Manion is a board-certified psychiatrist who was hired last January to treat marines returning from the occupations. It did not take him long to see what was going on. He grew alarmed at what he witnessed of the military's inability to give sufficient treatment to returning soldiers, and even more so at the reports of outright abuse meted out by some commanders to lower-ranking soldiers who sought help.

He realized that the condition of an overburdened, overstressed, understaffed, and ill-equipped military mental-health-care system is exponentially worsened for being administered by career military personnel woefully ill-trained to provide the complex psychiatric expertise necessary to effectively treat psychologically impaired soldiers from both occupations.

According to him, psychotherapy for soldiers returning with severe, complex, combat-related psychological trauma and new-onset, deployment-related mental health problems is the psychological equivalent of neurosurgery.

He found to his dismay that instead of receiving any such care the troops had to bear the brunt of pervasive harassment and often outright psychological abuse from superiors who refused to acknowledge the validity, much less the severity, of their problems.

I quote his reaction: "I felt like I was witnessing child abuse. These courageous and fit men go through boot camp, and combat, and the incredible duress inherent in deployment, and then you come back and your mid-level command [calls you a goddamn loser] ... There is a tremendous amount of resentment that builds up there."

His constant words of caution to the authorities about the irrevocable consequences of this situation went unheeded. Finally they resulted in his abrupt firing when he complained of "complete disregard for ... implications for patient safety and well-being" on the part of officials at Camp Lejeune.

Let me reiterate what must be obvious even to a casual reader of this book. What started as my empathetic curiosity soon turned into a compulsion. Apart from the concern I felt for their plight upon returning home, my interviews and discussions with the veterans and soldiers added fresh dimensions to my understanding of the occupation.

I have now become a member of the miniscule band of authors, journalists, alternative media people, and legal and medical workers who are trying to bring to the conscientious segments of the American public stories of resistance within the ranks to the occupations of Iraq and Afghanistan. I continue to hope along with them that veterans and soldiers who have chosen to resist will get visibility and support and that in the not-too-distant future the number of dissenters will increase steadily and sufficiently to end the occupations.

◆   ◆   ◆

On December 3, 2009, March Forward! issued a press release in response to President Barack Obama's announcement on December 1 to deploy thirty thousand additional troops to Afghanistan. It said:

March Forward! calls on all service members to refuse orders to deploy to Afghanistan and Iraq. We offer our unconditional support and solidarity. Join us in the fight to ensure that no more soldiers or civilians lose their lives in these criminal wars ...

On December 1, we got a clear order from President Obama. For many more years, we will be sent to kill, to die, to be maimed and wounded, in a war where "victory" is impossible, against a people who are not our enemies. For over eight years, we have come home in coffins, in wheelchairs, with our skin burned and with our days and nights haunted by the trauma of war. We return home to a VA whose services are so inadequate that active duty soldiers who succumb to suicide outnumber those killed in combat ...[1]

Michael Prysner, a former corporal and veteran of the Iraq occupation who served from 2001 to 2005, co-founded March Forward! along with another Iraq war veteran, James Circello, in 2008. Their organization "supports the right of all service members to refuse illegal and immoral orders."[2]

It is their contention that "Orders to deploy to Afghanistan and Iraq are just that: illegal and immoral. We have no reason to fight in these wars, and we have every right to refuse to be a part of them. [Our] aim is to unite all those who have served and who currently serve in the U.S. military, and who want to stand up for our rights and for that which is right."

Of soldiers being obligated to follow orders, no matter what, Prysner says,

Yes, people do sign a contract to follow orders, but [what if] those orders are wrong and unlawful. We want to educate people to the fact that these are immoral orders, and they [soldiers] are being used as muscle for corporations, to colonize the developing world, and it's not legitimate. People who join and take this oath seriously, think they are in [the military] to defend the United States. This is not what we are being used for in the military today.

In their 2009 book *Rules of Disengagement: The Politics and Honor of Military Dissent*, Marjorie Cohn, president of the National Lawyers Guild, and Kathleen Gilberd argue that every U.S. war since Second World War has been illegal. Article 51 of the UN Charter only permits the "right of individual or collective self-defense if an armed attack occurs against a Member ... until the Security Council has taken measures to maintain international peace and security."[3]

In addition, Article I, Section 8, Clause 11 (the war powers clause) of the U.S. Constitution authorizes only both houses of Congress, not the president, to declare war. However, that process has been followed only five times in our history and the last time was on December 8, 1941, after Japan attacked Pearl Harbor.

Of his experience in Iraq, Prysner writes,

> ... there was no computer screen separating me from the suffering civilian population. I spent 12 months in Iraq, doing everything from prisoner interrogations, to ground surveillance missions, to home raids. It was this firsthand experience that radicalized me. I believed I was going to Iraq to help liberate and better the lives of an oppressed people, but I soon realized that my purpose [of being] in Iraq was to be the oppressor, and to clear the way for U.S. corporations, with no regard for human life.[4]

Being part of the U.S. occupation of Iraq taught him that "I still had the same drive to fight for freedom, justice and equality as I did when I joined, and I understood that fighting for those things meant fighting against the U.S. government, not on behalf of it."[5]

He summarily dismisses those who call him and his organization anti-American and unpatriotic. "I would say that I have more in common with my sisters and brothers in Iraq and Afghanistan than I do with these people in D.C. who've sent us to war," Prysner told me. "If that's unpatriotic, then yes, I am. Patriotism and racism are the only things the military has, to fall back on, to convince people to do the things we are being asked to do today."[6]

His comrade in resistance, James Circello, joined the military in 2001. In April 2007 he left his base in Vicenza, Italy, and went AWOL. In November of the same year he turned himself in at Fort Knox and was discharged within three days. He has remained very active in his work against U.S. foreign policy, working first with Iraq Veterans Against the War and Courage to Resist before co-founding March Forward!

Circello's decision to go AWOL was his way of refusing to deploy to Afghanistan. He says,

> I had been fighting myself internally after my time in Iraq, about whether to deploy again. I ended up back in my old unit that was preparing to deploy, so at that moment I took it into my hands, and decided I wasn't going to go kill Afghans that had done nothing to me, or the American people. It was a defining moment for me ... During the occupation of Iraq, the truth about what the United States government has done to the country of Iraq became more apparent. Open wastewater flowed through neighborhood streets where children played soccer. Families were thrown out of their homes because of simple accusations from others. Vehicles were taken on sight by the military if individuals couldn't provide proper documents claiming they own the vehicle. These events and others helped in strengthening my opposition to the so-called "War on Terror."

He believes that those who consider it unpatriotic to encourage soldiers to refuse deployment orders are guilty of demonizing re-sisters and dissenters. His argument is straightforward:

> The corporations profiting in these wars don't care about America or the American people. Is providing mercenaries to kill innocent peo-ple overseas, and bombs to kill innocent people, is that American and patriotic? The people who use these terms are demagogues. We can't forget that America was a land of institutionalized slavery, slavery was American, and folks like Dr. Martin Luther King, when they stood up to racism, were called un-American ... so the same thing happens today. When you protest war, or call on soldiers to desert, based on their own interest, you are called un-American.[7]

In sharp contrast to this is the American Legion, defined on its website as "a patriotic, war-time veterans' organization devoted to mutual helpfulness." Its communication director, John Raughter, states emphatically that his organization does not in any way support AWOL soldiers or those who refuse to deploy to Iraq or Afghanistan.

> We have an all-volunteer force. These are not draftees. They swore an oath to obey the orders of the Commander in Chief. Within reason, the military should be able to enforce obedience. Obedience and order are critical for the military to do its mission. People can't pick and choose which orders to obey and which not to [obey]. If it's a lawful order, they are obliged to obey. If they are ethically opposed to wars in Iraq and Afghanistan, [they] should have never joined the ranks. Most of these people have enlisted or reenlisted since the be-ginning of the war. These wars were occurring when they made this oath of enlistment. It should have come to their minds.[8]

It is baffling, to say the least, that in a country with a proclaimed literacy rate of 99 percent a large segment of the population seems perfectly content in its ignorance of the oath people swear allegiance to when the join the military, and their adherence to lawful orders, not the whims of their Commander in Chief. That even a small percentage of men and women in the armed forces have been pushed into a closer examination of our government at severe risk to their careers and well-being cannot be applauded enough.

◆   ◆   ◆

As readers may have gathered from accounts in this book, the Veteran's administration—or VA, as it is commonly known—has displayed what can at best be described as inexcusable degrees of callousness toward the medical needs of returning vets and active-duty soldiers. Lack of funds, infrastructure, and autonomy only exacerbate matters. Complete lack of transparency on the part of the establishment and an obliging media help to keep the American public largely unaware of these facts.

Veterans having to seek unaffordable health care from other sources have been driven to penury, subsequent marital separations, and suicide. Families that have had to directly deal with all this have been unable to reconcile with the rampant apathy at the highest levels in addressing this enormous problem.

In June 2010 I had occasion to interview the wives of these soldiers at the NTC, along with wives of other soldiers at Fort Hood, who, despite having medical profiles that should have prohibited them from further military training, were sent to the National Training Center (NTC) at Fort Irwin, California.

For fear of official reprisal most of them wished to remain anonymous, since what they all had to report can only be considered highly indicting evidence against the military establishment. They were all given to understand that they would be offered the best medical facilities at the NTC, which turned out to be entirely untrue.

For individuals with severe cases of PTSD not to have access to psychiatric counseling is bad enough. In most of these cases even medication refills were withheld or unavailable.

Fort Hood doctors could not continue to treat their patients who had been moved to Fort Irwin and doctors at the new facility would not treat patients who were not permanent base members.

At Fort Hood Captain Ryan McDonald heads the Third Armored Cavalry Regiment (ACR), a unit with at least fifty-five members with medical profiles that are supposed to exclude them from combat training and being around weapons and ammunition, all of whom were sent to the NTC along with others.

Among the largest bases in the United States, Fort Hood has sent out the heaviest deployments to both occupations. It also accounts for more soldier suicides than any other army post since the U.S. invasion of Iraq in 2003.

On the outskirts of the base in Killeen, Texas, is Under the Hood Café, a place that tries to provide support for soldiers and their families. Cynthia Thomas, who runs the café, reports, "There are dozens of spouses here at Fort Hood whose husbands are diagnosed with PTSD, traumatic brain injury (TBI), and other problems and they are being sent to NTC anyway, even though their doctors are telling them they can't be around live fire or weapons or be given combat training."

The wives are aware that Captain McDonald, commander to most of these soldiers, has misled their doctors to believe that they will be given medical treatment at the NTC.

Brandi Owen, the wife of an Iraq vet, holds the commander responsible for pressuring the of many of the Third ACR soldiers into allowing them to be sent to the NTC. Her husband's psychiatrist at

Fort Hood gave him a last-minute clearance because the commander told him that he would receive the same medical treatment at the NTC. The truth is that he did not even get his medication there, although it is a known fact that patients tend to get suicidal when taken off those meds abruptly.

Outraged at the lack of medical treatment for her husband, Brandi Owen contacted her congressman, John Carter of the Thiry-first District of Texas, and was told that there had already been twenty-six congressional complaints about the soldiers' being sent to the NTC. Her attempts to get answers have only been met with frustration:

> I've talked to all of his chain of command, the generals here and at Ft. Irwin, they always transfer me to someone else, or say they can't help me or there is nothing they can do. I have a notebook full of numbers they refer me to, or tell me to make an IG [Inspector General] complaint, which I do, but I still haven't heard from any of them. The Chain of Command doesn't do anything. He's going on two and a half months without seeing a doctor. He needs meds! He needs a doctor! NTC has given him flashbacks from Iraq. He can't sleep and can't eat. Now I'm worried about what he'll be like when he gets back. It's going to be worse than when he left.

The NTC describes itself as "The World's Premier Training Center for the World's Finest Military."

Another Iraq veteran I interviewed for a story in June 2010 told me,

> About three days before I was told I was leaving for NTC, I went home to pack and flipped out and tore my house apart. I went to the ER, they talked about putting me in the psych ward, but they put me on homicide watch because they feared I would kill my chain of com-

mand. They sent me out here, supposedly with a thirty-day supply of narcotics, but I ran out. I went four days without my meds and they didn't even fill one of them.

His time in Iraq haunts him. He finds it unbearable to be around simulated combat. "But I'm here on a FOB, there are .50-caliber machine guns and ammo everywhere and I have access to all this and nobody in my chain of command gives a shit. I can't sleep at night. It's ruthless shit out here. I haven't seen anything like this before."

The soldier believes he is not going to be deployed because his medical profile lists him as being "non-deployable."

So why was he sent to the NTC?

I got sent out here because they get $8,000 per head for every soldier out here for their budget. You have people here on respirators, people with cervical cancer, it's not just me ... There are about fifty soldiers here that should not be here, just from my unit, Third ACR. There're about 5,500 soldiers in the regiment right now and about fifty of us that are absolutely not supposed to be out here, period.

Crystal Hess, herself a veteran of two tours in Iraq and two in Afghanistan, was dismayed when her husband, Specialist Cory Hess, was sent to the NTC, also at the behest of Captain McDonald, despite a broken hand and PTSD. As of this writing, he was slated to be deployed to Iraq in August 2010.

Crystal says, "He's got anger and depression issues. He's been blown up multiple times in Iraq, he has issues with his knees, back, shoulder, and I'm pushing for him to be screened for TBI, because he has persistent headaches."

She has tried talking with commanders, asking them to take care of this, because it's affecting their home life. She forced them, by calling the Department of Army inspector general, to send her husband home on grounds of imminent surgery. However, even six days after his return, he had been given no medicine and was in acute pain because of his broken hand, with no assurance in sight.

Something a flag-waving, "patriotic" nation that swears by family values may never comprehend is that soldiers may be driven by those same family values in rejecting the life of warfare.

According to Cynthia Thomas, Captain McDonald was not deployed with the soldiers in the Third ACR but took command of the unit after they came back from Iraq in January 2009. He isn't known to possess leadership skills and is not married, which may be a possible reason for his being dismissive of the concerns of the spouses. But the problem obviously extends beyond him to the entire chain of command at Fort Hood.

Stephanie Wallin and several other wives who have had husbands with non-deployable medical profiles sent to the NTC are not convinced by the PR lies and have reason to believe that the military is unconcerned about the soldiers and their families.

The women have pleaded with a military chaplain for help. Stephanie has talked to everyone: generals, chaplains, commanders. The commander apparently told the soldier, "Why don't you have your wife on a leash?" and later tried to punish him for Stephanie's wanting to help, even claiming that she was trying to get him into trouble.

For these wives, managing families singlehandedly while dealing with homicidal or suicidal husbands who have little to no medical support and are faced with the constant threat of deployment, the army lost its glory and glamour a while back.

Stephanie's words echo the feelings of many others like her:

It's really hard on me. My husband has homicidal thoughts and I have three kids. So I don't know how he's going to deal with the kids. I want to know why the chain of command lies. I don't know why they say they are all about soldiers and families and they'll make sure they'll get the help they need. They don't. It's very, very hard. I'm very, very stressed out. My husband is not the man I married. They pushed him until he broke and then they've pushed him beyond that … The army is not what it says it is. Recruiters make it sound so good, but once you sign up, you're screwed. My kids wonder what they did wrong because of what the army is doing to their father. They feel like they've lost their father. I don't know what to do anymore. There's a whole bunch of soldiers who need this story out. They need help.

If these conditions had greater visibility, what would be the American public's response to those distant wars?

Would they continue with their hollow patriotic platitudes or would they demand accountability of their government?

What will it take for the proverbial last straw to break the hold that a ruthless establishment has on the men and women who serve it?

◆   ◆   ◆

If personal factors like family and well-being are calling into question the credibility of the military establishment and its agenda, ideological and ethical issues are contributing in no small measure to the further disenchantment of veterans and soldiers.

More people today are joining the military out of economic necessity rather than for ideological or patriotic reasons. That the military today comprises an all-voluntary force is cited by war critics as one of the factors responsible for resistance not spreading as fast as it did during the Vietnam War.

But as readers may have gathered from this book, men and women can be governed by considerations other than economic when it comes to dissent and resistance. Sometimes it can be a fundamental instinct for survival. There have also been instances of sheer mental and physical exhaustion with the combat conditions.

However, for a growing number dissent has become a deep moral and ethical compulsion.

On April 5, 2010, video footage from Iraq on WikiLeaks.org showed the unprovoked slaughter of twelve people, including two children, by soldiers aboard a military Apache helicopter in July 2007. Among the dead were two Reuters staff, photographer Namir Noor-Eldeen and driver Saeed Chmagh.

The U.S. military confirmed the authenticity of the video.

The Pentagon announced that two investigations had cleared the air crew of any wrongdoing as they had acted appropriately and followed the ROE.

Testifying at the Winter Soldier hearings in Silver Spring, Maryland, in 2008, Corporal Jason Washburn said,

I remember one woman walking by. She was carrying a huge bag, and she looked like she was heading toward us, so we lit her up with the Mark 19, which is an automatic grenade launcher, and when the dust settled, we realized that the bag was full of groceries. She had been trying to bring us food and we blew her to pieces.

The ROE in Iraq, he admitted, were constantly and arbitrarily changed depending on the prevailing threat levels. They were lax to the point of being virtually nonexistent and soldiers were not only permitted but also expected to respond without restraint.

At the same Winter Soldier event Hart Viges, of the Eighty-second Airborne Division, reported one occasion when they received radio orders to fire on all taxicabs because the enemy was using them for transportation. When one of the snipers asked, "Excuse me? Did I hear that right ... fire on all taxicabs?" the lieutenant colonel responded with "You heard me, trooper, fire on all taxicabs." After that, the town lit up, with all units firing on cabs.

Others described how they had emptied bullets into cities without identifying targets, run over corpses with Humvees, taken pot shots at cars driving by, and collected "trophy" photos of dead bodies.

For those who are interested in the truth, it is not difficult to find out that such behavior by U.S. soldiers in Iraq has been the norm rather than the exception. I have had several soldiers tell me about horrific inflictions by the U.S. occupation forces.

Veteran Kelly Dougherty, the executive director of IVAW, said in 2008, "The abuses committed in the occupations, far from being the result of a 'few bad apples' misbehaving, are the result of our government's Middle East policy, which is crafted in the highest spheres of U.S. power."

Corporal Michael Leduc said his orders before entering Fallujah during the 2004 November siege were as follows: "You see an individual with a white flag and he does anything but approach you slowly and obey commands, assume it's a trick and kill him."

Scott Ewing admitted that units gave candy to Iraqi children for reasons other than winning hearts and minds: "We used the kids as human shields [knowing that] if the kids were around our vehicles the bad guys wouldn't attack."

Dr. Stjepan Mestrovic, a professor of sociology at Texas A&M University, has written three books on U.S. misconduct in Iraq: *The Trials of Abu Ghraib: An Expert Witness Account of Shame and Honor*, *Rules of Engagement?: Operation Iron Triangle, Iraq*, and *The "Good Soldier" on Trial: A Sociological Study of Misconduct by the US Military Pertaining to Operation Iron Triangle, Iraq*. His books meticulously document how the U.S. Army as an institution has become dysfunctional, and how illegal ROE are issued by officers and politicians at the top of the army's hierarchy but only low-ranking soldiers are punished for carrying out those same rules and orders. As an example, in one of the several hearings Dr. Mestrovic has attended as an expert witness, U.S. soldiers openly admitted they had shot a seventy-five-year-old man who had emerged unarmed from his house, but because the soldiers were following the rule to shoot all "military aged males," neither they nor their officers were charged for that death.

Jason Wayne Lemieux, who served three tours in Iraq, was told by his commander on his first deployment to kill those who needed to be killed and save those who needed to be saved. Soon the ROE changed, and Iraqis who were out after curfew or happened to be carrying a shovel or standing on a rooftop talking on a cell phone were to be killed. By the time of his third tour Lemieux says, "We were told to just shoot people, and the officers would take care of us."

There is enough evidence to establish that the ROE were no more than a joke.

If the mainstream media, instead of ignoring the testimonies offered at the Winter Soldier events, had been half as conscientious in its reportage of the reality of the occupation as experienced by the soldiers as it has been in parroting the establishment propaganda, would the American public still be offering tacit support or ignorant indifference to "wars" that are not really wars at all?

◆   ◆   ◆

I was in Baghdad in November 2004 when my Iraqi friend and interpreter, Abu Talat, was caught in the Abu Hanifa mosque raid by U.S. and Iraqi soldiers during Friday prayers.

Abu Talat described to me over the phone the horrific situation inside the mosque: "Everyone started yelling 'Allahu Akbar' [God is the greatest] because they were frightened. Then the soldiers started shooting the people praying! They have just shot and killed at least four of the people praying ... At least ten other people are wounded now. We are on our bellies and in a very bad situation."

This type of indiscriminate killing has been typical of the invasion from the outset. Iraq war veteran Jason Moon told me in an interview,

> While on our initial convoy into Iraq in early June 2003, we were given a direct order that if any children or civilians got in front of the vehicles in our convoy, we were not to stop, we were not to slow down, we were to keep driving. In the event an insurgent attacked us from behind human shields, we were supposed to count. If there were thirty or less civilians we were allowed to fire into the area. If there were over thirty, we were supposed to take fire and send it up the chain of command. These were the rules of engagement. I don't know about you, but if you are getting shot at from a crowd of people, how fast are you going to count, and how accurately?

Moon brought back a video that shows his sergeant declaring, "The difference between an insurgent and an Iraqi civilian is whether they are dead or alive."

In other words, when you kill a civilian you retroactively make that person a threat.

On December 27, 2009, in the eastern Kunar region of Afghanistan, ten people, eight of whom were schoolchildren, were dragged from their beds and shot by U.S. forces during a nighttime raid. Afghan government investigators said the eight students were eleven to seventeen years old.

The list of such atrocities U.S. military personnel have carried out in the occupation of Iraq and Afghanistan is seemingly endless.

Article 48 of the Geneva Conventions speaks to the "basic rule" regarding the protection of civilians: "In order to ensure respect for and protection of the civilian population and civilian objects, the Parties to the conflict shall at all times distinguish between the civilian population and combatants and between civilian objects and military objectives and accordingly shall direct their operations only against military objectives."

Iraq veteran Garret Reppenhagen said of the WikiLeaks footage,

> There are so many incidents like this that happen in Iraq, it's bound that eventually one of them hits the vein of public attention. Film helps, video and film documentation helps draw public attention. It's sad that these instances happen but they are occurring and it has to do with how we conduct ourselves in this conflict—clearly there are things that need to be done for soldiers to adhere to the Geneva Conventions.

He doubts that the media uproar caused by the leaked video would change how soldiers in Iraq and Afghanistan conduct themselves. "I still doubt enough support will be garnered to change how we operate in theater. Eventually I hope there'll be a critical mass of people coming out and telling their stories about these things."

I have written about what psychiatrist Robert Jay Lifton calls "atrocity-producing situations." Considering the alarmingly high instances of brutal behavior by the forces it would be no exaggeration to claim that the occupations are doing little other than creating atrocity-producing situations.

I refer the reader back to veteran Jason Hurd's testimony:

With this occupation we're disrupting not only the lives of Iraqis but also the lives of our veterans. If a foreign occupying force came here to the United States, do you not think that every person that has a shotgun would come out of the hills and fight for his right for self-determination? Ladies and gentlemen, that country is suffering from our occupation, and ending that suffering begins with the total and immediate withdrawal of all of our troops.

◆   ◆   ◆

For anyone serious about putting an end to these occupations it is imperative that they seek out the sites of resistance where individuals and at times entire units have refused to submit to atrocity-producing situations and instead have rebelled against those that doctor them.

In May 2009, on a counseling statement—a punitive U.S. Army memo—Specialist Victor Agosto wrote: "There is no way I will deploy to Afghanistan. The occupation is immoral and unjust. It does not make the American people any safer. It has the opposite effect."

Ten days later, on refusing a direct order from his company commander to prepare to deploy, he was issued a second counseling statement on which he declared, "I will not obey any orders I deem to be immoral or illegal."

Shortly thereafter he told a reporter, "I'm not willing to participate in this occupation, knowing it is completely wrong. It's a matter of what I'm willing to live with."

On active duty at Fort Hood in 2009, Agosto had already served in Iraq for thirteen months. He reveals, "It was in Iraq that I turned against the occupations. I started to feel very guilty. I watched contractors making obscene amounts of money. I found no evidence that the occupation was in any way helping the people of Iraq. I know I contributed to death and human suffering. It's hard to quantify how much I caused, but I know I contributed to it."

Clearly he is prepared to face the consequences of his decision:

> Yes, I'm fully prepared for this. I have concluded that the wars [in Iraq and Afghanistan] are not going to be ended by politicians or people at the top. They're not responsive to people, they're responsive to corporate America. The only way to make them responsive to the needs of the people is for soldiers to not fight their wars. If soldiers won't fight their wars, the wars won't happen. I hope I'm setting an example for other soldiers.

On May 27, rejecting an Article 15—a nonjudicial punishment imposed by a commanding officer who believes a member of his command has committed an offense under the Uniform Code of Military Justice—Agosto demanded to be court-martialed. He was to receive the harshest court-martial possible for his decision—one that would land him in jail for up to one year, followed by a dishonorable discharge.

However, within hours of the publication of a story about his case in the online journal Truthout in July 2009, he received word from the military that his court-martial had been reduced and that he was to be recommended for a summary plea deal.

Justifiably filled with hope, Agosto refers to the efforts that went into his release: "I think it's great. It shows what a determined group of people can do. The power of the alternative media is evident.

In September 2004 when Specialist Jeff Englehart blogged: "We get awards and medals that are supposed to make us feel proud about our wicked assignment ..." he was perhaps not even aware of the reaction he would generate in other soldiers.

The truth is that in response to such feelings, some American soldiers have come up with ingenious ways to express defiance or dissent on our distant battlegrounds and at home.

♦   ♦   ♦

Instances of resistance may seem isolated, but their implications cannot be ignored as an increasingly overstretched military plunges into an expanding Afghan War even as its war in Iraq continues.

Acts of defiance and dissent have been little noted in the mainstream media, and when they do surface, officials in the Pentagon or in Washington brush them aside as "bad apple" incidents in the same vein that they tend to use when explaining war crimes that get exposed.

"Search and avoid" missions are a common avoidance strategy in the field. As Sergeant Eli Wright told me when I interviewed him for this book, "Oh yeah, we did search and avoid missions all the time. It was common for us to go set camp atop a bridge and use it as an overwatch position. We would use our binoculars to observe rather than sweep, but call in radio checks every hour to report on our sweeps."

Private First Class Clifton Hicks was candid enough to confess that these missions had the backing of a senior officers: "Our platoon sergeant was with us and he knew our patrols were bullshit, just riding around to get blown up. We were just sick and tired of going out on these stupid patrols."

Sergeant Geoff Millard, whom I also interviewed for the book, told me that he still had friends in Iraq performing "search and avoid" missions as of December 2008. Corporal Bryan Casler, Staff Sergeant Ronn Cantu, and several others have described in detail variations and versions of the tactic of avoidance.

As a Stryker armored combat vehicle commander in Iraq, Sergeant Seth Manzel had figured out a way to fabricate on screen the movement of their patrol and so could run computerized versions of a "search and avoid" mission.

Counterintelligence agent and former sergeant Josh Simpson confirmed that he had witnessed instances of faked movement: "There's no doubt that people did it."

Dissent, according to Corporal Casler, starts as simple as saying "This is bullshit. Why am I risking my life?"

To this day, troops in Iraq continue to be plagued by equipment and manpower shortages, long hours in an extreme climate, and inordinately high stress levels. Anxieties only rise higher with regular news from home of veterans returning to separations and divorces, and an inconceivably underequipped and unwilling Veterans Administration unable to provide appropriate physical and psychological care to veterans.

My interviews with those back from Iraq after the after the Obama administration was ushered in indicated that levels of despair and disappointment were on the rise among troops and that hopes of an early withdrawal have evaporated.

Under these conditions, dissent and resistance are unlikely to abate. In addition to small numbers of outright public refusals to deploy or redeploy, troops are going AWOL between deployments, and actual desertions may once again be on the rise.

The unprecedented numbers of soldiers committing suicide are certainly one strong indication that despair is growing. The army's official suicide count was 133 in 2008, up from 115 in 2007, itself a record since the Pentagon began keeping suicide statistics in 1980. Two thousand and nine was another record year of suicides in the army, and 2010 is on a pace that indicates another grim record will be set.

Chuck Luther, a two-time Iraq veteran with twelve years of military service behind him founded the Soldier's Advocacy Group of Disposable Warriors in 2007. Based on his insider's knowledge of the military's continued attempts to mask the true number of suicides in the ranks, along with an ongoing refusal to make the radical policy changes necessary to properly treat soldiers and psychiatric care providers exposed to secondary PTSD, Luther fears the worst for the future.

A 2008 court case in California brought to light a VA email that revealed one thousand veterans receiving care from the VA are attempting suicide every single month, and eighteen veterans kill themselves daily.

Though seldom perceived in a context other than that of an act of despair, suicide is also a form of refusal, an extreme, individual way of refusing to comply, saying no, or simply "no more."

These understated acts of rebellion were often survival strategies as well as gestures of dissent, as the troops were invariably undertrained and ill-equipped for the job of putting down an insurgency.

◆   ◆   ◆

Former sergeant Josh Simpson had described to me how the feeling of discontent and opposition creeps up on you while you're on duty

> [When it] doesn't make any sense. You realize that the whole system is flawed and if that is flawed, then obviously the whole war is flawed. If the basic premise of the war is flawed, definitely the intelligence system that is supposed to lead us to victory is flawed. What that implies is that victory is not even a possibility.

When he was called up for redeployment, he says, "I thought to myself, I can't do this anymore. First of all, it's bad for me mentally because I'm doing something I loathe. Second, I'm participating in an organization that I wish to resist in every way I can."

So he simply dissociated from the military.

He is among the very few fortunate ones who have not been brought to heel and he has paid a small price of uncertainty for it. "I don't know if technically I'm still in the reserves. I don't know what my situation is, but I don't really care either. If I go to jail, I go to jail. I'd rather go to jail than go to Iraq."

U.S. Army Specialist André Shepherd was trained in Apache helicopter repair and was in Germany before being sent to Iraq from November 2004 to February 2005, after which he was returned to Germany, where he went AWOL in April 2007 and lived underground until applying for asylum in November 2008. This made him the first Iraq veteran to apply for refugee status in Europe.

He, too, has refused further military service because he feels morally opposed to the occupation of Iraq. As he awaits word from the German government, he remains technically AWOL. He is being supported by Courage to Resist.

Adam Szyper-Seibert, counselor and administrative associate at the organization, discloses that in the months following Barack Obama's being sworn in as president, there was a dramatic rise of nearly 200 percent in the number of soldiers that have contacted Courage to Resist.

He suspects this has to do with the decision of the Obama administration to dramatically increase efforts, troop strength, and resources in Afghanistan. "We are actively supporting over fifty military resisters. They are all over the world, including André Shepherd in Germany and several people in Canada. We are getting five or six calls a week just about the Individual Ready Reserve [IRR] recall alone."

The typical military contract mandates four years of active duty followed by four years in the Individual Ready Reserve, though variations on this pattern exist. IRR members live civilian lives and are not paid by the military, but they are required to show up for periodic musters. Many have moved on from military life and are enrolled in college, working civilian jobs, and building families.

At any point, however, a member of the IRR can be recalled to active duty. This policy has led to the nonvoluntary reactivation of tens of thousands of troops to fight the ongoing wars in Iraq and Afghanistan.

Ironically, under a new commander in chief whom many voters believed to be antiwar, the army is continuing its IRR recalls. Sarah Lazare, project coordinator for Courage to Resist, says,

> The IRR recall has not seen any change since Obama became president. It's difficult to predict what the Obama administration's policy will be in the future regarding the IRR, but definitely they haven't made any moves to stop this practice. Needing boots on the ground, the military continues to fall back on the Ready Reserve system to fill the gaps since these are experienced troops, many of them have already served tours in Iraq and Afghanistan. When Obama announced his Afghanistan surge, we got a huge wave of calls from soldiers saying they didn't want to be reactivated and to please help them not go.

It would seem in several instances that the process and experience of dissenting has often transformed the consciousness of "bad apples" and converted them to a more inclusive and compassionate worldview, both toward their own and the loathsome other.

◆   ◆   ◆

In August 2009 I wrote a story about Sergeant Travis Bishop. He served fourteen months in Baghdad. In early 2009, when his unit deployed to Afghanistan he went AWOL from his station at Fort Hood, Texas. It was the combined effect of his time in Iraq, the illegality of the occupation, and a moral awakening that led to his decision to refuse to deploy.

He was affected by the disjunction between the reality in Iraq and the one projected in the news at home but insists that morality and religion played a role as well. On receiving orders to deploy to Afghanistan, Bishop says, "I started reading my Bible to get right with my creator before going. Through my reading I realized all this goes against what Jesus taught and what all true Christians should believe. I had a religious transformation, and realized that all war is wrong."

He felt that it would be unethical for him to deploy to support an occupation he opposes on moral grounds. On his blog, he put his position this way:

> I love my country, but I believe that this particular war is unjust, unconstitutional and a total abuse of our nation's power and influence. And so, in the next few days, I will be speaking with my lawyer, and taking actions that will more than likely result in my discharge from the military, and possible jail time … and I am prepared to live with that … My father said, 'Do only what you can live with, because every morning you have to look at your face in the mirror when you shave. Ten years from now, you'll still be shaving the same face.' If I had deployed to Afghanistan, I don't think I would have been able to look into another mirror again.

I spoke with him briefly after he turned himself in at his base in early June. He said he had been inspired by Specialist Agosto's example of refusal, and was willing to accept the consequences of his actions. He, too, hoped others might follow his lead.

Agosto, for his part says, "I already feel vindicated for what I'm doing by his actions. It's nice to see some immediate results."

He is convinced that his actions have affected the way his fellow soldiers are now looking at the war in Afghanistan. Prior to his discharge, while still at the base, Agosto had soldiers ask him, "What are we doing in Afghanistan? Why are we there?" It was important, he felt, that people were compelled to bring this up in his presence. Even those that disagreed with his stance agreed that what he was doing required courage that they lacked. Almost all his peers started treating him with respect.

During his court-martial in August 2009, Bishop had stated that his decision to file for conscientious objector status had been based on his conviction that it would be unethical for him to deploy to support an occupation he opposed on both moral and legal grounds. A CO may be given an honorable discharge by the military.

Bishop was sentenced to twelve months in the notorious Northwest Joint Regional Correctional Facility at Fort Lewis, Washington. Amnesty International took up his case and while in confinement he received support from hundreds of people around the world who wrote to him, along with appeals to Lieutenant General Robert Cone, the commanding general of Fort Hood, to get him released.

As a result of a successful clemency application Bishop was granted a three-month reduction in his sentence by General Cone and released in March 2010.

Agosto and Bishop are hardly alone. In November 2007, the Pentagon revealed that between 2003 and 2007 there had been an 80 percent increase in overall desertion rates in the army. Desertion refers to soldiers who go AWOL and never intend to return to service. Army AWOL rates from 2003 to 2006 were the highest since 1980. Between 2000 and 2006, more than forty thousand troops from all branches of the military deserted, more than half from the army, which alone saw a 42 percent jump in desertion rates between 2006 and 2007.

What is remarkable is that regardless of the origin of discontent in the dissenting soldiers, in most cases it has led to a close examination of the credibility of the entire war machinery, the largely unpatriotic and anti-people motives of the establishment, inexcusable degrees of ineptitude and blundering at higher levels, and an unconscionable malaise of unaccountability among sworn upholders of the nation's ideals.

◆   ◆   ◆

Bishop's case brought to light the important issue of the soldiers' ability, while serving, to follow their consciences during a time of war.

This became the theme of a conference held at Riverside Church in New York City in March 2010. The conference brought together a Truth Commission comprised of war veterans and religious, academic, and advocacy leaders with the aim of honoring and protecting freedom of conscience in the military. It featured testimony from recent veterans and national experts on the moral, psychological, and legal dimensions of conscience and war.

According to a press release about the event, "The [March 21] public hearing will launch the Commission's eight-month campaign to bring national attention to decisions of moral and religious conscience facing American service members, culminating with the Veterans Day release of the Commission's Final Report."[10]

In an interview at the time of his court-martial, Bishop had stated emphatically that on the basis of his religious beliefs, he was opposed to all war. His belief is that, "as a real Christian, I must be opposed to all violence, no matter what, because that is what Jesus taught."

The chair of the Truth Commission, Reverend Dr. Kaia Stern, who is also the director of the Pathways Home Project at the Charles Hamilton Houston Institute for Race and Justice at Harvard Law School, submitted to the commission: "The United States of America is founded on principals of political and religious freedom. When we punish the soldier who heeds his or her moral compass, our democracy is in grave danger."

Ian Slattery, a member of the planning committee for the commission, and an associate producer of the nationally broadcast film *Soldiers of Conscience*, says Bishop's story is "a good example of service members' consciences not being honored."

He elaborated, "From our point of view, Travis's story is indicative of something that is a broader issue, and that is that every service member has a conscience. At the meeting in New York and in subsequent meetings we look at stories across the board that service members are experiencing. His story is like some of the other COs we've seen, who've had their claims denied or approved. These are folks who have chosen the harder road—to follow the call to conscience they've heard within themselves."

One of the main points James Branum, Bishop's civilian lawyer, made in his defense during the court-martial was that Bishop had never been given proper training that would have informed him of the CO option. When I interviewed Branum he explained, "Travis was never told about his option of conscientious objector status. If an enlisted soldier isn't informed that he has a right, then he effectively does not have that right. Just one to two days before he was set to deploy, in the midst of moral questions, he heard about CO status."

During the trial, the defense called Private First Class Anthony Sadoski and Specialist Michael Kern as witnesses. Both active-duty soldiers at Fort Hood confirmed that they, too, had never been informed that filing for CO status was an option.

The judge, Major Matthew McDonald, dismissed the point as immaterial, saying, "If every soldier in the army who disobeyed an order could claim it was because they weren't notified of conscientious objector status, we probably wouldn't have a military anymore."

Branum was insistent: "We want to change the law, and I would argue that when soldiers are informed of their deployment, which is generally two to six months in advance, they should be given training about CO status. I will argue that if you don't do the training, you can't deploy."

The Truth Commission hopes to bring these issues to the national stage and the public consciousness.

Slattery laid out the plan:

> With two conflicts in the last nine years, hundreds of thousands of service members have come home, and we've yet to bring matters of conscience to the table to talk about. The commissioners who met at the conference will be working together in the coming months to release a report on Veterans Day, that may include recommendations on policy and policy changes that will better protect the consciences of people like Travis and those to come in the future.
>
> One of the ironies of the all-volunteer army is that the only way we'll recognize their conscience is if they are a CO ... but Travis's story teaches us that justice is a part of war, and when they attempt to exercise that conscience, they are only recognized if they are opposed to all war. We want to bring all this into a discussion, and do so without being accused of being unpatriotic, but we owe it to service members to respect their conscience and their choices.

In *Soldiers of Conscience*, the film Slattery helped produce, we hear Iraq veteran Camilo Mejia, the first service member to publicly refuse to return to Iraq, articulating the core spirit of the Truth Commission and of COs like Bishop: "There's no higher assertion of freedom than to follow your conscience."

Reverend Dr. Rita Nakashima Brock, project director of the Truth Commission, said in her speech at the conference, "In his Nobel acceptance speech, President Obama argued that nations will at times 'find the use of force not only necessary but morally justified.' We are asking: What happens when service members are asked to fight in a war they believe is not morally justified?"

VA Secretary Eric Shinseki confirmed in January 2010 that young male veterans are committing suicide at an increasing rate—losses that go uncounted as casualties of the current U.S. wars. At the same time, new VA research on "moral injury" highlights the lasting moral and psychological harm of violating one's sense of right and wrong in war.

The Truth Commission addressed these aspects of the war, along with the need to respect not just COs but also "selective conscientious objection." The commission's honorary host, Reverend Herman Keizer Jr., a retired army chaplain, Vietnam veteran, and former chair of the National Conference on Ministry to the Armed Forces, is an outspoken leader in a growing movement for "selective conscientious objection," or the right to object morally to a particular war.

Current military regulations only recognize objections to "war in any form." In a recent letter to President Obama, Keizer argued, "The conscience of the selective objector deserves the same respect as the conscience of the pacifist."

Prior to his release, in a letter from prison, Bishop had written, "I can't wait to get out of here, if only to tell people, 'Hey! Look at me! If I can do it, surely more people can too!!'" Now that he is free,

Bishop plans to continue to speak out about conscientious objection and work as an advocate for other COs.

Meanwhile, Branum, his lawyer, plans to force the issue with the military to have CO training better represented within the military. He intends to take the result of Bishop's trial to the military court, the U.S. Army court of criminal appeals, the U.S. Military court of criminal appeals, and for habeas review, after which he would take it to a civil court—then, if necessary, to the Supreme Court.

"It sends a message to be bold," Branum explained.

> There is a high likelihood that being bold helps your own case. Be smart, of course, but the army screws people over by keeping it 'in house.' My challenge is to be bold, shine the light. When the military is confronted with it, they are sometimes stunned by their own injustice. Appeal to their humanity and conscience, and if that doesn't work, scare them.

◆   ◆   ◆

At the time of writing this, "combat troops" have been withdrawn from Iraq but fifty thousand remain and the ravaged nation boils on at still dangerous levels of violence, while the war in Afghanistan (and across the border in Pakistan) only grows, as does the U.S. commitment to both. It's already clear that even an all-volunteer military isn't immune to dissent. If violence in either or both occupations escalates, if the Pentagon struggles to add more boots on the ground, if the stresses and strains on the military, involving endless redeployments to combat zones, increase rather than lessen, then the acts of Agosto, Bishop, and Shepherd may turn out to be pathbreaking ones in a world of dissent yet to be experienced and explored by larger numbers in the military.

If dissatisfaction and discontent at home is factored in, and American treasure continues to be poured into an Afghan quagmire, public support for a GI resistance movement may surface as well. If so, then the early pioneers in methods of dissent within the military will have laid the groundwork for a movement.

To repeat the words of First Lieutenant Ehren Watada, the first commissioned officer to publicly refuse a combat deployment to Iraq, "If we want soldiers to choose the right but difficult path, they must know beyond any shadow of a doubt that they will be supported by Americans."

I'm aware that my observations will not endear me to a vast section of my countryfolk but I have reason to believe that there are others who are more than willing to look at the irrevocable disasters accruing from my country's policies at home and abroad. Among them will be lawmakers as well as homemakers, teachers as well as artists, activists and not-so-active opinion makers.

My sincere hope is to see a sufficient buildup in that mass of Americans so that our government can be held accountable for its omissions and commissions.

INTRODUCTION

1. See Just Foreign Policy, "Iraq Deaths Due to U.S. Invasion," http://www.just-foreignpolicy.org/iraq/iraqdeaths.html and Opinion Business Research, "September 2007 – More than 1,000,000 Iraqis Murdered," http://opinion.co.uk/Newsroom_details.aspx?NewsId=78.

2. Many people now argue that while there is no longer a draft, there remains an "economic conscription" where poverty is driving people to join the military.

3. See resource appendix for current GI support groups.

4. Ira Katz, "FW: Not for the CBS News Interview Request," e-mail to Ev Chasen, VA spokesperson, February 13, 2008. Plaintiff's Exhibit P-1269, Veterans for Common Sense et al. v. Peake, United States District Court, Northern California, Case No. C-07-3758; Ira Katz, "Re: Suicides," e-mail to Michael J. Kussman, Undersecretary of Health, Veterans Health Administration, December 15, 2007, Plantiff's Exhibit P-1283, Veterans for Common Sense et al. v. Peake, United States District Court, Northern California, Case No. C-07-3758.

5. For an overview of the prospects for veterans' medical care, including mental health, see Linda Bilmes, "Soldiers Returning from Iraq and Afghanistan: The Long-term Costs of Providing Veterans Medical Care and Disability Benefits," Paper presented at ASSA meeting, Three Trillion Dollar War site, January 2007, http://threetrilliondollarwar.org/2008/04/22/soldiers-returning-from-iraq-and-afghanistan-the-long-term-costs-of-providing-veterans-medical-care-and-disability-benefits/.

6. Katz, "FW: Not for the CBS News Interview Request," and Katz, "Re: Suicides."

7. Veterans for Common Sense v. Peake, Northern District of California, United States District Court Trial Transcript Final, April 30, 2008, 1369, 1372.

8. Department of Veterans Affairs, "Analysis of VA Health Care Utilization

Among U.S. Global War on Terrorism (GWOT) Veterans," March 25, 2008, and "VA Benefits Activity: Veterans Deployed to the Global War on Terror," April 16, 2008. Obtained by Veterans for Common Sense using the Freedom of Information Act.

9.   Defense Manpower Data Center, "CTS Deployment File Baseline Report for Operation Enduring Freedom and Operation Iraqi Freedom as of October 31, 2007." Obtained by Veterans for Common Sense using the Freedom of Information Act.

10. Amy Fairweather, *Risk and Protective Factors for Homelessness among OIF/OEF Veterans* (San Francisco: Swords to Plowshares, 2006).

11. "U.S. Soldier in Iraq Shoots Dead Five Comrades," Reuters, May 11, 2009.

12. Greg Zoroya, "US Deploys More than 43,000 Unfit for Combat," *USA Today*, May 8, 2008.

13. Mark Thompson, "America's Medicated Army," *Time*, June 5, 2008.

14. Pauline Jelinek, "Officials: Army Suicides at 3-Decade High," Associated Press, January 29, 2009.

15. Tony Perry, "Marine Suicides in 2008 at a Yearly High since Iraq Invasion," *Los Angeles Times*, January 14, 2009.

16. Rick Maze, "Bill Would Pay Extra for Stop-Loss Service," *Army Times*, May 25, 2008.

17. Defense Manpower Data Center, "CTS Deployment File Baseline Report for Operation Enduring Freedom and Operation Iraqi Freedom as of October 31, 2007."

18. Staff Sgt. Stacy L. Pearsall, "The Army Raises Enlistment Age to 42," Army.com, June 22, 2006.

19. Michelle Singer, "Military Lowers Standards to Fill Ranks," *CBS Evening News*, July 30, 2007.

20. Dave Alsup, "Convicted Soldier: 'You Probably Think I'm a Monster,'" CNN.com, May 11, 2009, http://www.cnn.com/2009/CRIME/05/11/us.soldier.iraq.killings/index.html.

21. Lolita C. Baldor, "Recruitment Costs Rise 25% for Army, Marines," Associated Press, October 3, 2008.

22. "251 Soldiers Become U.S. Citizens," Associated Press, March 4, 2009.

CHAPTER ONE: RESISTANCE IN IRAQ

1.   Camilo Mejía, "Regaining My Humanity," Common Dreams, February 24, 2005, http://www.commondreams.org/views05/0224-22.htm.

2.   Camilo Mejía, *Road from ar Ramadi: The Private Rebellion of Staff Sergeant*

Camilo Mejía: An Iraq War Memoir, (Chicago: Haymarket Books, 2008), 157–58.

3. Ibid.

4. Lolita C. Baldor, "Army Desertion Rates Rise 80 Percent since Invasion of Iraq in 2003," Associated Press, November 16, 2007.

5. Ibid.

6. Due to the fact that the United States is a signatory to the Geneva Conventions, any violation of the Geneva Conventions is by definition a violation of the U.S. Constitution.

7. Neela Banerjee and John Kifner, "Reservists Who Refused Order Tried to Persuade Superiors," *New York Times*, October 19, 2004.

8. Eric Ruder, "Soldiers Refuse to Be Cannon Fodder," *Socialist Worker*, October 22, 2004.

9. Kelly Kennedy, "Blood Brothers," *Military Times*, December 17, 2007.

10. Ibid.

11. Ibid.

12. Kelly Kennedy, "U.S. Soldiers Stage Mutiny, Refuse Orders in Iraq Fearing They Would Commit Massacre in Revenge for IED Attack," interview by Juan Gonzales and Amy Goodman, *Democracy Now!*, December 21, 2007.

13. Ibid.

14. Mejía, *Road from ar Ramadi*, 168.

15. Ibid, 173–74.

16. Ibid, 176.

17. Ibid, 176–177.

CHAPTER TWO: QUARTERS OF RESISTANCE

1. Lieutenant Ehren Watada was the highest-ranking enlisted soldier to publicly refuse deployment to Iraq.

2. See Iraq Veterans Against the War and Aaron Glantz, eds., *Winter Soldier: Iraq and Afghanistan: Eyewitness Accounts of the Occupations*, (Chicago: Haymarket Books, 2008).

3. Mike Ferner, *Inside the Red Zone: A Veteran for Peace Reports from Iraq* (Westport, CN.: Praeger, 2006); Norman Solomon, *War Made Easy: How Presidents and Pundits Keep Spinning Us to Death* (Hoboken, NJ: Wiley, 2006); Robert Persig, *Zen and the Art of Motorcycle Maintenance* (New York: Morrow, 1974).

4. David Hackworth and Julie Sherman, *About Face: The Odyssey of an American Warrior* (New York: Simon and Schuster, 1989).

CHAPTER THREE: SPEAKING OUT

1. Thom Shanker, "Military Chief Warns Troops About Politics," *New York Times*, May 26, 2008.

2. Casler references the September 10, 2007, report submitted to Congress by David Petraeus, then the general of the Multinational Forces in Iraq. Petraeus, along with U.S. Ambassador to Iraq Ryan Crocker, claimed progress was being made by occupation forces. Petraeus suggested that the so-called surge forces could be withdrawn by July 2008.

3. Warrior Writers Project is a group that aims to transform Iraq veterans' trauma by helping them write down their experiences and share them with other veterans.

4. The Winter Soldier testimonies were where veterans from Iraq and Afghanistan testified publicly to the crimes they committed and observed in both occupations. The hearings took place in Silver Spring, Maryland, in March 2008.

5. Combat Paper Project is an art project that seeks to transform the veterans' trauma by having them turn their old uniforms into paper and writing down their experiences on them to share with other vets, as well as the public.

6. To learn more about Appeal for Redress, visit their website at http://www.appealforredress.org/.

7. *Countdown with Keith Olbermann*, MSNBC, October 24, 2006.

8. "GIs Petition Congress to End Iraq War," *60 Minutes*, CBS News, February 25, 2007.

9. The Under Other Than Honorable Conditions (OTH) discharge from the U.S. military is the most severe form of administrative discharge. They are usually meted out to service members convicted by a civilian court where a sentence of confinement has been adjudged or when the conduct leading to the conviction brings discredit upon the military. OTH discharges bar the recipient from reenlisting into any branch of the armed forces, including the reserves, and they are not eligible for veteran's benefits, including the Montgomery GI Bill and VA health-care benefits.

10. Quoted in Kirsten Scharnberg, "Veterans: Military Curbing Free Speech," *Chicago Tribune*, June 24, 2007.

11. Heather Hollingsworth, "Marines Drop Case Against Iraq Veteran," Associated Press, June 29, 2007.

12. Winter Soldier events, smaller in scope but in the spirit of the original event held in Silver Spring, Maryland, in March 2008, have become common across the United States. The goal of these ongoing events is to increase public awareness of the occupations of Iraq and Afghanistan.

13. In February 2007, the Bush administration announced the so-called "surge"

strategy for Iraq, where thirty thousand additional soldiers were sent to Iraq. The two stated goals of the surge were to decrease violence and to create a climate where reconciliation could occur within the Iraqi government.

14. Simon Jeffery and Jason Deans, "U.S. Tank Shell Hits Media Hotel," *Guardian* (London), April 8, 2003.

15. "*Democracy Now!* Exclusive: Fmr. Military Intelligence Sgt. Reveals US Listed Palestine Hotel in Baghdad as Target Prior to Killing of Two Journalists in 2003," interview by Amy Goodman, *Democracy Now!* May 13, 2008, http://www .democracynow.org/2008/5/13/fmr_military_intelligence_officer_reveals_us.

16. Ibid.

17. Polytrauma is a new term used by doctors to describe multiple traumatic injuries that U.S. soldiers have upon returning home from serving in the occupations of Iraq and Afghanistan.

18. "GIs Petition Congress to End Iraq War," interview by Lara Logan, *60 Minutes*, CBS, February 25, 2007.

19. "U.S. Troops in Iraq: 72% Say End War in 2006," Zogby International, February 28, 2006.

CHAPTER FOUR: ABSENT WITHOUT LEAVE

1. "Agustín Aguayo Speaks Out Against War in Pacific Northwest," Courage to Resist, http://www.couragetoresist.org/x/content.

2. Quoted in Lori Hurlebaus, "Army Spc. Agustín Aguayo's Fight Against War," Courage to Resist, March 29, 2007, http://www.couragetoresist.org/x/content/view/265/36.

3. "Soldier Allegedly Stages Shooting to Avoid Return to Iraq," Associated Press, February 26, 2008.

4. Alec Castonguay, "American Deserters, a Case of Canadian Conscience," *Le Devoir*, June 4, 2008.

5. Stop-loss is the involuntary extension of the enlistment contract of members of the U.S. military. The policy serves the government, as it allows the military to retain service members beyond their initial end of service date.

6. Baldor, "Army Desertion Rates."

7. Ibid.

8. "GI Faces Charges in Alleged 2006 Desertion," Associated Press, March 31, 2008. This report states that army desertion rates "peaked in 2007." See also "U.S. Army Desertion Rate Drops 24 Percent," Strategypage.com, November 30, 2008, http://www.strategypage.com/htmw/htatrit/20081130.aspx.

9. Maggie Farley, "Canada's House Backs War Resisters," *Los Angeles Times*, June 4,

2008.

10.   "Most Canadians Would Grant Permanent Residence to U.S. Military Desert-
       ers," Angus Reid Poll, June 27, 2008, http://www.angusreidstrategies.com/
       polls-analysis/opinion-polls/angus-reid-poll-most-canadians-would-grant-
       permanent-residence-us-milit.

11.   "Facing Years in U.S. Prison, Iraq War Resister Jeremy Hinzman Ordered De-
       ported from Canada," interview by Juan Gonzales and Amy Goodman,
       Democracy Now!, August 15, 2008.

12.   Amnesty International, "Canada: Possible Prisoner of Conscience: Jeremy
       Hinzman (M)," September 11, 2008.

13.   Michelle Shephard, "U.S. Deserter Feared Torture Orders: Arabic-speaking
       Soldier May Prompt Canada to Wade into Legal Debate," *Toronto Star*, Sep-
       tember 7, 2008.

CHAPTER FIVE: ORGANIZED RESISTANCE

1.   During the April 2004 siege of Fallujah, where I personally witnessed women
      and children shot by U.S. snipers, doctors at Fallujah General Hospital had
      reported that of the 736 deaths, more than 60 percent were civilians. See
      Dahr Jamail, *Beyond the Green Zone: Dispatches from an Unembedded Jour-
      nalist in Occupied Iraq* (Chicago: Haymarket Books, 2007).

2.   Robert Jay Lifton, "Conditions of Atrocity," *Nation*, May 13, 2004.

3.   Quoted in "Iraq Veterans: It's Our Turn to Tell Our Stories," IVAW press re-
      lease, February 11, 2008.

CHAPTER SIX: RESISTING SEXISM

1.   Work to keep young adults from joining the military.

2.   "Spc. Suzanne Swift Signs Statement with Military After Harassment Claim,
      AWOL Status Lead to Court Martial," *Democracy Now!*, December 11, 2006.

3.   Cited in "Sexual Assault in Military Draws Attention," Associated Press, July
      23, 2008.

4.   Helen Benedict, "Women at War Face Sexual Violence," BBC News,
      http://news.bbc.co.uk/2/hi/americas/8005198.stm.

5.   Patricia Tjaden and Nancy Thoennes, *Prevalence, Incidence, and Consequences
      of Violence Against Women: Findings from the National Violence against
      Women Study* (Washington D.C.: NIJCDC, November, 1998), 3.

6.   Katie Couric, "Sexual Assault Permeates U.S. Armed Forces," CBS News, May

22, 2009, http://www.cbsnews.com/stories/2009/03/17/eveningnews/main48 72713.shtml.

7.　See the Official April Fitzsimmons website, http://www.aprilfitzsimmons.com.

8.　"Suicide or Murder? Three Years After the Death of Pfc. LaVena Johnson in Iraq, Her Parents Continue Their Call for a Congressional Investigation," interview with Dr. John Johnson, Linda Johnson, and Ann Wright by Amy Goodman, *Democracy Now!*, July 23, 2008.

9.　"Suicide or Murder?" *Democracy Now!*.

10.　Quoted in Marjorie Cohn, "Military Hides Cause of Women Soldier's Deaths," Truthout, January 30, 2006, http://ww.truthout.org/article/military-hides-cause-women-soldiers-deaths.

11.　Ibid.

12.　"Sexual Assault in Military 'Jaw-Dropping,' Lawmaker Says," CNN.com, July 31, 2008, http://www.cnn.com/2008/US/07/31/military.sexabuse/#cnn,STCText.

13.　Ibid.

14.　Ibid.

15.　Col. Ann Wright, "Sexual Assault in the Military: A DoD Cover-Up?," Truthdig, August 1, 2008, http://truthdig.com/report/item/20080801_sexual_assault_in_the_military_a_dad_cover_up/.

16.　"Harman Introduces Bipartisan Bill to Halt Rape and Sexual Assault in the Military," Press Release, July 29, 2008, http://www.house.gov/apps/list/press/ca36_harman/July29_MST.shtml

17.　"Oversight Hearing on Sexual Assault in the Military—Part 2," video of the hearing, September 10, 2008, http://nationalsecurity.oversight.house.gov/story.asp?ID=2183.

CHAPTER SEVEN: RESISTING DESCRIMINATION

1.　"Don't ask, don't tell" is the common phrase describing the policy about homosexuality in the U.S. military mandated by federal law. The policy prohibits anyone who "demonstrate(s) a propensity or intent to engage in homosexual acts" from serving in the armed forces of the United States, because it "would create an unacceptable risk to the high standards of morale, good order and discipline, and unit cohesion that are the essence of military capability." U.S. Code Title 10, Subtitle A, part II, chapter 37, § 654 details the policy concerning homosexuality in the armed forces. See Cornell Law School website at http://www.law.cornell.edu/uscode/10/654.html.

2.　Martin Smith, "Learning to Be a Killer: Remembering Marine Corps Boot Camp," *International Socialist Review*, September–October 2006.

3. While the contractors were portrayed by most mainstream media outlets as "soldiers" or even "American civilians," they were, in fact, four Blackwater mercenaries who were killed in Fallujah.

4. "American Civilians Killed in Iraq," interview by Paula Zahn, *Paula Zahn Now*, CNN, March 31, 2004.

CHAPTER EIGHT: SUICIDE:
THE RESISTANCE OF DESPERATION

1. Holly G. Prigerson, PhD, Paul K. Maciejewski, PhD, Robert A. Rosenheck, MD, "Population Attributable Fractions of Psychiatric Disorders and Behavioral Outcomes Associated with Combat Exposure Among US Men," *American Journal of Public Health* 92, no 1 (January 2002): 59–63.

2. Armen Keteyian, "VA Hid Suicide Risk, Internal E-Mails Show," CBS News, April 21, 2008, http://www.cbsnews.com/stories/2008/04/21/cbsnews_investigates/main4032921.shtml. Eighteen veterans a day are committing suicide in the United States, while an average of one to two soldiers are killed each day in the occupations of Iraq and Afghanistan.

3. Cited in Pauline Jelinek, "Army Suicides Highest in 26 Years," Associated Press, August 16, 2007.

4. Cited in Pauline Jelinek, "Officials: Army Suicides at 3-Decade High," Associated Press, January 29, 2009.

5. Tony Perry, "Marine Suicides in 2008 at a Yearly High Since Iraq Invasion," *Los Angeles Times*, January 14, 2009.

6. Lizette Alvarez, "Army Data Show Rise in Number of Suicides," *New York Times*, February 5, 2009.

7. Amy Tan, "Army Sees Significant Rise in January Suicides," *Army Times*, February 9, 2009.

8. RAND Corporation, "One in Five Iraq and Afghanistan Veterans Suffer from PTSD or Major Depression," press release, April 17, 2008.

9. Aaron Glantz, "The Truth About Veteran Suicides," Foreign Policy in Focus, commentary, May 9, 2008, http://www.fpif.org/fpiftxt/5219.

10. Christopher Lee, "Official Urged Fewer Diagnoses of PTSD," *Washington Post*, May 16, 2008.

11. Quoted in Les Blumenthal, "Senator: VA Lying About Number of Veteran Suicides," McClatchy Newspapers, April 23, 2008, http://www.mcclatchydc.com/244/story/34718.html.

12. Glantz, "Truth About Veteran Suicides."

13. Cited in Lizette Alvarez, "After the Battle, Fighting the Bottle at Home," *New*

York Times, July 8, 2008.

14. Mark Thompson, "America's Medicated Army," *Time*, June 5, 2008.

15. Damien McElroy, "U.S. Troops in Iraq and Afghanistan Turning to Anti-Depressants in Record Numbers," *Daily Telegraph* (London), June 6, 2008.

16. Gregg Zoroya, "U.S. Deploys More than 43,000 Unfit for Combat," *USA Today*, May 8, 2008.

17. Thompson, "America's Medicated Military."

18. Robert Bryce, "A Death Reconsidered: Was Col. Ted Westhusing's Death in Iraq Something More Sinister than Suicide?" *Texas Observer*, February 8, 2008.

19. Quoted in Megan Greenwell, "Reservist Due for Iraq Is Killed in Standoff with Police," *Washington Post*, December 27, 2006.

20. Quoted in Megan Greenwell, "Distant War May Have Claimed Md. Soldier: Veteran Slain in Police Standoff Was Devastated by Call-Up, Family Says," *Washington Post*, December 29, 2006.

21. Quoted in Meredith May and Matthew Stannard, "No Clear Motive in Marine's Killing of Police Officer: Shooter's Friends Believe He Suffered from Combat Stress," *San Francisco Chronicle*, January 12, 2005.

22. Ibid.

23. Quoted in Andrew Buncombe and Oliver Duff, "The Life and Death of an Iraq Veteran Who Could Take No More," *Independent*, January 25, 2006.

24. Ibid.

CHAPTER NINE: CYBER RESISTANCE

1. Adrian Stanley, "Mightier than the Sword: Inspired by Overwhelming Emotion, Local Veterans Turn to the Healing Power of Poetry," *Colorado Springs Independent*, December 20, 2007.

2. David Montgomery, "Far from Iraq, a demonstration of a War Zone," *Washington Post*, March 20, 2007.

3. David Montgomery, "Antiwar to the Corps; Marine Reservist-Protestors Face Discipline," *Washington Post*, May 31, 2007.

CHAPTER TEN: ART AS RESISTANCE

1. *Warrior Writers: Move, Shoot and Communicate*, Lovella Calica, ed. (Burlington, VT: Iraq Veterans Against the War and The People's Republic of Paper, 2007).

2. *Warrior Writers: Re-making Sense*, Lovella Calica, ed. (Burlington, VT: Iraq Veterans Against the War, 2007).

3. Lovella Calica, Iraq Veterans Against the War, from the Green Door Studio web-

site, available at http://www.greendoorstudio.net/exhibits/remakingsense/
workshop/writers.html.

4. Available on the Green Door Studio website at http://www.greendoorstu-
dio.net.

5. Combat Paper Project, http://www.combatpaper.org/.

6. Tatyana Safronova, "In Your Words: Aaron Hughes," *Buzz Magazine*, May 4,
2006.

7. Aaron Hughes, http://aarhughes.org/.

8. Joshua Key and Lawrence Hill, *The Deserter's Tale: The Story of an Ordinary
Soldier Who Walked away from the War in Iraq* (New York: Grove Press, 2007),
69–70.

9. Quoted in Aaron Glantz, "Revelations of an Abu Ghraib Interrogator," Inter
Press Service, September 4, 2008.

10. Quoted in Ed Pilkington, "Iraq Veteran Wins Blog Prize as U.S. Military Cuts
Web Access," *Guardian* (London), May 15, 2007.

11. See the Official April Fitzsimmons website, http://www.aprilfitzsimmons.com.

12. See The Eyes of Babylon website, http://theeyesofbabylon.com.

13. Mehadi Foundation mission statement, http://www.mehadifoundation.org.

14. Brian Stelter, "TV News Winds Down Operations on Iraq War," *New York
Times*, December 29, 2008.

CHAPTER ELEVEN: STANDING UP

1. Quoted in Nicholas Riccardi and DeeDee Correll, "Obama Camp Meets with
Iraq War Veterans Protesting at Democratic Convention," *Los Angeles Times*, August 28, 2008.

2. Alex Kane and Jessica Lee, "Standoff with Police as Iraq Vets Demand to Meet
with Obama Campaign," *Indypendent*, September 5, 2008.

3. Quoted in Liliana Segura, "As Vets Take to the Streets to Protest the War, Mc-
Cain Snubs IVAW at the RNC," AlterNet, September 6, 2008, http://www.al-
ternet.org/waroniraq/97812/as_vets_take_to_the_streets_to_protest_the_
war,_mccain_snubs_ivaw_at_the_rnc_/.

4. Ibid.

5. S. Amdt. 3642 to H.R. 4939, vote 98, April 26, 2006, http://projects.washing-
tonpost.com/congress/109/bills/h_r_4939/.

6. The footage is available as "Adam Kokesh Protests McCain at RNC 09/04/2008"
on YouTube.

7. Adam Kokesh, interview with Dana Goldstein, "Tapped: The Group Blog of
The American Prospect," posted September 4, 2008.

8.   Jeremy Brecher and Brendan Smith, "Watada's Double Jeopardy," Zmag.org, http://zmag.org/znet/viewarticle/15604.

AFTERWORD

1.   "Veterans and Active Duty Service Members Respond to Obama's Speech on Afghanistan War Escalation," March Forward! Press release, December 3, 2009, www.answercoalition.org/march-forward/statements/veterans-and-active-duty.html.
2.   Ibid.
3.   Marjorie Cohn and Kathleen Gilberd, *Rules of Disengagement: The Politics and Honor of Military Dissent* (Sausalito, CA: Polipoint Press, 2009).
4.   "Meet Michael Prysner," March Forward!, www.answercoalition.org/site/News2?page=NewsArticle&id=9020&news_iv_ctrl.
5.   Ibid.
6.   Dahr Jamail, "Veterans Group Calls of Soldiers to Refuse Deployment Orders," Truthout, December 14, 2009, http://dahrjamailiraq.com/veterans-group-calls-on-soldiers-to-refuse-deployment-orders.
7.   Ibid.
8.   Ibid.
9.   Protocol 1, Additional to the Geneva Conventions, 1977, "Article 48: Basic Rule," http://deoxy.org/wc/wc-proto.htm.
10.   "First Truth Commission on Conscience in War to be Convened at the Historic Riverside Church," Press release, March 9, 2010, www.conscienceinwar.org/TruthCommission_Release.pdf.

ACKNOWLEDGMENTS

This book would not have been possible were it not for the courageous soldiers, both active duty and veterans, who chose to speak with me. Knowing better than anyone what the risk of doing so involved, they chose to speak their truth, danger be damned.

Karin Fleming, your tireless efforts in transcribing literally dozens upon dozens of hours of interviews and your research assistance made this book possible. For your efforts and professionalism, I owe a tremendous debt of gratitude.

Bhashwati Sengupta, for your editing suggestions I am once again obliged.

The Lannan Foundation generously provided me a Writing Residency Fellowship, during which the manuscript of this book coalesced. Your support is deeply appreciated.

Mikki Smith, Rachel Cohen, Dao Tran, Julie Fain, and Eric Ruder at Haymarket Books—your professionalism helped make this book what it is.

I also want to thank Karen Houppert, for your generous assistance in sharing research and suggestions.

Erika Blumenfeld, in deepest gratitude, for your ever-present light.

INDEX

ALSO FROM HAYMARKET BOOKS

Winter Soldier: Iraq and Afghanistan

Iraq Veterans Against the War and Aaron Glantz • In the spring of 2008, Iraq Veterans Against the War gathered veterans outside Washington, D.C., to tell the truth about the occupations of Afghanistan and Iraq. Here are the powerful words, images, and documents of this historic event. • ISBN 9781931859653

Winter Soldiers: An Oral History
of the Vietnam Veterans Against the War

Richard Stacewitcz • In all that has been written about the war, rarely do the worlds of the Vietnam veteran and the antiwar demonstrator come together. Yet in an articulate and determined organization known as Vietnam Veterans Against the War (VVAW), the two made common cause. Winter Soldiers recovers this moving chapter in the history of the Vietnam War era. • ISBN 9781931859608

Road from ar Ramadi: The Private Rebellion
of Staff Sergeant Camilo Mejía: An Iraq War Memoir

Camilo Mejia • Staff Sergeant Camilo Mejía became a leading voice for the antiwar movement when he applied for discharge from the army as a conscientious objector. In this stirring book, he argues passionately for the end to an unjust war. As New York Times columnist Bob Herbert writes, "The issues [Mejía] has raised deserve a close reading by the nation as a whole.... He has made a contribution to the truth about Iraq." • ISBN 9781931859530

Soldiers in Revolt: GI Resistance During the Vietnam War

David Cortright, introduction by Howard Zinn • Soldiers in Revolt documents one of the least known and most important aspects of the Vietnam War: the rebellion among U.S. soldiers opposed to the war. • ISBN 9781931859271

Beyond the Green Zone:
Dispatches from an Unembedded Journalist in Occupied Iraq

Dahr Jamail • Jamail's critically acclaimed, indispensable account of life in Iraq under U.S. occupation, now available in paperback, with a new afterword. This widely read account offers lyrical journalism, personal reflection, incisive analysis, and groundbreaking reportage, including previously unpublished details of the first years of occupation. • ISBN 9781931859615

ABOUT HAYMARKET BOOKS

Haymarket Books is a nonprofit, progressive book distributor and publisher, a project of the Center for Economic Research and Social Change. We believe that activists need to take ideas, history, and politics into the many struggles for social justice today. Learning the lessons of past victories, as well as defeats, can arm a new generation of fighters for a better world. As Karl Marx said, "The philosophers have merely interpreted the world; the point, however, is to change it."

We take inspiration and courage from our namesakes, the Haymarket Martyrs, who gave their lives fighting for a better world. Their 1886 struggle for the eight-hour day, which gave us May Day, the international workers' holiday, reminds workers around the world that ordinary people can organize and struggle for their own liberation. These struggles continue today across the globe—struggles against oppression, exploitation, hunger, and poverty.

It was August Spies, one of the Martyrs targeted for being an immigrant and an anarchist, who predicted the battles being fought to this day. "If you think that by hanging us you can stamp out the labor movement," Spies told the judge, "then hang us. Here you will tread upon a spark, but here, and there, and behind you, and in front of you, and everywhere, the flames will blaze up. It is a subterranean fire. You cannot put it out. The ground is on fire upon which you stand."

We could not succeed in our publishing efforts without the generous financial support of our readers. Many people contribute to our project through the Haymarket Sustainers program, where donors receive free books in return for their monetary support. If you would like to be a part of this program, please contact us at info@haymarketbooks.org.

Order these titles and more online at www.haymarketbooks.org or call 773-583-7884.